FROM UTOPIA TO APOCALYPSE

FROM UTOPIA

TO APOCALYPSE

Science Fiction and the Politics of Catastrophe

PETER Y. PAIK

 University of Minnesota Press *Minneapolis London*

Published by the University of Minnesota Press
111 Third Avenue South, Suite 290
Minneapolis, MN 55401-2520
http://www.upress.umn.edu

Library of Congress Cataloging-in-Publication Data

Paik, Peter Yoonsuk.
    From utopia to apocalypse : science fiction and the politics of catastrophe / Peter Y. Paik.
        p.   cm.
    Includes bibliographical references and index.
    ISBN 978-0-8166-5078-1 (hc : alk. paper) — ISBN 978-0-8166-5079-8 (pbk. : alk. paper)
    1. Science fiction—History and criticism.   2. Utopias in literature.
3. Apocalypse in literature.   4. Politics in literature.   5. Politics and literature—History—20th century.   I. Title.
    PN3433.6.P35   2010
    809.3'8762—dc22   2009016789

Printed in the United States of America on acid-free paper

The University of Minnesota is an equal-opportunity educator and employer.

17 16 15 14 13 12 11 10   10 9 8 7 6 5 4 3 2 1

FOR MY PARENTS
KYUNG-SOO PAIK AND JU EUN PAIK

MYSTERIES,
AFTER THEY HAVE BEEN REVEALED,
DO NOT CEASE TO HAUNT US.

CONTENTS

THE GOD THAT SUCCEEDED

The disbelief of the stars comes down to establish an unbalanced
heretical light

— ROBERTO JUARROZ, "SECOND VERTICAL POETRY," NO. 17

(TRANSLATED BY W. S. MERWIN)

The corruption in things is not only the best argument for being
progressive; it is also the only argument against being conservative. The
conservative theory would really be quite sweeping and unanswerable
if it were not for this one fact. But all conservatism is based upon the
idea that if you leave things alone you leave them as they are. But you
do not. If you leave a thing alone you leave it to a torrent of change.

— G. K. CHESTERTON, *ORTHODOXY*

This book is a study of revolutionary change. Inasmuch as it focuses on a
set of narratives belonging predominantly to the genres of science fiction
and fantasy, this study undertakes to examine the hypothetical transformations and imaginary upheavals overtaking fictitious individuals and
societies. Yet the underlying contention of this work is that science fiction
and fantasy, in particular narratives drawn from media often dismissed as
unserious and trivial, such as the comic book and the science fiction film,
are capable of achieving profound and probing insights into the principal
dilemmas of political life. Indeed, this book explores such themes as the
foundation of new political orders, the endeavor to realize utopia, the exigencies underpinning tyranny, the relationship of a saintly politics to the
practice of *realpolitik,* and the potential and limitations of radical politics

in the present age. Science fiction proves to be eminently constructive for reflecting on these far-reaching questions, thanks in considerable measure to its roots in the practice of philosophic speculation. Many works of the genre are after all distinguished by the effort to imagine a fundamentally different world, one that, though it might be drastically divergent from the really existing world in its laws, mores, and technologies, nevertheless exhibits the consistency and coherence of actuality. Science fiction can accordingly serve as a vital instrument for the investigation of the contingencies governing political life, the forces that structure and dissolve collective existence, by providing the reader with visions in which familiar realities are destabilized and transformed. By compelling us to imagine a different order, science fiction cultivates in us the capacity to conceive of our contemporary situation in a dynamic manner, whether in terms of its disintegration or rejuvenation, making it the literary genre that perhaps most actively fosters a sense of historical as well as—in the Nietzschean sense—unhistorical consciousness in the present.

The work of literary speculation, to be sure, can be mobilized toward the depiction of an ideal social order as much as it can result in the creation of a society with flaws and limitations distinct from our own, a collective in which the ideals and repressions of our society have become, as it were, dislodged and reshuffled before cohering into another, possibly utopian, hierarchy of values. Leading academic critics of science fiction, such as Darko Suvin, Fredric Jameson, and Carl Freedman, have focused on the utopian orientation of the genre, invoking Thomas More's *Utopia* as its prototype and Ernst Bloch as its presiding theorist.[1] The approach I take in this book emphasizes by contrast what might be called the expository aspects of literary speculation. Whereas More's text generates the image of a society already established and governed according to more rational and enlightened principles, the texts on which this study concentrates deploy the speculative mode in order to explore the dynamics whereby a social and political order is transformed. Thus, the book takes as its imaginative paradigm not More's dialogue but rather Plato's *Republic*, which portrays the play of forces and desires—on a sweepingly collective as well as on an intimately personal scale—whereby one type of social and political organization transforms into another. In a discussion of the evolution of the five regimes, Socrates shows the just city, once it is completed in speech, undergoing a process of cumulative decline and disintegration until it becomes the worst of all regimes. Plato's dialogue thus proves to be disarmingly candid in these late passages about the fate of the ideal city after it has been founded upon that perennial stumbling block of liberal thinkers, the Phoenician tale or noble lie.

The idea of utopia has, nevertheless, provided the conceptual horizon for science fiction scholarship; the genre's emphasis on the technologically advanced future makes it, in the words of Istvan Csicsery-Ronay, a significant repository of "critical utopian imagining."[2] Science fiction, according to Darko Suvin, manifests its utopian character through the operation of cognitive estrangement. A text portraying a society in which the political institutions, social norms, economic system, and ways of life are superior—i.e., more harmonious, reasonable, virtuous, enlightened, and pleasurable—than those of the author's own society serves to estrange the reader by underscoring for her or him the bitter gulf that exists between the injustices and oppressions plaguing the society she or he inhabits and the more humane and enlightened political order on display in the fiction.[3] Science fiction, in its most progressive incarnations, advances a form of enlightened social critique, as inaugurated by More in his "great discovery" of the capacity of human powers to abolish "misery, sickness, and injustice" by means of the transformation of "sociopolitical institutions and norms."[4] The utopian element of science fiction thus enunciates the imperative to bring the status quo closer to the fictional ideal, albeit with the disclaimers that "the actual place" in question is "not to be taken literally" and that "it is less significant than the orientation toward a better place somewhere in front of the orienter."[5] Carl Freedman continues this line of thought when, following Ernst Bloch, he asserts that "the transformation of actuality into utopia constitutes the practical end of utopian critique and the ultimate object of utopian hope."[6]

This is not to say that Freedman and Suvin underrate the diagnostic powers of science fiction. As Freedman observes, the possibilities of social critique in the genre rely on the effort to "account rationally for its imagined world and for the connections as well as the disconnections of the latter to our own empirical world."[7] Yet, not surprisingly, the Marxist critics of science fiction have not themselves managed to transcend the fundamental aporias and bedeviling contradictions of Marxist ideology. As much as they might insist on the anticipatory character of what they deem as authentic science fiction, on the basis that the articulation of the wish for a better future sets in motion a process that brings reality closer to the wish, their assertion of a genetic relation between utopia and science fiction nevertheless truncates, if not suppresses, questions of how a utopia might be founded in the first place. Indeed, More himself gives the foundation of his imaginary island kingdom a noticeably cursory treatment: the founder, King Utopus, had conquered a part of the continent, thereupon bringing "its rude and uncouth inhabitants to... a high level of culture and humanity," and then had his soldiers and slaves dig a channel to separate his kingdom from the continent.[8] War is mentioned, but More provides scant detail about the policies and measures whereby these unruly and barbaric peoples were subdued, unified, and disciplined into achieving a level of culture and humanity surpassing that of other nations. Such reticence or discretion, one suspects, is indicative of an ongoing repression of foundational violence amid the praise lavished upon the wisdom of Utopian institutions and their achievement of socioeconomic equality.

For political philosopher Eric Voegelin, More's representation of an ideal society depends on the expurgation of pride and its disordering effects from the life of his imaginary commonwealth.[9] More deliberately excludes a vital and ineradicable aspect of human life and thus produces a necessarily false and distorted image of a social order. But even a counterfeit image of peace and harmony finds itself deformed by the implicit violence of its successful exercise of force, a violence that reverberates through the torpor and homogeneity of the description of the political ideal. Voegelin locates the source of this unsettling rhythm in the attitude of the Utopians regarding the conduct of war. The Utopians are said to detest wars, fighting them only for self-defense or for aiding allies invaded by aggressors. Raphael Hythlodaeus, the primary speaker in the dialogue, adds that they also embark on offensive wars to liberate oppressed and enslaved peoples. Although these stipulations regarding warfare sound quite humane and rational, the explicit principles by which warfare is constrained to magnanimous or necessary purposes mark the opening by which an exterminating violence makes itself an ordinary instrument of policy. The apparent humanitarianism of the Utopians prefigures the rigidly moral—and murderous—universe of modern totalitarianism. For anyone who is on the opposing side of the Utopians' just wars is automatically unjust, since the "carrier of the ideal can only act morally," having appointed himself as the "party, judge, and executor" of his necessarily immoral enemies.[10] Voegelin concludes that the Utopian state—as well as those ideological movements that proclaim themselves to be the defenders of human well-being and dignity—develops in principle into a "brutal attack on the historical realization of all values that do not happen to be incorporated in the ideal," whereby "anybody who wants to lead his own way of life, unmolested by the idealist, is a criminal."[11]

Voegelin's critique of More centers on the irony whereby the rational, ostensibly peaceful, internally harmonious social order ends up confronting the outside world in an unremittingly antagonistic posture of perpetual war and imperial expansion. In that regard, his stance parallels that of Carl Schmitt in *The Concept of the Political*, in which the erstwhile apologist for the Third Reich defines a liberal capitalist form of imperialism that masks its brutal wars of economic exploitation as crusades on behalf of human rights.[12] Indeed, Voegelin effectively traverses the gulf between utopia and praxis, over which left-wing theorists suspend themselves for the sake of keeping up the practice of dialectical criticism. More's abolition of pride among the Utopians effectively displaces its disordering energies onto the "formation of the ideal." The will to domination accordingly exposes itself when the narrator of the discourse most emphatically insists on the marvelous justice of this spiritually amputated society. Of course, critics of revolutionary politics, whether of the political Right or not, often make the charge that the radical Left tends to underestimate the depth and strength of the underlying factors shaping social conditions. Left-wing progressives, in this view, find themselves resorting to brutal and disastrous measures because of their reliance on high-minded sentiment and their optimistic conceptions of history, which work against the awareness of the gap between the revolutionary ideal and historical actuality. As even Georges Sorel, a thinker of the activist bent so vociferously denounced by Voegelin throughout his long career, argues in his introduction to *Reflections on Violence*, the disappointed optimist poses great dangers to society should he come to power. Frustrated by the setbacks and obstacles hindering political reform, he blames the people he governs for the failure to eliminate the evils and injustices afflicting them. The optimist thus blunders into terror as he becomes "tempted to get rid of people whose ill will seems to him to be a danger to the happiness of all."[13]

The charge that left-wing movements invariably become shipwrecked on their utopian delusions has a lengthy history, to be sure, and risks becoming something of a caricature, although one could attack the ideologies of the nationalist and imperialist Right, on more or less identical grounds.[14] An elementary axiom of political realism, after all, is that access to utopia, like the Kingdom of Heaven, is closed to purely human effort. Accordingly, ideological programs seeking to establish "universal freedom and prosperity," whether it takes the form of Soviet communism or neoliberal capitalism, are doomed to inflict bloodshed on a massive scale in the name of peace and liberty.[15] Theorists of utopia, on the other hand, frequently insist on the sharp demarcation of authentic utopian longings from the murderous policies of totalitarian and imperialist states, as well as their straightforward adoption of *realpolitik*. For utopia is said to be "never fully present in the here-and-now, and necessarily eludes all attempts to locate it with complete empirical precision."[16] According to Bloch, utopia represents an "all-surpassing *summum bonum*," the happiness and freedom for which all people yearn in the innermost depths of their being.[17] Its traces thus reside almost everywhere, in the desires and wishes aroused by everyday phenomena (fashion, architecture, dancing, sports, fairy tales, films, advertising, and daydreams), yet utopia remains at best intangible, premonitory of a better future.

From the standpoint of the realist, such efforts to distinguish or extricate utopia from the unforgiving dilemmas of political upheaval cannot but reek of evasion. To exempt utopian wishes from the sphere of political action is to rig the game in advance, so that one may retreat into the ideal, or the sheer wish for an ideal, and thereby avoid having to confront the harsh exigencies inherent to any process of far-reaching sociopolitical change. The idea of utopia as theorized by Bloch finds its logical destiny in Hegel's "beautiful soul," which, in clinging to its sense of moral purity, shrinks from accepting real political responsibility.[18] One is reminded on this score of Reinhart Koselleck's stinging assessment of the moralistic self-deceptions of the French bourgeoisie during the time of the Revolution: the bourgeois revolutionaries, claiming themselves to be wholly occupied in the "non-political" practice of virtue, sought to "rule indirectly through the moralisation of politics" and thereby ended up taking "refuge in naked force."[19] For the realist view of political change can be summed up in Sorel's point that "social conditions" form a "system bound together by an iron law which cannot be evaded, as something in the form of one block, and which can only disappear through a catastrophe which involves the whole."[20]

For what if the main blind spot of utopian thought in the present postpolitical era lay not in its complicity with mass ideological movements but rather in a lack of determination in imagining the irresistible pressures unleashed by political upheaval, a loss of nerve in confronting the intractable forces of social equilibrium that make genuine change impossible without a "catastrophe" befalling the entire society? For example, in his analysis of Ursula Le Guin's novel *The Dispossessed,* Freedman contends that while Le Guin provides a nuanced and balanced view of several different types of sociopolitical order—"bourgeois capitalism," "aristocratic conservatism," and "Stalinist communism," her novel nevertheless takes the clear stance that the "anarcho-communism" of her protagonist's home planet of Anarres is definitively "superior" to the aforementioned alternatives.[21] Le Guin, to be sure, mounts a "critique of anarchism" that Freedman judges to be "remarkably thoroughgoing," portraying the stifling conformism and xenophobic prejudices that come to take hold in the everyday life of a society founded by revolutionary anarchists. But it is the "self-critical" character of the critique of anarchism that according to Freedman elevates it above its rival sociopolitical systems. Whereas the nation of A-Io, the capitalist power on the planet Urras, from which the revolutionary dissidents originally immigrated to Anarres, "never acknowledged the claims of justice," and the bureaucratic socialist regime of Thu gives lip service to these claims but has "systematically betrayed them," only the isolated society of Anarres genuinely aspires to justice, even if its actual inhabitants frequently fall short of the democratic and egalitarian ideals of their founder, the anarchist philosopher Odo.[22] For the culture of Anarres exhibits a "self-reflexive capacity for self-correction," according to which the revolt of the novel's protagonist, the physicist Shevek, against the narrow conventions and rigid utilitarianism of his society must be regarded as the fulfillment of the founder's original vision.

The positive valuation accorded to self-criticism is not by any means exceptional, as such ideological hair-splitting has long enabled Western Marxists to denounce capitalist liberal democracy while protesting the inhuman violence as well as the pitiless statecraft practiced by the leaders of really existing socialist regimes. But in making the case that self-criticism constitutes the central dynamic of Le Guin's novel, Freedman neglects to consider the extent to which Shevek's protest might be conditioned by the peculiar and arduous circumstances of Anarres's isolation as well as the social upheavals certain to ensue from the unconstrained pursuit of truth and scientific knowledge. For life on Anarres takes the form of a difficult, unending struggle in an inhospitable, arid environment in which famine and scarcity pose a constant threat. Personal property is for the most part forbidden, and most of the people are engaged in some form of demanding physical labor. It does not occur to Freedman that the very harshness of life on Anarres, the unceasing need of its people to struggle for necessities on a daily basis, might actually constitute the most effective means for preserving the sparks of revolutionary fervor across multiple generations. Instead, the "self-criticism" that Freedman attributes to Le Guin is aimed at remedying the stifling "provincialism" and "economic underdevelopment" of the inhabitants, whose bigotry and narrow-mindedness have stunted their emergence as revolutionary subjects. Citing the late studies of Leon Trotsky, who concluded that the socialist project required an economy of abundance and that building a socialist state under conditions of scarcity would lead to the "reemergence of competition, privation, and bureaucracy," Freedman implies that "wealth" would in fact enable Anarres to achieve a more enlightened sociopolitical status, alluding to the utopian possibility of building socialism not on one planet but on all planets.

The betrayal of revolution and disappointment in its consequences have tended to reinforce the circular doctrine that the entire world must become communist in order for communism to succeed. The very impossibility of this demand, at once totalitarian and naïve, has the unfortunate effect of rendering less intelligible the vital and decisive factors governing political change. The self-criticism of revolutionary society might point logically to a higher third in which capitalist abundance is to be combined with socialist egalitarianism, but to place one's hopes in such an outcome is to overlook the danger of a society that would combine the mediocrity of socialist egalitarianism with the unrestrained competition inherent to capitalism. Freedman's analysis makes no mention of the traditional republican suspicion of luxury, the conviction that abundance invariably not only breeds in the citizens but also promotes destructive forms of competition over trifling distinctions. He moreover discounts the transformative character of the changes that Shevek's exercise of self-criticism might bring about. For Shevek's devotion to scientific truth can be said to contain the seeds of a challenge to the egalitarianism that reigns on Anarres, if not its outright demise. Just as the conquest of scarcity, and the end to the perpetual state of emergency, is certain to introduce inequalities on Anarres between the conservative purists and the ambitiously forward-looking, the sovereignty of scientific advancement likewise emancipates not only the truthful but also the enterprising from the bonds of modesty and restraint. The pressure of social conformity and the tyranny of conventional opinion, which prevent Shevek from carrying out his research in mathematical physics and drive him away to the economically stratified world of Urras, are indissoluble from the egalitarian convictions and democratic voluntarism of his people.

I would argue that the conventionalized gesture of affirming self-criticism displays a far greater compatibility with the established values of liberal bourgeois society—and its crushing dread at the prospect of sweeping, coercive change—than with any genuinely revolutionary political stance.[23] Inasmuch as such an affirmation typifies the ideal of criticism elaborated by Jacques Derrida as a "procedure ready to undertake its self-critique,"[24] it leaves intact the basic prerogative on which liberal capitalist society depends: the idea of negative freedom, defined as the absence of constraints. For while the call for perpetual critique presents itself as an enlightened form of moral vigilance, it consigns the substance of this very morality to an indefinite—and therefore comfortably postponed—future. As Koselleck puts it, the proper theological model for the practice of perpetual, open-ended critique is not a leap of faith but an "unsecured loan."[25]

Poststructuralist and deconstructionist theory thus tends to act as a factor reinforcing the existing order by reducing dissent to a safely foredoomed possibility rather than as a shattering intervention that imposes ineluctable duties and forced choices in clearing the way for the establishment of a new law and the foundation of a new order.[26] Furthermore, not only does poststructuralist deconstruction ultimately deprive any radical politics of its genuinely disruptive potential, but it also denies the tragic nature of political life, exposing thereby its underlying harmony and congruence with the technologist fantasy of permanently banishing conflict and contradiction from human existence.

For does not the appeal to an open and unspecified future seek to avoid the traumatic character of societal upheaval, to look away from the likelihood of calamities that are as unbearable as they are inevitable? In the superhero comic *Miracleman Book 3: Olympus* (1990), by British writer Alan Moore, the reader is confronted with an almost intolerable sense of closure at the end of the narrative. The supervillain enemy has been vanquished after a brutal, hard-fought battle that has left much of London in ruins. The heroes proceed to rebuild the shattered city in which tens of thousands have been brutally slaughtered. But the superpowered beings do not stop there. They rid the earth of all its nuclear weapons by transporting them to the sun. They regenerate the deserts of Africa into verdant farmland, introduce gases from a distant planet to neutralize emissions trapped in the atmosphere, and heal the environment from the ravages of industrial pollution. This clique of superhumans and their extraterrestrial allies impose their will in political and economic spheres as well, eliminating poverty and currency at one stroke, legalizing all drugs, and administering pacifying medications to sociopaths and other dangerous personalities. The erstwhile masters of the world are summarily herded into group therapy sessions where they work through their fantasies of omnipotence and feelings of inadequacy.

The earth soon becomes a paradise in which no one goes hungry, there are no shortages of vital resources, and war has become a memory. Eugenics and bioengineering bring superhuman abilities within the reach of ordinary human beings, and even the recently dead are revived in artificial bodies provided by alien technology. There are a few scattered malcontents, to be sure: survivalists hiding out in the mountains, and Christian and Islamic fundamentalists, who have joined forces against the superheroes that now rule the world and fitfully register their largely futile dissent through acts of self-immolation. But the narrative closes with a tone of growing unease and gnawing disquiet over the implications of what these living demigods have accomplished. The protagonist Miracleman might have created a perfect world with his companions, but their indisputable improvements and reforms display an ominously irrevocable character. At the end, he wonders why his human wife, who has become estranged from him in part because of his infidelities with a superpowered companion, has refused his offer to endow her with superhuman abilities. He muses over this question while striking a pose that is suggestive of a despot receiving homage from his subjects: his hand is being kissed by a grotesque flower, transplanted from a distant galaxy, that sprouts human lips.

The startling impact of this comic book narrative arises of course from the fact that Moore aggressively violates the fundamental generic conventions of the superhero narrative. As Umberto Eco observes in his analysis of Superman, the superhero comic is governed by rigid limitations on the superpowered being's use of his or her powers and thus on the range of his or her actions. Although Superman is "practically omnipotent" in his physical and mental abilities, the narrative limits him to performing acts of charity on the "level of the small community," in which evil generally takes the form of "an attempt on private property."[27] He might be a godlike being from whom "one could expect the most bewildering political, economic, and technological upheavals in the world," but the fantastic system of causality operating in the superhero comic proscribes the narrative from venturing out into the quasi-divine orbit of the consequences that such power would logically necessitate.[28] Eco's analysis is a bit one-sided to be sure, as it does not take into account the changes that the iconic character has undergone over the decades, as well as some of the more overtly political topics that the comic has explored even in its early years (most notably, the evils of racial prejudice and the struggle against fascism). But the rhetorical questions he raises enumerate the codes of artifice through which Moore's revisionist narrative makes its breakthrough.

For a superpowered being to make full use of his or her powers would, of course, place him or her on the path of becoming a global tyrant, however unselfish and beneficial his or her exercises of power. Moore displays impressive foresight in formulating a scenario that leaps in advance of the strategic deadlock that marked the Cold War years. For the narrative leash that restrained superheroes from intervening actively in the realm of geopolitics is fastened to the particular anxieties and yearnings of that period, corresponding on the one hand to the fear of nuclear conflagration and on the other to the desire to be reassured of the steadiness of the liberal democratic order against its ideological adversary. *Miracleman: Olympus,* completed shortly before the collapse of the Soviet Union, envisions the predicaments and crises that would follow when an interminable stalemate gives way, when the sources of catastrophe have become more elusive and thus more alarming and ominous. Moore's shattering of the geopolitical taboo accordingly serves to give flesh to the ineluctably revolutionary dream of unconstrained expansionism and unlimited power that has been dreamt—and become magnified—within liberal democratic society. Indeed, the abandonment of geopolitical restraint, on the grounds that the United States is the "indispensable nation," sets out after all to make actual a casually brutal fantasy of globalizing exceptionalism inherent to the assurance that the United States can always avoid any severe setback or stave off excessive hardships by availing itself of its overwhelming military might.

The fantasy of putting annihilating omnipotence to beneficial effect surfaces in the works of other creators of superhero comics, such as Mark Millar *(Red Son),* Warren Ellis *(The Authority),* and Frank Miller. For Miller, who takes an affirmative view of vigilantism, one striking political correlative to the costumed adventurer operating beyond the law takes the form of a U.S. president who feigns a vindictive readiness to engage in nuclear war to force the Soviets into peace talks.[29] Though presented as something of a parody, this narrative twist points ahead to the unsettling temptations that arise from altered geopolitical circumstances, when the possession of a massive and unchallengeable military arsenal may come to confer psychologically and ideologically reassuring effects. For global supremacy can be permanently achievable—and all geopolitical problems (access to natural resources, the flow of finance capital, and so on) thereby rendered soluble—if one is ready to make good on the implicit threat of deploying weapons of mass destruction. Moore's revisionist comic, by contrast, strikes directly at the largely unspoken prejudice that overwhelming technological and military superiority makes both drastic changes and dramatic setbacks inconceivable. Indeed, the scenario that the imaginary of a narrative such as *Miracleman* unreservedly rules out is that of prevailing historical conditions continuing indefinitely in their present form. Moore pursues a ruthlessly realist logic to portray the shattering eruption of the fantasy of geopolitical omnipotence into a social order that regards itself as final, unsurpassable, and posthistorical. At such a level of the advancement or decay of bourgeois modernity, when it believes itself beyond the reach of revolution and catastrophe, it comes as little surprise that not only the dream of transformation but also the denial of its inevitability will necessarily assume apocalyptic proportions.

In Moore's incendiary exploration of the political implications of the superhero genre, the costumed heroes go beyond the traditional function of merely serving as the guardians of an imperfect and decaying social order to take direct control of the planet from its small-minded and exasperating rulers and govern it themselves. While it is easy to compare them to tyrants and dictators, however sensible and compassionate their policies, the superhumans regard themselves in even more exalted terms, accounting for their arrival into history as the very point of transition from the human to the divine. In a startling poetic monologue, *Miracleman* pronounces the apocalyptic significance of the figure of the superhero:

> Oh, earth, look up and see your gods at celebration. See the things that frightened you when you were in your caves; the things you named, and dedicated idols to; the things you rendered up burnt offerings to appease . . . *They are as you, and in their great mercy have decreed that you should be as they.* Oh, earth, look up . . . (emphasis mine)
>
> Look up: we have repealed the laws of gravity, torn off the ceiling of the world that was so very low. The skies are ours, new beaches made of cirrus-cloud, new valleys made of strato-cumulus. Lift up your heads! You were not made to gaze at gutters, mud and puddles

all your lives, but have not dared to raise your sights in case the thing you longed for was not there. Look up and see it now, the shape that's haunted human dreams and legends since we first peered from the jungles long ago and wondered what might dwell upon those blue and distant hills, upon those mountains there.[30]

The superhumans have arrived to fulfill the destiny of humankind, to step before the world and make known to them at last whose mercy they implored, whose fury drove them into throes of panic and despair, and before whose dread and astonishing majesty they cowered in awe and ter-ror throughout the millennia. *God* is a word whose true meaning has at last become revealed. There thus dawns a new law, granted to humanity through the beneficence of really existing divine beings who abolish the elemental constraints on human ambition and power. The paradise that these gods create maintains, to be sure, a horrifying and tragic reminder of the old world: a memory park that commemorates the climactic battle between the lords of light and the prince of darkness, where the visitor may gaze upon "coral reefs of baby skulls and far worse." But they cannot help nor halt their unchallengeable power from embalming the world they rule. The manifestation of divine wonder becomes reduced in this untroubled and uneventful globe to the spectacle of its enlightened rulers copulating across the night-sky, to the perfunctory applause of the numbed and invulnerable masses below.

The revolutionary transformations introduced and imposed by the superhumans would fulfill the highest potential of any radical political program by founding a new order and a new epoch in human history. Their actions, furthermore, take effect on a transcendent scale and alter the very fabric of social reality. As such, one must account for the vast and irresistible changes brought about by these new masters of the world according to the terms of the categories of political theology, for their exercise of sover-eignty is nothing short of religious in magnitude and intensity, far exceed-ing the parameters of what secular liberal thought defines as encompass-ing political life. For the superheroes enact—and rule by—nothing short of miracles. In the work of Carl Schmitt, the last century's most infamous theorist of political theology, the divine intervention of the miracle finds its equivalent in jurisprudence in the form of the exception. The God who demands unconditional obedience is mirrored by the sovereign who decides the exception, i.e., determines when laws and norms can be suspended. As Schmitt puts it, "all significant concepts of the modern theory of the state are secularized theological concepts not only because of their historical development—in which they were transferred from theology to the theory of the state, whereby, for example, the omnipotent God became the omnipotent lawgiver—but also because of their systematic structure."[31] As much as the idea of an omnipotent God might recede from the secular culture advanced by Enlightenment modernity, Schmitt contends that the figure that occupies the position of God in the realm of political life cannot vanish insofar as it carries out the function of binding together the very constitutional order; there is thus no equivalent to deism in the theory of the state. The modern state, including liberal democracies, cannot evade the elemental problem of sovereignty, which consists of the need to decide "whether there is an extreme emergency" and what courses must be taken to address it.[32]

Schmitt's political theology centers on the role of the sovereign in defending a given or existing moral and political order. The superheroes portrayed by Moore, by contrast, are lawgivers who create new norms and thus direct the properly miraculous work of sovereignty toward radically divergent ends. Whereas Schmitt emphasized or idealized the sovereign in the role of the "restrainer"—what he calls the *katechon* or *Aufhalter* who strives to hold back the outbreak of apocalyptic disorder[33]—the superhero in *Miracleman* emerges as a political innovator, that is to say, as the demiurgic creator of a new social reality. Within Schmitt's schema, the figure of the revolutionary demiurge can only appear as the demonic counterfeit of the sovereign, an engineer of human souls presiding over the bestial kingdom of postpolitical darkness. Yet, as Heinrich Meier points out, the totalism of Schmitt's political theology, the all-encompassing nature of the struggle between obedience and rebellion, has the effect of laying bare every other political stance, whether pagan, heterodox, or secular, as a theological position; even the denial of the theological attests to its inescapable character.[34] Likewise, a sworn enemy of authority, such as the anarchist Mikhail Bakunin, is compelled to reproduce the unconditional and uncompromising character of political theology in fighting against it. Although the figure of the political revolutionary as demiurgic innovator is left undeveloped in Schmitt's *Political Theology*, it is clear that such a conception fits into his account as the necessary and ineluctable outcome of the decision made against God. Indeed, the revolutionary leader as demiurge, one might say, arises once a revolutionary political program has absorbed and integrated the lessons of political theology—the need to "penetrate the innermost core of men" and restructure political life by creating a new social reality.[35]

Although lacking in any explicit reference to the idea, there is perhaps no more profound an exploration of political theology as it takes expression within the revolutionary Left than Boris Groys's remarkable study of socialist realism, *The Total Art of Stalinism*. A work that has as its object of analysis a vast and comprehensive project to transform social life according to a "unitary artistic plan," Groys's book comes to focus on the figure of the demiurge and his creation of a new sociopolitical reality as the abiding theme of Stalinist social realist art and literature.[36] According to Groys, socialist realism, far from being hackneyed and vulgar kitsch, a crude and degraded reversion to classical aesthetics, in fact strove after and achieved the objective of the avant-garde to organize "the life of society" according to "monolithic artistic forms" (9). Socialist realism developed among the intellectual and artistic elite as the solution to the impasse of the avant-garde, once artists such as Kazimir Malevich and Velimir Khlebnikov had claimed for themselves unlimited power to realize their projects (21). Such a demand, in the Soviet context, resulted in the spillover of struggles over questions of aesthetics into the sphere of politics, especially once the avant-garde began calling openly for the state to crush their opponents as counterrevolutionaries. As Groys observes, the inner logic of the avant-garde, which sought to transform the world by liquidating tradition, brought the artist into a usurpatory relationship vis-à-vis the revolutionary state. The avant-garde "constructor of a new world" was therefore compelled to abdicate this ambition to the state, and was "succeeded by a military and political leader ruling over the whole of 'reality saturated with art'—the mystical figure of that 'great corporal of the guard' soon to be incarnated in the figure of Stalin" (28).

One of the most contentious aspects of Groys's study is his characterization of Stalin as a demiurgic sovereign who achieves a consummate unity of aesthetic theory and political practice in his leadership over the revolutionary state. The avant-garde's world-making ambitions, once they had been appropriated by the party, meant that demiurgy would become the predominant theme of artworks that would depict and unfold in a social reality transformed by revolutionary willpower (64–65). The figure of the demiurge becomes thematized in socialist realist art as the struggle between the "Divine Creator and his demoniacal double" (62). But, as Groys notes in terms that strikingly resemble the narrative conventions of American superhero comics, the struggle between the "positive hero" of Bolshevism and the counterrevolutionary "wrecker" is a conflict that unfolds on a transcendent plane, in which material reality is reduced to a mere staging ground for their superhuman battles. For the literary hero of Stalinism, reflecting the indomitable will of the leader, could "cure tuberculosis by willpower alone, raise tropical plants in the open air of the tundra, paralyze their enemies by the power of their gaze," and "without any additional technology... increase labor productivity manifold" (59–60). His counterrevolutionary adversary likewise draws on transcendent powers, being able to spread lethal diseases, poison food, and poison wells on a "superhuman, unimaginable scale, accomplishing the most titanically destructive feats in many places at the same time but without any technical or organizational assistance (since that would eliminate their individual guilt), and by willpower alone (since they were the whole time working for the party and under its supervision)" (61). As Groys argues, the archetype of a gratuitously malevolent adversary was necessitated by the show trials of the 1930s, which demonstrated that ostensibly loyal Bolshevists and otherwise ordinary citizens were capable of acts of astonishing subversion and appalling destructiveness.

Not only do the Stalinist heroes and Western superheroes share superhuman capabilities and engage their no less extraordinary adversaries in struggles charged with cosmic significance, but Stalinist art and American superhero comics are also obliged to confront the challenge of providing a reassuring and identifiable face to essentially godlike personages, that is to say, to humanize the inhuman. Groys notes the frenetic character of the gestures by which the creators of socialist realism sought to endow their icons with familiar and soothing characteristics in terms that could apply, without revision, to American superhero narratives:

Its heroes . . . must thoroughly resemble people if people are not to be frightened by their true aspect, and this is why the writers and artists of socialist realism constantly bustle about inventing biographies, habits, clothing, physiognomies, and so on. They almost seem to be in the employ of some sort of extraterrestrial travel bureau planning a trip to Earth—they want to make their envoys as anthropomorphic as possible, but they cannot keep the otherworldly void from gaping through all the cracks in the mask. (63)

The need to give a disquietingly powerful demigod a minimally identifiable, all-too-human identity is of course in the Western instance resolved through the convention of the superhero's secret identity, the disguise of a banal, often inept alter ego. The dream of omnipotence cannot be staged directly, lest the cataclysms triggered by his annihilating limbs awaken the dreamer. But the repression of the "otherworldly void" in such superhuman characters means that their representation must take the form of a self-conscious hagiography, in which the technologized self has no choice but to become idolized once it lays claim to the prerogative to reshape the "laws that govern cosmic and social forces" (65).

One could accordingly speak of an identity in the content of the fantasy life of both Soviet communists and liberal democratic capitalists, an ideological symmetry that betrays in turn their shared faith in technology, whether in the form of sociopolitical engineering or of an infinitely expanding global market, to eliminate forever the historically intractable afflictions of poverty, scarcity, and war.[37] For the largely unspoken religion of globalizing modernity is the progressivist and technicist denial of tragedy, a cult that finds its messiah in the demiurge who not only reforms political and economic structures but also conjures forth through superhuman effort a new social reality. Indeed, the collective desires evoked by revolutionary socialism and neoliberal capitalism cannot be satisfied by the conventional, unglamorous role of a sovereign that merely protects and seeks to preserve the relative safety and well-being of a given social and political order. One need not assent to Schmitt's political itinerary to recognize the merits of a politics based on the restraint of the appetites and the checking of ambitions, not least in an era of unconstrained greed, natural resource depletion, and looming environmental catastrophe. For the denial of any limits on human ambition, whether in the name of ceaseless superhuman labor, an infinite and borderless rapacity, or the doctrine of the constructed nature of reality, clears the way for a demiurgic program of world-making whereby one becomes cursed to substitute oneself for the god that one has murdered and compelled to simulate the veracity that one has discredited.

With regard to the texts discussed in this book, it is incorrect to say that they comprise direct and unmediated attempts to assert or affirm the values contained in political theology, whether of revolutionary socialism or neoliberal capitalism. Rather, the fictional narratives by Alan Moore, Kurt Vonnegut, Jang Joon-Hwan, Hayao Miyazaki, and others take the path that, in spite of their outwardly fantastic character, has traditionally been regarded as antithetical to the spirit of theology as well as to modern ideology as a whole—the approach of realism. The reader will note that I am not speaking of realism in the sense of the nineteenth-century novel and its representational conventions, but rather in terms closer to how it is understood in the realm of political philosophy. Realism in this latter sense constitutes a discourse which analyzes in an impartial and dispassionate manner the workings of power. It arises out of the awareness that the wellsprings of political conflict generally lie in the tragic struggle between two irreconcilable forms of the good. For the works of Moore, Vonnegut, Jang, and Miyazaki do not seek to create new myths or to reinforce existing theologies but rather to display, with unblinking candor and rigorous equanimity, the violence committed in the name of founding new modes and orders as well as for the sake of destroying unjust regimes. Their narratives accordingly may open under the sign of a brutal exigency, that is to say, under the shadow of its clear and logical resolution, but then tend to close with a bedeviling ethical dilemma. Rather than settling the issue in favor of one set of ideological values or another, they accord to the reader or viewer the prerogative of judgment, compelling them to decide on both the justice and the efficacy of the actions undertaken by the characters. Thus, one might say that these fictions invert the process whereby the demiurge becomes the theme of ideologically affirmative works of art, for, in taking political theology as their principal theme, these narratives serve to unmask with unflinching directness the brutal impact of the world-making projects of its demiurges as well as the harsh necessities that call forth these undertakings in the first place. In portraying the upheavals wrought by political theology, they lay bare its mechanisms.

For example, in *Miracleman,* Moore shows how the act of liquidating the power of the established authorities brings the superheroes into theological warfare, which generates new theologies that build on the rubble of the all-too-human faiths. Yet the reader is not given an account of these new theologies from within the subjective position of the believer but is rather invited to evaluate them from the outside, that is to say, to treat them as myths. Furthermore, the skeptical appraisal of the political theologies within the narrative is performed by Miracleman himself, through his own interior narration. His survey of the sects that have arisen in the wake of the apocalyptic battle against the murderous and diabolical Kid Miracleman subtly underscores how acts of theological-political interpretation ineluctably contaminate the most decisive events in human history. There is the school of "trans-time integrationists," who assert that Miracleman gained the strength necessary to defeat his vastly more powerful opponent by traveling through time to fight against his former and future selves.[38] On the other hand, the "witnesses of the conspiracy" hold that the superhumans sold the earth to an alien race in order to govern it as their satraps. A dissident sect within the "rational brethren" maintains that the entire world in which the superhumans have seized power is a hallucination unfolding in the mind of the insane scientist who engineered Miracleman and the superpowered individuals in the first place. The gnostic "knights of the Warpsmith resurrected" imagine the apocalyptic confrontation as a chess match in which the alien ally of the superhumans tears out his own heart for Miracleman to use as a piece when all seems lost. Finally, the "church of the deicide" asserts that the superhumans slew the decadent gods of the old world—Gabriel, Shiva, and so on—and usurped their power.

After giving a brief description of each school of thought, Miracleman, far from refuting or dismissing these newborn illusions, instead openly concedes their truth content. Indeed, in the most damning of instances, he praises the insight and ingenuity of his accusers. "Who knows," he muses, perhaps the "witnesses of the conspiracy" are correct in their accusation that he and his companions now administer the world in the service of alien overlords. It is in a sense undeniable, he muses, that the revolutionary changes wrought by the superhumans are but the deranged fantasy of a malevolent and impotent scientist. The disarming candor of the superhero's reflections extend to his own personal account of the titanic battle in a recitation, which, it is clear, is intended to be kept off any public record: "My apologists have claimed that the first car I threw at Bates (the alter ego of Kid Miracleman) was empty, those who'd been inside having all previously escaped. I'm sorry, but that isn't true."[39] There is something relentlessly disquieting about the tone of this confession as well as its explicit content, for it foregrounds uncomfortably those very details that have been hitherto suppressed within the genre of superhero fantasy— massacred bystanders, cruel expediencies, and the furious destruction unleashed by the self-proclaimed defenders of the innocent and vulnerable. Yet, it is within the exaggerated scaffolding provided by the fantasy, within the frame of a fundamentally implausible fiction, that the mechanisms that measure and sanction political violence can become properly visible. For the interpretation of prestigious literary forms is more liable to fall prey to the reader's moralistic impulses, whereby the recognition of a text detailing inhuman acts as a historical document almost automatically confers upon it the blinding glare of moral authority. Such authority has had the unfortunate effect of allowing the reader to disavow rather too easily instances of historical violence as inexplicable and incomprehensible acts of inhuman evil, or, as G. K. Chesterton put it, as remote from their everyday realities as the lives of "apes in a forest ten thousand miles away."[40] But when one speaks of fictional atrocities, when the victims belong to imaginary societies or alternate realities, the gaze of the perpetrator, as well as that of the beneficiaries of his or her violence, more easily infiltrates the perspective of the interpreter, who tears down, as it were, the ramparts of his or her moralizing judgments to welcome the strange gift of an imaginable apocalypse.

Science fiction and fantasy, in dispelling the aura of moral interpretation, become capable of following myth up to the precise moment of its forgetting, when it seals itself within its own contrived universe. On the other hand, the realist impulse that encompasses inflammatory speculations about the nature of authority and depicts the terrifying exigencies whereby political order takes root proves to be subversive of both the goal of utopia and the desire to secure the continuance of the established order. A realist depiction of a transformed world, after all, is one that does not omit the horrors that accompany its foundations. These acts of literary speculation thus confront us with the harsh truths evaded or repressed by liberal and progressive thought. It is perhaps only such a fantastic realism that is at present capable of opening up a critical space for reflection between the alternatives of an enlightened obedience to a devouring and deteriorating beast and a headlong embrace of fate that masquerades as a godlike freedom. In that sense, the uncompromising political vision of an author like Moore, in carrying out a withering critique of repressed religion, explores and elucidates the relationship between liberal and totalitarian politics in terms of a demiurgic continuity, preordained in both cases by the lure of a posthistorical salvation. The realist imperative, whether it provokes the metaphors of political philosophers or the imaginary worlds of science fiction writers, reflects the determination to achieve wakefulness through the exercise of the literary imagination.

1 UTOPIA ACHIEVED
The Case of *Watchmen*

We need greater virtues to bear good rather than evil fortune.

— LA ROCHEFOUCAULD

It was the belief of Charles Atlas that muscles could be built without
bar bells or spring exercisers, could be built by simply pitting one set
of muscles against another.

It was the belief of Bokonon that good societies could be built only by
pitting good against evil, and by keeping the tension between the two
high at all times.

— KURT VONNEGUT, *CAT'S CRADLE*

THE TALE OF THE LAW

Cadmus throws the stone. The throng of armed men, sprung forth from
the dragon's teeth that the hero has sown into the earth, accuses each other
of having hurled the rock and soon come to blows. Most of the *spartoi* are
killed in the ensuing melee, but a handful of the badly wounded survivors
are nursed back to health by the Phoenician prince. The survivors accept
Cadmus as their ruler and help him to found the city of Thebes.

The mythical account of the origin of Thebes contains the elements
that political thinkers such as Plato and Machiavelli have come to associate
with the founding of new orders—the killing of the innocent, the deception of the ruled, the apodictic institution of authority, and the unpunished
crime of the founders. The story of Cadmus manifests its pivotal significance in Plato's *Republic* when Socrates makes the unity and cohesion of

the inhabitants of the just city depend on the deliberate promotion of a falsehood regarding a shared autochthonous past. Myths, or at least lies, are required to ground and sustain a new state, not least by transmuting the violence committed by its founders into the less disruptive forms of coercion imposed by laws and constitutions. In this respect the Phoenician tale appears to be more than merely a repugnant counsel recommending the authorities to avail themselves of fraud in order to maintain their hold on power. For Plato as for Machiavelli, the establishment of new orders is an undertaking that far exceeds the scope of any secular or liberal definition of politics. In the *Republic*, the formation of the just city is indissoluble from the development of a new theology that is explicitly at odds with the tales of Homer and the other poets. In *The Prince*, the daunting task of introducing and successfully implementing political innovation is associated with those distinguished by a supernatural level of *virtù*, the armed prophets, the favored exemplars of which are Moses, Cyrus, Romulus, and Theseus. The overwhelming difficulty and unpredictable perils of such an undertaking mean that the activity of the prophet and legislator will be demiurgic in nature.[1] For the giving of new laws is tantamount to the creation of a second nature, just as the republic, "being the precondition of virtue in man," must "be created by a virtue more than human."[2]

Thus, while the ends of Machiavellian *realpolitik*—the establishment of a new and enduring order—might appear modest in comparison to the utopias dreamt by modern revolutionaries, Machiavelli demands far more of his founders, who are to be prophets and legislators aided by divine inspiration, than do Marx and his followers of the workers mobilized to carry out the task of liquidating the old regime. The discrepancy between the fantasy of universal abundance achieved through the rational and self-interested activity of the proletariat and the more modest goal of a stable political order instituted by the daring and craftiness of an extraordinary individual (or group of individuals) reflects the distance between the optimism that dooms itself in the name of necessity to increasing the frequency of its brutalities and the pessimism that endeavors to limit its exercise of violence over the course of time. Indeed, the advantage of "realism" over utopian ideology is not exclusively a practical or tactical one— the impulse to censure Machiavelli's harsh teachings regarding the uses of cruelty and deception must be tempered by the understanding that

Machiavelli provides such instruction regarding the "power not to be good" within the framework of what Paul Ricoeur calls an "economy of force" or an "ethic of limited violence."[3] Machiavelli's candid analyses of the bitter realities of power, the unflinching character of which sets him apart from his predecessors as well as from the humanists of the Enlightenment, prove to be far more productive of political insights than an "eschatology of innocence" that supposes and insists that the correct distribution of material goods will give rise to a society without antagonism.[4] The question of political innovation, contra Marx's famous dictum regarding the need to change the world instead of merely interpreting it, demands an analytical framework that would countenance the upheaval of the revolutionary act as well as the process of corruption that would inevitably take hold afterward, as in Plato's account of the series of displacements of desires and passions that results in the best regime becoming progressively corrupted into the worst. The abdication of Marx and his followers, on the other hand, in engaging these questions would play no small role in dooming the communist regimes to impose upon their peoples an attenuated and interminable process of founding that stretched into a moribund and stagnant status quo marked by corroding mendacities and dispiriting frustrations.

Simone Weil, one of Marx's severest and at the same time most sympathetic critics, reproaches him for failing or refusing to address such fundamental issues as "why oppression is invincible as long as it is useful," "why the oppressed in revolt have never succeeded in founding a non-oppressive society, whether on the basis of the productive forces of their time, or even at the cost of an economic regression which could hardly increase their misery," and, finally, what constitute the "general principles of the mechanism by which a given form of oppression is replaced by another."[5] The task, then, of the authentically political imagination is to conceive of the transformation of the social order without recourse to an eschatological fantasy that denies and conceals the fundamental and ineradicable conflicts that constitute the realm of politics. One must, in other words, examine the shift from one type of social order to another without the distorting effects of such euphemisms as "progress" or "utopia." In the realm of speculative fiction, the endeavor to capture the ambiguities of revolutionary change is to be found in counterutopian narratives that provide an account of sociopolitical transformation resulting not in the abolition of oppression but rather in its redistribution, not in the end of thymotic striving but rather in its becoming coerced into pursuits other than those of war or wealth, and not in a peace that is equated with justice but in a peaceableness that is enforced by the terrors of a most outrageous form of injustice. In Kurt Vonnegut's science-fiction satire *The Sirens of Titan* and Alan Moore's metafictional superhero comic *Watchmen*, we are confronted with tales portraying the salvation of humanity and the planet, but through means that can only be recognized as horrifying. For in both narratives, world peace is won not only through deception and genocide, but also extorted by means of myths concocted by the very perpetrators of the slaughter, imposing new illusions that effectively blackmail the world into abstaining from its violence.

SUPERHERO GEOPOLITICS

"Nothing ends, Adrian. Nothing ever ends." So runs the enigmatic reply to a question about whether a certain morally questionable deed will eventually be vindicated by its results. The dialogue is, however, complicated by the fact that the act in question refers to the deliberate killing of three million people, as well as by the detail that the response is uttered by an indestructible and immortal superhuman entity possessed of a virtually omniscient consciousness. The latter is a blue-skinned superhero named Dr. Manhattan, who has, as is typically the case, acquired his powers in a freak laboratory accident, while his interlocutor, Adrian Veidt, alias Ozymandias, is a former masked hero who has just executed a horrifying conspiracy to avert nuclear war and usher in a new age of global peace. For in the days leading up to Ozymandias orchestrating what appears to be an alien attack on New York, an attack that in spite of its being a hoax nevertheless takes the lives of half of the population of the city, tensions between the United States and the Soviet Union had escalated to the point where the two adversaries have begun active preparations for nuclear strikes against each other. The shock of the ensuing carnage and mass death in Manhattan has its intended effect, as the superpowers draw back from the precipice of mutual annihilation with pledges of peace and mutual assistance in the face of this unforeseen and unprecedented threat to the human species. Yet Ozymandias derives no comfort from his superhuman interlocutor's total knowledge, as from Dr. Manhattan's transcendent perspective, the concern with human survival is merely an anthropocentric prejudice. As even Ozymandias himself has earlier said of Dr. Manhattan, whose active involvement in promoting the expansionist and militarist policies of the United States has triggered the geopolitical crisis threatening to unleash the war to end the world, the ideological dilemma posed by left-wing and right-wing rivalries is for him akin to choosing between red ants and black ants.

Watchmen, written by Alan Moore and drawn by Dave Gibbons, is perhaps the most ambitious and ground-breaking narrative in the history of superhero comics, a work renowned for the unprecedented depths of its thematic complexity, historical reflection, and visual lyricism. A limited series that appeared in twelve installments starting in 1986 and subsequently collected into a graphic novel, *Watchmen* frequently avails itself of metafictional devices to reflect on the genre of superhero fantasy, but it investigates the medium by placing its costumed adventurers in a realistic world governed by power politics, rather than the juvenile, idealized universe of moral certitudes in which the upholders of truth and justice do battle against the forces of darkness. Although the initial purpose of the superhero team, called the Minutemen, is to combat urban crime, the activities of these masked vigilantes come to blur into the netherworld of covert operations, presidential conspiracies, imperialist wars, and, finally, the aforementioned plot to prevent nuclear holocaust by staging an extraterrestrial attack on Manhattan. Indeed, it is impossible to say with any certainty whether the costumed adventurers in *Watchmen* are to be considered heroes or villains, as they either serve or are otherwise forced to come to terms with the brutal and feverishly expansionist policies of a belligerent American administration, which makes full use of the strategic advantages provided by superheroes in prosecuting its wars and fomenting coups against uncooperative governments. Moore turns the familiar comic book icon of Superman, the noble and indomitable hero who defends truth and justice, on its head with the premise that if superheroes really existed, their powers would be made to advance the interests of the state in its pursuit of geopolitical power, unless, of course, these super-human beings were to turn on the ruling authorities and make themselves the masters of the world.[6]

The major characters in *Watchmen* include the Comedian, a violent and sadistic government agent; Rorschach, an unhinged vigilante whose draconian zeal for punishing criminals has made him wanted by the law; Nite Owl, an ornithologist in retirement from crime fighting; the Silk Spectre, a woman who was compelled by her mother, a famous ex-heroine, to train in martial arts and take up the profession; Ozymandias, a self-made industrialist and renaissance man whose companies have a stake in almost every sector of the economy; and finally Dr. Manhattan, the only character in the novel who actually possesses superhuman abilities, having acquired near-omnipotent powers in a nuclear accident. Moore modeled these characters after the superheroes featured by Charlton Comics in the 1940s, who present a representative cross-section of the familiar archetypes of the genre—the patriotic crime-fighter and war veteran (the Peacemaker), the hero who makes use of futuristic technology (the Blue Beetle), the invulnerable champion with godlike powers (Captain Atom), the female warrior (Nightshade), the martial artist trained in the mystical wisdom of the East (Thunderbolt), and the street-wise vigilante who conceals his face behind a mask (the Question). Although these characters have been long overshadowed by their more familiar counterparts such as Marvel Comics' patriotic hero Captain America, the technology-powered Iron Man, and the most familiar figures from the universe of DC Comics (Superman, Wonder Woman, and Batman), Moore's revisionist realism endows these archetypes with a density of characterization and a striking array of idiosyncrasies that achieve a novelistic complexity. For example, Rorschach is haunted by his childhood as the bullied son of a prostitute, the vicious and ruthless Comedian loses his triumphal swagger when he discovers a joke at which even he cannot laugh, the humane and scholarly Nite Owl is plagued by self-doubt and a sense of helplessness, and the Silk Spectre finds that leaving behind a career that she had always resented has only led to a different form of imprisonment as the consort of a god. Dr. Manhattan, after becoming publicly exposed as a cancer threat, exiles himself from the world and begins to look back on his achievements and betrayals with regret and sorrow.

Thanks to the interventions of its superhero agents, the United States enjoys a series of untrammeled successes in its struggle against its communist adversaries. The major crises of the Cold War are given outcomes quite different from what took place in real life, working for the most part to the benefit of Richard Nixon and his administration. The Viet Cong are routed by Dr. Manhattan, with a conquered and unified Vietnam becoming the fifty-first state, and the journalists investigating the Watergate scandal are murdered by the Comedian, who also rescues the American hostages from Tehran and helps topple a series of leftist governments in South America. The beginning of the story finds an increasingly frustrated and demoralized Soviet Union protesting U.S. military incursions into Afghanistan. One of the few reversals for an aggressive and triumphant Pentagon mentioned in the course of the narrative is the public exposure of a scheme to unleash lethal diseases upon the population of Africa.[7] Real-world historical personages such as John F. Kennedy, Gerald Ford, Henry Kissinger, Alexander Haig, and G. Gordon Liddy make appearances, sharing jokes with the fictional protagonists, awarding them medals, and weighing the advantages of a nuclear first strike against their Cold War rivals. Richard Nixon himself is able to serve five terms as president, thanks to the victory in Vietnam and to the strategic superiority accorded the United States by the presence of his blue-skinned, divinely powerful operative. Such revisions of real-world history, which are often conveyed by seemingly innocuous and easy-to-overlook subsidiary details, such as a piece of graffiti or the front page of a newspaper (the headlines of which are often partially obstructed by the frame or by some everyday object like a coffee cup), come together to form an astonishingly detailed sociopolitical backdrop for the main storyline.

The narrative itself commences with a mysterious homicide. A man falls to his death after being thrown out of a luxurious high-rise in New York City. The police are dismayed by the clues at the scene: the victim had worked in some diplomatic capacity, and a photograph in his living room shows him standing next to Vice President Ford. Furthermore, the deceased, named Edward Morgan Blake, possessed a robust, well-muscled frame and had to be thrown hard enough against the window to shatter reinforced glass. Fearing the intervention of vigilantes into their investigation, one detective suggests to his partner that they pass the crime off to the public as the work of the drug-addled thugs who terrorize the streets of Manhattan. It is left to the fugitive crime fighter Rorschach to unravel the alter ego of the homicide victim as the Comedian. Masked vigilantes having been made illegal eight years earlier in response to a strike by law enforcement officers, Rorschach's stubborn and relentless effort to punish criminals has made him into an outlaw hunted by the police. The Comedian, on the other hand, was, along with Dr. Manhattan, an exception to the Keene Act, being exempted from mandatory retirement on the basis of his working exclusively for the government. Concluding that the likeliest explanation for the Comedian's death is a conspiracy targeting current and retired costumed adventurers, Rorschach sets out to warn his former teammates from the Minutemen that their lives might be in danger. He visits in turn his former partner Dan Dreiberg, alias the Nite Owl, now a solitary, middle-aged bachelor leading a life of quiet anxiety; Adrian Veidt, alias Ozymandias, a much-admired celebrity philanthropist who retired and revealed his identity before the police riots that forever tainted the costumed vigilante in the eyes of the public; and finally Dr. Manhattan and his lover Laurie Juspeczyk, the former Silk Spectre, who reside on the grounds of a military research center. None of Rorschach's former teammates, knowing him to be both paranoid and jingoistic, are particularly pleased to see him, or inclined to give much credence to his mask-killer hypothesis.

Yet little more than a week later, an assassin makes an attempt on Veidt's life, and, after failing to gun him down, dies from swallowing a cyanide capsule before he can be interrogated. The same night Rorschach himself is led into a trap and captured by the police, who act on information regarding his whereabouts from an anonymous phone call. But most significantly, for its potentially apocalyptic consequences, Dr. Manhattan, during a TV interview, is confronted with evidence that he has given terminal cancer to his friends and associates. Reeling from this public humiliation, the superhuman with annihilating powers quits the earth for a solitary exile on Mars. The departure of the living weapon responsible for American strategic supremacy emboldens the Soviets, who, seeing the opportunity to reverse their setbacks, promptly mount a full-scale invasion of Afghanistan. Shaken by this double blow, Nixon and his advisors begin drawing up plans for a nuclear strike, in the ludicrous hope that a preemptive attack might destroy enough of the Soviet arsenal to spare a few sections of North America from utter destruction.

The rest of the narrative thus unfolds with the world teetering on the brink of nuclear Armageddon. Moore uses secondary characters to convey the atmosphere of collective dread and anxiety that takes hold as events escalate toward a nuclear conflagration. An elderly newspaper vendor provides a running commentary on the standoff as it deteriorates from one day to the next, with reports of tanks massing in Eastern Europe followed by those of Soviet forces crossing over into Pakistan, while detectives Fein and Bourquin, who investigate the Comedian's murder and apprehend Rorschach, brace themselves for a rash of killings driven by an all-devouring despair; they are called in to handle a murder-suicide, in which a father has killed his daughters before taking his own life. Stung by his sense of helplessness in the face of this crisis and conjecturing that the real object of the attacks on costumed heroes was the removal of Dr. Manhattan, perhaps in order to ignite World War Three, Dreiberg decides to defy the law and reassume his costumed identity as the Nite Owl, so as to continue the investigation begun by his former partner. Assisted by the Silk Spectre, he breaks Rorschach out of prison. The two men, acting on the information that every one of the associates of Dr. Manhattan who had fallen ill with cancer was at one time employed by the same company, are able to piece together enough evidence that points to Veidt, a professing pacifist and humanitarian, as the mastermind behind the attempts to murder his fellow masked adventurers and the perilous escalation of geopolitical hostilities.

They confront Ozymandias at his retreat in Antarctica, only to be roundly beaten by the preternaturally agile overman and self-styled disciple of Alexander of Macedon and Ramses II. Having subdued his visitors, Ozymandias matter-of-factly explains to his former teammates his plans for ushering in a new age of peace. Realizing that the unrelenting antagonism of the superpowers would doom them to mutual annihilation, and that a world economy based on the ceaseless production of arms made such a catastrophic outcome increasingly unavoidable while destroying the environment in the process, Ozymandias has arrived at the conclusion that any solution to this dismal impasse would have to be commensurable with the extreme and intractable nature of the problem itself. In the manner of his predecessor, Alexander, who, when confronted with an unsolvable enigma in the Gordian knot, simply cut it with his sword, he would save the earth from nuclear holocaust by means of "history's greatest practical joke," teleporting a genetically engineered monster into New York City, to fool the nations of the world into believing that they are all threatened by the invasion of an alien species. Rorschach reminds Ozymandias of the latter's admission that his corporation had not succeeded in making teleportation a viable means for transporting living bodies across space, to which Ozymandias breezily answers:

> It works *fine,* assuming you want things to *explode* on arrival. Teleported to New York, my creature's death would trigger mechanisms within its massive brain, cloned from a human sensitive ... the resultant shock wave killing half the city (emphases mine). (XII: 26)

Nite Owl cannot bring himself to believe Veidt's story and asks him when his insane scheme was to be set in motion. Moore makes Ozymandias's reply an occasion for self-referential irony—the Machiavellian *Übermensch* states that he is not the clichéd evil genius found in juvenile adventure stories who boasts about his plans just before their execution, giving the heroes the opportunity to save the day at the last minute: "Dan, I'm not a *Republic* serial villain. Do you seriously think I'd explain my masterstroke if there remained the slightest chance of you affecting its outcome? I did it thirty minutes ago..."

UTOPIA PLUS MASSACRE

The panels that follow are remarkable for depicting the horrific carnage unleashed by the materialization of an enormous tentacled creature in midtown Manhattan by means of a strikingly unorthodox layout. On the final page of the narrative's penultimate chapter unfolds a series of six narrow frames, all but one of which show the linked pairs of all the significant noncostumed and fictional (i.e., nonhistorical) secondary characters on a city street at midnight being taken aback by the sudden manifestation of a blinding radiance. On the page's next row six more frames portray an elderly news vendor and a boy being driven into each other's arms as they are overwhelmed by the devouring light (XI: 28). The bottom of the final panel is left fully blank, next to which is a citation of the final lines from Percy Bysshe Shelley's poem, "Ozymandias" ("Look on my works, ye mighty, and despair!"). The concluding chapter begins with seven pages that are each filled by a single large panel—the first is of blood running down a clock, followed by a frame showing two mounds of corpses, a crowd of fans felled in the middle of a violent punk rock concert at Madison Square Garden, the arms of those about to stab or strangle now draped over the bodies of their would-be victims in a permanent gesture of assault (XII: 1). Drawing back from the stadium to the street in a manner that mirrors the movements of a tracking shot in film, a garishly purple tentacle becomes visible above the shattered windows of the stadium (a banner indicates that one of the bands is called "Krystalnacht") and corpses strewn over the street, lying in pools of blood. Three more full-page panels show the dead bodies of the secondary characters—a street peddler selling wristwatches, detectives Fein and Bourquin, a prominent criminal psychologist and his wife, a butch taxi driver and her estranged girlfriend—before framing the still-smoking bodies of the news vendor and the adolescent boy clinging to each other (XII: 3–6). Above them loom the hulking remains of a massive squidlike creature, its single unblinking eye and circular mouth obscenely mimicking the shape of the human clitoris and vagina (XII: 6). Greenish fluid seeps from its tentacles, which puncture the concrete and are impaled on the streetlights, like the grotesque and insatiable tendrils of a weed boring through a gravestone.

Yet what might be most unsettling about this portrayal of mass death is the haunting atmosphere of absence and muteness it creates. There is not a single word or thought bubble in the full-page panels; the reader is confronted by a landscape filled by the objects of human production that have become voided of any living human presence, as inert and detached as the evidence at the scene of a crime. Although pieces of concrete and broken glass litter the streets, the buildings remain intact, as is reckoned to take place after the detonation of a neutron warhead. In the background of the third panel, an airship can be seen having crashed into a building, its tail wings protruding from the damaged edifice like an unexploded bomb. Behind the airship looms a skyscraper, made visible against the night

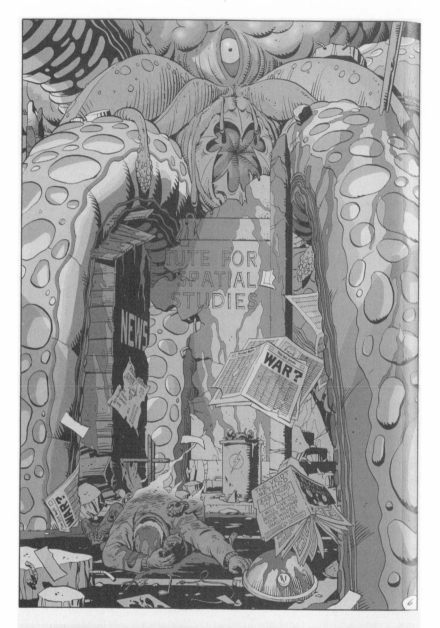

A STRONGER LOVING WORLD

The fake alien, engineered by Ozymandias and teleported into New York, kills half of the city's inhabitants. From *Watchmen;* copyright 1986, 1987 DC Comics; all rights reserved; reprinted with permission.

sky by its lights. The only signs of movement are the reddish smoke that rises in thin streams from the buildings and the water that gushes out of a broken hydrant. Newspapers flutter in the air above the faces recognizable as those of the secondary characters, their alarming single word headline, "War?" now taking on a cruelly mocking resonance.

And yet we are invited to read this extended scene of death and destruction as the signifiers for the near-miraculous founding of a new and peaceful order, a golden age of international cooperation and solidarity, and regard the three million victims as a necessary and unavoidable sacrifice, the price to be paid for rescuing humanity from extinction. Indeed, the costumed heroes who track Ozymandias to his Antarctic lair find themselves trapped by a supremely fiendish version of the pallid dilemmas one finds in undergraduate ethics textbooks: Is it ever right to lie? Should one commit murder if that person's death will result in a cure for lethal diseases? Would you allow an act of injustice to go unpunished if the lives of billions depended on it? As might be expected, Ozymandias's former comrades are brought around without much difficulty into consenting to keep secret the truth behind the slaughter in New York. As Dr. Manhattan, who has teleported back to Earth, concludes, "exposing this plot, we destroy any chance of peace, dooming earth to worse destruction," while the Silk Spectre, after being the first along with her former lover to witness the horrors in the city, rationalizes, "all we did was fail to stop him saving earth" (XII: 20). The only one among them who does not accede to Ozymandias's proposition is Rorschach ("Not in the face of Armageddon. Never compromise"), who is shortly afterward incinerated in the Antarctic snows by Dr. Manhattan before he can set out on the long voyage back to the United States to expose the truth and punish the crime.

This is not to say that the narrative finally endorses, however cautiously, the methods by which Ozymandias coerces the nations of the world to embrace the path of peace or the decision of the other heroes to refrain from pursuing justice or revenge, whether for the murder of one or for the slaughter of millions. Although the closing pages of the graphic novel portray a world still flush with elation and delight at having been delivered from the destructive forces it has itself unleashed, the narrative strikes a final note not of closure or resolution associated with the dawning of a new age of universal peace, but of disconcerting openness. A dull-witted assistant, aptly as well as ironically named Seymour, at a rabidly right-wing magazine is told by the editor to reach into the "crank file" of unsolicited materials to pad out the upcoming issue, their customary rants against the Soviets having become taboo with the onset of an era of international reconciliation. His hand hovers over a stack of correspondence in which Rorschach's journal, documenting the course of the investigation that led him and Nite Owl to Ozymandias, sits quite prominently. Indeed, Veidt's chosen *nom de guerre,* in recalling Shelley's famous poem, unavoidably pronounces the ultimate futility of any human undertaking, the unbending exigency of oblivion that greets conqueror and slave alike across the wastes of time.

Further cracks appear in the artifice of Ozymandias's utopia when he lies to his former teammates about the fate of his Vietnamese servants. Although Nite Owl and Rorschach do not even bring up the subject, Ozymandias assures them that the three men—political refugees from the fifty-first state to whom he had provided asylum—had become drunk and died of exposure after opening the roof of his tropical greenhouse, when in fact Veidt had poisoned them. It is difficult to overlook the incongruity of an overman who orchestrates the murder of millions yet feels the need to lie about the deaths of three individuals, but such an apparently minor discrepancy is suggestive of the moral abyss above which the residents of utopia must levitate if they are to disprove the fact of their survival as a miracle. For the disconcerting sense of open-endedness that closes the narrative arises less from the terrible consequences of the public learning of the truth behind their survival than with the dissolution of truth by survival itself. The vicious dilemma with which Moore closes the narrative—the choice that opposes truth, war, and the annihilation of the Earth on the one side to lies, peace, and the well-being of the world on the other—evokes those severe and insoluble antinomies, associated with Plato but also found in Melville and Dostoevsky, that illuminate by virtue of their uncompromising harshness the inexorable and merciless character of the unwritten laws of the world. In *Watchmen,* as in Melville's *Billy Budd* or Dostoevsky's "Grand Inquisitor," we find no less striking examples of what Hannah Arendt calls "goodness beyond virtue" in Rorschach's unconditional fidelity to his vocation and "wickedness without vice" in the salvation achieved by Ozymandias's act of mass slaughter.[8]

Ozymandias, in comparison to the noticeably "ethnic" features of the wiry and baby-faced Rorschach or the rotund and self-effacing Nite Owl, not to mention the forbidding and unearthly Dr. Manhattan, incarnates the costumed hero as a Homeric or Aryan ideal—he is fair-haired, handsome, charming, and charismatic, a star in his own right who is much admired for his humanitarian work and known for his left-wing politics. It strikes one as almost redundant that the actor who is reputed to be seeking the presidency in the new and peaceful world that Ozymandias has brought into being—Robert Redford—is the celebrity whose good looks and political orientation make him as likely a model as any for the former masked hero himself. Ozymandias's given name, Adrian Veidt, brings into play a very different series of associations, evoking on the one hand the mercurial Roman emperor Hadrian, noted by Edward Gibbon for his equal aptitude for wise leadership and tyrannical excess, and on the other the German film actor Conrad Veidt, whose career was distinguished by his portrayal of such sinister characters as Cesare Borgia, Dr. Jekyll and Mr. Hyde, Ivan the Terrible, and the devil, and whose fearfully grimacing expression in *The Man Who Laughs* served as the inspiration for the Joker, the primary antagonist in the *Batman* comics.[9] It is, furthermore, noteworthy that the role for which Veidt is most famous is that of Cesare, the somnambulist who is hypnotized into carrying out a series of murders in the expressionist film classic *The Cabinet of Dr. Caligari*. The gesture of linking the cunning puppeteer of world history with a mesmerized, blank-faced killer whose consciousness is trapped in a perpetual twilight between sleep and wakefulness adds a further layer of irony to the contrast between Ozymandias, the superhero most admired by the Left, and his counterpart on the Right, the Comedian, the emblem of American militarism and expansionism whose revered status allows him to give free rein to his most vicious desires and brutal impulses.

Whereas the cruel and sneering Comedian is shown taking immense delight in butchering enemy combatants or gunning down his pregnant Vietnamese mistress in a fit of rage after she has slashed his face for trying to abandon her, the violence committed by Ozymandias, with the exception of his murder of the Comedian, is cold and detached, on the order of pressing a button that results in the deaths of millions. Yet, does not the catastrophic upheaval he engineers make actual the left-wing progressivist dream of a peaceful and enlightened sociopolitical order? Doesn't Ozymandias fulfill the paradigm of the successful revolutionary leader, whose unyielding determination to create a new society and to impose a new historical epoch leads him to contemplate and carry out a series of actions from which most other human beings would shrink with horror and revulsion?[10] He is, after all, willing to acknowledge fully the grievous human cost involved in achieving his goal of rescuing human civilization from the devastating consequences of its technological mastery and its insatiable drive for power. It is as though Moore, through his character Ozymandias, says to the liberal sympathizers of progressive revolutionary change, you long for a peaceful and humane political order but remain too tender-hearted to come to grips with the harsh truth that revolution is warfare and entails violence. If such an undertaking is to succeed, it will involve the deaths of innocents. So why not confine the inevitable butchery to a single horrifying event, the incalculably beneficial outcome of which will be the abolition of war? Like the fascist who contends that true patriotism consists of the willingness to commit a crime on behalf of one's country, the sacrifice of one's morality being more arduous than merely giving up one's own life,[11] Ozymandias justifies his humanitarian act through the perverse ethical framework of an unavoidable duty to engage in evil: "someone had to take the weight of that awful, necessary crime" (XII: 27).

Unlike those who dream of a revolutionary transformation of social conditions without taking into view the bloody cataclysms entailed by such a sweeping undertaking, Ozymandias refuses to divorce utopia, as most utopians do, from the terrors of the apocalypse but grants it its proper place within the latter's overarching framework of rejuvenating destruction and shattering deliverance. This authentically harsh political innovator realizes that he cannot entrust the implementation of his program to the automatic improvement of productive forces, nor can he rescue the nations from their destructive entanglements by offering incentives in the form of unalloyed benefits; rather, what is needed is a mixture of overpowering intimidation and inexplicable generosity, a gesture of astonishing cruelty that simultaneously satisfies the deep-seated desires of those whom such an act is intended to terrorize. As in Machiavelli's account of how Cesare Borgia secured the favor and won the stunned gratitude of the inhabitants of Romagna by arranging for the brutal murder of his ruthless and effective lieutenant, Remirro de Orco, once the latter had succeeded in his task of pacifying the anarchic and unruly province, Ozymandias manages at first to "stupefy" his former comrades with the spectacle of the murder of millions and then "appease" them with the prospect of universal peace as the direct consequence of that slaughter.[12]

Ozymandias's plot resembles in its elements the world-historical contrivances of the time-traveling lawgiver and philosopher-king Winston Niles Rumfoord in Kurt Vonnegut's *The Sirens of Titan*. Rumfoord, a Newport, Rhode Island, patrician who has come into possession of the most powerful source of energy in the cosmos, uses it to assemble a deliberately ineffectual and woefully ill-equipped army on Mars to mount an invasion of the Earth. According to Rumfoord's plan, his army, recruited from among the pitiable and the thwarted, lamentable failures in their worldly ambitions, is to be massacred all over the globe by enraged and indignant populations rising up to defend themselves. To their shock and consternation, the peoples of Earth soon discover that they have annihilated a pathetic and poorly armed invasion force, which includes in its ranks sizeable numbers of unarmed women and children who thus never posed any real threat to them. As guilt overtakes the winners of this lopsided war, Rumfoord launches the second phase of his program—to use the killings as the foundation for a new religion to ensure the peace of the world: "Earth's glorious victory over Mars had been a tawdry butchery of virtually unarmed saints, saints who had waged a feeble war on Earth in order to weld the peoples of that planet into a monolithic Brotherhood of Man."[13] As Rumfoord himself puts it in his own chronicle of the war, "Enough of these fizzles of leadership, in which millions die for nothing or less. . . . Let us have, for a change, a magnificently-led few who die for a great deal."[14]

Rumfoord draws on his predictive powers to introduce a religion of universal guilt that roots out the autonomous, self-affirming subject of liberal modernity and puts in its place the self-scourging and self-mortifying subject resembling that of the Middle Ages. In place of selfish individual freedoms and the preoccupation with maximizing one's opportunities for self-gratification, the people in this new golden age are instead intimidated or encouraged into becoming relentlessly absorbed in limiting and thwarting their natural advantages, whether physical, emotional, or intellectual, by "handicapping" themselves. Those who are vigorous and healthy burden their bodies with iron weights and chains, those who are blessed with physical beauty hide their features under thick glasses or masks, while the erudite take into wedlock the determinedly anti-intellectual and those with strong amorous desires pledge lifelong fidelity to their physically unappealing spouses. Humanity becomes unified and consoled under the warmth provided by a universal and collective hair shirt.

The very grotesqueness of Rumfoord's revolutionary order speaks to its greater truth value over the more conventional utopias associated with the progressive political ideologies, not least insofar as it recognizes the inestimable merit of mobilizing hardship for the purposes of securing lasting social harmony. For Rumfoord can be said to take to heart the Hobbesian tenet that felicity consists of "a continual progress of desire, from one object to another," and thus that no political order can endure if it does not arrive at the proper management of human restlessness.[15] If, as E. M. Cioran observes, the yearning for utopia arises out of the calamitous denial of the principle that the "disadvantages of satiety" are "incomparably greater than those of poverty," Rumfoord's utopia remedies human insatiability—and the stagnation that stimulates the craving for the "novelty and spice of disaster," by imposing upon its inhabitants a new (and medieval) way of life that is both strenuous and demanding.[16] By channeling competitive desire, through the mediation of a collective and insurmountable guilt, into an inoffensive asceticism that concentrates its violence upon the self, his new order, more so than the ones dreamt of by tender-hearted or murderous utopians, solves the problem of human happiness, at least for a few centuries. For the competitive nature of handicapping enables Rumfoord to preserve that vital element that the managers of dystopia are always accusing revolutionary collectives of ignoring or repressing—the category of individuality.

Like Rumfoord, Ozymandias calibrates his solution of saving the human race from annihilation according to his recognition of the limits of humanity's moral imagination, as manifested in his endorsement of Hitler's dictum that "people swallow lies easily, provided they're big enough" (XI: 26). Unlike Rumfoord, Ozymandias does not go so far as to introduce a new religion for the sake of safeguarding the decision he coerces humanity into making by repudiating evermore "the darkness in its heart" (XII: 17). If his answer strikes the reader as less stable than that of Rumfoord, it is because, for this invisible conqueror, religion has become incapable of performing its once-salutary function of preventing society from lapsing into a "state of perpetual unrest" or the terrors of a "constant and ubiquitous repression."[17] Rather than yoking the truth to the unceasing and politically salutary consciousness of guilt, Ozymandias dispenses with the truth altogether with respect to his foundational act, calculating that the desire for naked self-preservation, even at the price of one's active and knowing subservience to falsehoods, will trump all other demands. Ozymandias, no less than Rumfoord, might be said to exhibit the paradoxical qualities assigned by Machiavelli to his ideal liberator, insofar as he is the "good man ready to use bad methods,"[18] but the stability and perdurability of Veidt's utopia depends on repeating the wager of Dostoevsky's Grand Inquisitor, who derives his authority from the readiness of the people to forsake their consciences in exchange for their physical and emotional well-being. Indeed, the cruelty that freezes Seymour's hand in mid-gesture over Rorschach's journal in the very last panel of the narrative stems largely from the likelihood that, were the public to be informed that the alien attack was indeed a hoax, they would be as little inclined as the masked heroes in acting on the truth and pursuing the claims of justice. The possibility of retaliatory or punitive violence thus recedes from view because its stakes are nothing short of apocalyptic; yet, the process of erasing the possibility of retaliation or punishment engenders that form of spiritual violence that is inflicted against those already dead—it carries out what Slavoj Žižek calls the "second death," although in this case the expunging of the symbolic identities of the victims of history takes the form of retroactively sacrificing them before the altar of necessity.[19] If the present age is to be enjoyed as a utopia, then the deaths of millions on the slaughterbench of history are merely the unfortunate but obligatory outlay for the purchase of a glorious and inescapable end.[20]

The pointed lack of resolution at the end of the narrative thus portends the inhuman redemption of the saved, a theme Moore explores in a more explicit manner in his graphic novel about the Whitechapel murders, *From Hell*. It tells the story of Sir William Gull, the personal surgeon of Queen Victoria, who methodically hunts down and kills a group of prostitutes who have been seeking to extort money from the crown with their knowledge of a secret marriage between her weak-minded grandson,

Edward Albert Victor, and a shop-girl, with whom he has fathered a child. Gull, who fears that traditional patriarchal authority is losing its grip over the irrational powers of the feminine, performs the killings as the enactment of a Masonic ritual aimed at keeping the black magic that has sustained the age of reason and the unchallenged rule of male deities from leeching away.[21] Standing over the unrecognizably mutilated and partially dismembered corpse of Mary Kelly, his final victim, he is given glimpses of the next century, into the world his legendary crimes are bringing into being. The avatar of the modern serial murderer undergoes a series of hallucinations, in which his surroundings transform around him from the dead woman's impoverished lodgings into the auditorium of a medical college, where he lectures on the properties of the liver, using his victim's body as a demonstration, to an audience that includes the notorious child murderers Ian Brady and Myra Hindley, as well as Peter Sutcliffe, the Yorkshire Ripper. The subsequent vision transports Gull and his victim into the sterile, fluorescent interior of an office building in the present day. Surrounded by computers and copy machines, Gull grows stricken and aghast after taking in the deadened, soulless gazes of the people who manipulate the shining implements of the age of high technology. The legendary slayer of women, driven to despair, rails in dismay and revulsion at the fate of the social order, which he has sacrificed his conscience as well as his sanity to preserve:

> It would seem we are to suffer an apocalypse of cockatoos.... Morose, barbaric children playing joylessly with their unfathomable toys. Where comes this dullness in your eyes? How has your century numbed you so? Shall man be given marvels only when he is beyond all wonder?...
>
> You are the sum of all preceding you, yet seem indifferent to yourselves. A culture grown disinterested, even in its own abysmal wounds. Your women all but show their sexes, and yet this display elicits not a flicker of response. Your own flesh is made meaningless to you. How would I seem to you? Some antique fiend or penny dreadful horror, yet *you* frighten *me*! You have not souls. With you I am alone (emphases in original).[22]

The triumph of scientific rationality has given rise to a world at once sterile and squalid, in which the carnage Gull has taken upon himself to wreak has become reduced to the indifferent triviality of spectacle. The division of day and night, symbolized by the cosmic victory of the god Marduk over the monster Tiamat, has given way to an undifferentiated twilight, in which the blood shed by the stabbings and hackings of a host of petty devils falls resoundingly short of rousing the collective from its hedonistic trance into a new reverence for the law. What alarms Gull, to the point where he tenderly and pathetically takes into his arms the corpse he has been mutilating, is not merely the ungratefulness of a profligate, hedonistic, and self-obsessed age that fails to acknowledge its indebtedness to the crimes and brutalities, not least those of a military and imperialist nature, that have enabled it to come into being, but also the fact that it finds such actions inconceivable in the first place, dismissing them as the pathologies of benighted epochs in the grip of malevolent superstitions.

Yet for Ozymandias, it is this very readiness of the postmodern and posthistorical subject to turn its back to the brutal deeds of the past that furnishes the conditions for his utopia. Such a callous and cold-hearted, though swift and efficient, approach to the construction of an ideal political order can be easily distilled from the philosophy of history conceptualized by Alexandre Kojève in his lectures on Hegel. Kojève, who fully acknowledges that the attainment of the peaceful order of posthistory exacts a harsh moral price, goes quite further than Marx and other ideologists of progress in presenting an account of the conditions that will prevail in human society after the completion of history. Whereas the latter have typically called for sacrificing one's own well-being and interests in the struggle against unjust and oppressive social orders, the apologist for global tyranny deduces that in the final and definitive regime, oppression and coercion will not so much be eliminated as simply cease to be matters of overriding concern to a satisfied and complacent population preoccupied with fulfilling their trivial gratifications. The state of contentedness and satisfaction experienced by posthistorical individuals thus depends on the one hand on their unconstrained enjoyment of abundance and security, which they no longer regard as objects to be achieved through toil and sacrifice, and on the other hand on their being rendered apathetic to the historical accumulation of injustices and grievances, which they reflexively disparage as the relics of a primitive and barbarous past, in accordance with the principle that the "wounds of the Spirit heal, and leave no scars behind."[23] The grievous price of achieving utopia thus ceases to be terrible once *Homo sapiens* reaches the stage at which it feels free to shrug off as unduly burdensome the moral reservations entailed by the sacrifices that have been committed for the sake of advancing the progress of history. If economic productivity and technological advancement solve the problem of human antagonism, it does so by abolishing the category of the human itself, hence Kojève's doctrine of the "annihilation of Man properly so-called" with the attainment of the realm of freedom and the arrival of the concord and unanimity enjoyed by pacified beasts.[24] Peace thus proves merely to be the excrescence of an excessive and slavish attachment to pleasure, which can only be safeguarded with the universal recognition that there are no causes for which it is worth living, let alone fighting.

THE CLANDESTINE PASSIONS OF DEMIURGY

Kojève unapologetically affirms the vital role of terror in bringing about the posthistorical order, on the basis that it is only through exposure to an indiscriminate and leveling form of violent death that equals are able to arrive at the mutual recognition of the other's value.[25] The contrivance whereby Ozymandias terrorizes the world into acting upon its universally endangered status is portrayed in tantalizingly cryptic details throughout the course of the narrative: a prominent painter draws a sketch of a bizarre, genetically engineered creature she believes is going to be used in a science-fiction film; there is a television news story concerning the search for a missing science-fiction writer; the ultra–right wing magazine *New Frontiersman* runs a story about the unexplained disappearances of several notable American artists and scientists, predictably accusing the Cubans of involvement; and, more dramatically, the Comedian breaks into the apartment of a former adversary, where he drunkenly babbles about an unsettling discovery he has made on an island in the Caribbean, a discovery that has driven him to a crushing reassessment of his life and career: "I mean I done some bad things. I did bad things to women. I shot kids! In

Nam, I shot kids . . . but I never did anything like, like. . . . Oh, mother. Oh, forgive me" (II: 23). Although the suspense plot requires that Ozymandias's conspiracy be disclosed only at the very end of the narrative, Moore and Gibbons resort to an ingenious metafictional technique to relate the overwhelming and inhuman horror associated with Veidt's plan to sacrifice the lives of the millions to avert the destruction of the entire world. Commencing in chapter III, they intersperse among the panels unfolding the main thread of the narrative the actual content of the comic books being read by one of the secondary characters, a young African American boy who spends his afternoons sitting beside a newsstand run by an elderly Jewish widower. The comic book within the comic is published under the title *Tales of the Black Freighter* and features a harrowing narrative of inexorable determination and miscarried revenge. Its author is the missing science-fiction writer Max Shea, who later turns up on Veidt's private island as one of the group of leading artists and scientists hired to work on the production of a top-secret, big budget "monster movie."

The narrative in the *Black Freighter* comic, told entirely from the first-person perspective in the form of an interior monologue, begins with its hero marooned on a deserted island, the sole survivor of an attack by the brigands manning the eponymous ship, reputed to be a vessel from the depths of hell itself. Agonized by the prospect of the infernal ship sacking his home port of Davidstown, and tormented by visions of his wife and children being hacked to death by its demonic crew, he resorts to the desperate measure of digging up the gas-distended bodies of his murdered fellow sailors to provide flotation for a makeshift raft. Setting out over the sea at nightfall, he undergoes a series of horrific tribulations, which his unshakable determination to reach his hometown at all costs enables him to overcome. But each success only plunges him more deeply into the inferno of his own revulsion. Crazed by hunger, he manages to seize with his bare hands one of the many seagulls that have been drawn to his craft by the human carrion lashed to its bottom. Shortly afterward, he vomits over the side of his craft after becoming sickened by the awareness of what he has eaten, and shrinks back in horror from the reflection of his deranged eyes and blood-caked face on the water. Assailed by sharks, which tear away at the bodies of his comrades, the protagonist drives the edge of a broken mast through the eye of the largest of their number, which has become entangled in his ropes. This massive beast, driven wild with pain, attempts to speed away from the craft, but instead drags it along in its wake until it at last dies. The sailor takes grim note of the irony in the reversal of the roles of predator and prey as he rends and eats the flesh of the creature, which has in the meantime brought him into calmer waters. Having lost his sail, he drifts over the murky depths, his mind consumed by images of his dead shipmates being gradually eaten away by fish and of his beloved family being butchered by the buccaneers who are certain to have laid waste already to Davidstown. After a long and listless spell during which he clasps the arm of one of his murdered comrades while bemoaning the wretchedness and futility of human life, he leaps into the abyss, but then is bewildered by what he takes to be a malicious miracle when the waters refuse to bear him down to his death: "What new torture was this? I stood upon the calm sea, a charnel messiah unable to sink beneath it to the oblivion I craved. . . . I lifted my uncomprehending eyes to the heavens . . . and saw instead the earth" (VIII: 26).

Believing the town to have been sacked by the freebooters in the service of the devil's ship, the sailor determines that the only course for him— the reason he survived not only the brutal attack that spared none of his companions but also the unthinkably perilous and harrowing journey back to Davidstown—is to avenge himself upon the fiends who have robbed him of all that he cherishes in life. Spying the town's moneylender riding on the beach with a female companion, he concludes that the wealthy man's survival marks him as a collaborator of the pirates, and so crushes his head with a rock, before strangling the woman. He dresses himself in the dead man's clothes and rides into town under the cover of darkness. Stealing into his own house, he assaults a figure he glimpses walking in the hallway, taking him to be a guard. A horror that exceeds even the grue-some ordeals he has already endured soon wells up as he recognizes the person he has knocked to the ground as his wife, who fearfully calls out his name. Aghast at the welling up of an "understanding so large" that it leaves "no room for sanity," the sailor flees back to the beach, pursued by a lynch mob that has gathered after discovering one of the murdered bodies (XI: 6). In the distance he recognizes the black freighter approaching the shoreline, and the realization dawns on him, as he swims out to the ship of the damned, that the everlasting servitude of his soul, and not the ephemeral riches of the town, had been the objective of the demonic crew all along. The single-mindedness of his drive to save his loved ones has paradoxically triggered the chain of events that, in effect, severs their lives irrevocably from his own: "The world I'd tried to save was lost beyond recall. I was a horror: amongst horrors must I dwell" (XI: 23).

The grisly tale of a man who, in seeking to avenge himself upon a group of devils, becomes thereby initiated into their company, serves as an example of the terrible irony whereby the ruthless actions and shocking cruelties committed on behalf of a good and noble cause work mischievously to wring from that cause its meaning and justification. The comic book within the comic is thus revealed in the end to be a proleptic correlative, ending as it does a mere four pages before Ozymandias explains the details of his scheme, to the inward struggles, the deliberations and nightmares, that a man or woman with the capacity to act on the world-historical stage might undergo while settling on a disquieting and revolutionary course of action. For it is precisely this dimension of inner turmoil and agony that is absent from Moore and Gibbons's portrayal of Ozymandias, who unveils his genocidal solution for putting an end to geopolitical conflict only after he has teleported his beast into New York City. Indeed, the first glimpse we are given of his inner life comes in the narrative's penultimate chapter, when he reminisces to his servants, whom he has just poisoned, about his youthful travels to Egypt and the lands conquered by Alexander the Great. Thus, the devouring fury and frenzied agony of the solitary mariner comes to serve as the zealous, feverish counterpoint to Ozymandias's imperturbable reserve, the impassioned and deeply human inversion of the world-historical puppeteer who calculates without prejudice and without compunction the source and nature of the threat of annihilation and coldly devises its inhuman remedy. The inverted symmetry between the avenging sailor and the Nietzschean superhero is established in the visuals by the images of the two standing in the same pose, but viewed from opposite directions—the vengeance-crazed mariner walks toward the land with the sun setting behind him, while the young Adrian Veidt wades into the sea in the direction of the rising sun. The sailor tenses his arms when it dawns on him that he is actually standing on a beach and not sinking into the depths as he had expected. Conversely, Veidt holds his arms in a similar gesture, but seen again from the back, as he casts aside his clothes under a starlit sky while drifting into a hashish-induced reverie that purportedly awakens him to the secrets of the Pharaohs.

Apropos of the controversial reputation and enigmatic ambitions of his former teacher, Alexandre Kojève, whose lectures on Hegel were attended by the leading thinkers in France, Stanley Rosen makes the following observation: "If a proper definition of a god is one who creates a world, then Kojève's intentions were divine."[26] The divinity to which Kojève laid claim, according to Rosen, arises from his determination to unify theory and practice, whether as the sage who brings to completion what can be considered to be characteristically human speech, leaving nothing more to say, or in his service as a high-ranking official in the ministry of foreign economic affairs and as the trusted advisor of French presidents de Gaulle and Giscard d'Estaing in implementing the aforementioned dialectico-speculative truth concerning the historical process. The work of actualizing philosophy and transforming thereby the established sociopolitical order is the labor of a demiurge, who is best exemplified in Kojève's account by the figure of the universal tyrant, such as Napoleon or Stalin. In *Watchmen*, the demiurgic prestidigitations of its armed lawgiver are not only dissected by the allegory of the deranged sailor but also paralleled by the exhaustive level of detail with which the authors depict their alternate world.

For Moore and Gibbons mirror the demiurgic scale of Ozymandias's aspirations by the exhaustive completeness with which their creation emerges. There is a startling myriad of small details that signify the separation of the universe of *Watchmen* from the real world: cigarettes are smoked through spherical glass pipes; chickens have been genetically modified so as to possess two extra legs in place of their wings; Heinz food products have 58, not 57, varieties; the New York *Gazette*, not the *Times* or the *Post*, is the city's most popular newspaper; airships fill the skies above Manhattan; automobiles run on electricity, thanks to the ability of Dr. Manhattan to synthesize lithium in mass quantities; tandoori is more common as fast food than hamburgers; lesbians are referred to as "gay women"; those in same-sex relationships casually express affection for each other in public places; Nazi emblems are pervasive in youth culture, especially among rock bands; the practice of tying one's hair into a knot resembling that of the medieval samurai has become fashionable among both sexes; the most popular drug on the street is a fictitious stimulant known as KT-28, with its users being called "katies" or "katieheads"; it is fashionable for men to wear helmets, manufactured by the Veidt corporation, with ventilation holes or radio transmitters on the sides (the narrative does not specify which); Veidt is also a popular maker of athletic shoes, marked by the distinctive "V" logo. Such inconspicuous minutiae, being easy to miss during a cursory first reading, derail in effect the rapid and oblivious scanning of the panels that focuses on the suspense plot into a paranoid immersion in each individual frame for the sake of detecting some askew element.[27]

The drive of the authors of *Watchmen* to create a stunningly complete alternate world leads them to go beyond merely referencing these frequently indiscernible details to reproduce between the chapters of the graphic novel a heterogeneous array of texts and documents, such as pages from fictitious books and magazines, psychiatric reports, and business letters. There are excerpts from a memoir written by a retired costumed adventurer, the contents of a prison psychiatrist's file on Walter Joseph Kovacs (the alter ego of Rorschach), a panegyric to the marvels of owls penned by Daniel Dreiberg (alias Nite Owl) for the fall 1983 issue of the *Journal of The American Ornithological Society*, the introduction to an academic study of the impact of Dr. Manhattan on the arms race between the superpowers, unfinished layouts from an upcoming issue of *The New Frontiersman* (complete with an editorial cartoon featuring racist and anti-Semitic caricatures as well as an amusingly discerning article lambasting the authorities for their lack of action in investigating the rash of disappearances of prominent American artists and scientists), a fawning celebrity profile of Ozymandias published in the leading leftist magazine *Nova Express*, and most astonishingly, a series of memos and ad copy from the Veidt Corporation, one of which details the phasing out of a popular line of fragrances marketed for a "time of stress and anxiety" when the "natural response is to retreat and withdraw from reality," and the impending roll-out of a new product that will be promoted by a marketing strategy "projecting a vision of a technological utopia" (X: iii).

What this letter neglects to mention, of course, is the imminent attack on New York City, while showing that Veidt's preparations for ushering in an age of global peace have not led him to neglect his financial interests, as he positions his companies to make a killing, in a more figurative sense, from the momentous historical shift that he is about to engineer. *Watchmen*, furthermore, deftly registers the displacements and repercussions of its revisions of real world history, giving rise to forking paths that twist into satirical inversions of their real-life correlatives. Thus, the "cowboy actor" who runs for president in the 1980s is not Ronald Reagan but Robert Redford. It is the Soviet Union, not the United States, that appeals to the international community to protest foreign adventurism in Afghanistan. The quote from the *Satires* of Juvenal, "who watches the watchmen," which in the comic is linked to the legislation outlawing vigilantism, will in our world come to be cited by the Tower Commission Report, which investigated the Iran-Contra scandal and published its findings in 1987, the year the entire series was completed.[28] Even the fact that the stories of pirates have become the narrative staple for comic books is the result of its masked superheroes having exited, as it were, from the pages of illustrated fantasy adventure tales to live and act in the world of reality.

Yet the cumulative effect of the astonishing level of attention with which Moore and Gibbons bring their world into being is a palpable sense of suffocation, in that the world of *Watchmen* ultimately takes shape in the form of a totality that has become wholly closed in upon itself. Its profusion of discourses and plural registers of meaning serve only to reinforce and bind ever more tightly the fabric of an unassailable and immutable reality, in which is ruled out any form of change other than an abrupt and global transformation of the very conditions of existence, such as would take place with the extinction of *Homo sapiens*. Accordingly, the remark by Dr. Manhattan that "nothing ever ends" may not so much be taken as words of consolation and fellow feeling than as a neutral observation of nonhuman fact, attesting, perhaps, to the vitality and dynamism of subatomic particles. Moore and Gibbons evoke the constricting nature of this mortified reality by means of the repetition of certain key motifs, to such an excessive degree that the proliferation of these images overflows into an unforgiving necessity beyond the materiality of chance. Indeed, the comic frequently mimics the cinematic technique in which the spoken reference to an object is paired with a visual that, while not identical to the referent, nonetheless relates to it in some way, usually signaling the viewer to convert the object into a metaphor or synecdoche. What is striking about

Moore and Gibbons's use of this rudimentary and hackneyed method for constructing meaning out of the juxtaposition of word and image is not the fact that they deploy it for the sake of parody, although the instances in which it appears are frequently humorous. Neither can they be said to be preoccupied with demystifying the inadequacies of symbolic interpretation in the face of the irreducible ambiguities of the sign. Rather, they move in a direction deliberately contrary to the complexities attributed by deconstructionist linguistics to the material signifier, that is to say, towards a blunt and brutal reductiveness. Thus, when Laurie Juspeczyk, alias the Silk Spectre, confides to Dan Dreiberg her reasons for leaving her lover, Dr. Manhattan, having become increasingly disconcerted by what she senses as his unearthly sense of detachment from human cares, she makes mention of how "the real world, to him it's like walking through mist, and all the people are like shadows...just shadows in the fog" (III: 9). In the panel that contains the dialogue bubble with the reference to "fog," steam is shown rising up from a kettle, obscuring her face.

The otherwise quotidian gestures of Dan handing her a mug of coffee and of Laurie staring at her reflection in the drink are repeated later in the narrative with gestures drawn in a nearly identical fashion—Dr. Manhattan's first lover, Janey Slater, offers him a glass of beer upon making his acquaintance, and the eyes of Laurie, as a young girl, appear reflected on a snow-globe during a reminiscence of a childhood trauma. The frame in which the famished mariner tears the flesh from the seagull that he has caught with his bare hands is followed by the image of Dan chewing on a chicken drumstick in a pose that nearly duplicates that of the avenging sailor, with an equivalent amount of flesh torn from the bone. Similarly, the most conspicuous motif in the work, the smiley-face button with a drop of blood splashed across its left eye, an image that appears on the cover of most editions, recurs throughout the narrative in a variety of distinct situations. The smiley-face button being the trademark of the Comedian, the particular image in question is shown on the very first page of the work, sitting on the sidewalk in a pool of the slain superhero's blood, after he has been hurled through the window of his high-rise apartment. The image of the smiley-face reappears to provide a humorous and alarming form of closure on the last page of the work, where it is shown on the t-shirt of the assistant at the *New Frontiersman,* who is taking a lunch break. Ketchup drips from his hamburger to cover the left eye of the smiley-face, in the exact spot marked on the Comedian's button by his blood. A smiley-face also appears on the landscape of Mars, over the left "eye" of which the ruins of the giant clocklike structure created by Dr. Manhattan comes to rest. The fact that Moore and Gibbons choose to depict Dr. Manhattan proclaiming to Laurie his change of heart over leaving the world to its fate while standing inside a crater shaped like a smiley-face icon provides, at the very least, a partial refutation of his affirmation of life on earth as the outcome of a wondrous and miraculous chain of accidents. When Ozymandias heaves the Comedian up over his head to throw him out the window, the area around his left eye is shown covered with his victim's blood forming the same telltale splash mark. Indeed, even in a scene in which the Comedian is shown alive, in this case gleefully engaged in slaughtering a group of Vietnamese with a flame-thrower, the sweat from his face can be seen dripping right onto the icon's left eye, over the exact spot that will be stained by his own vital fluids.

Such instances of repetition compel the reader to suspect that almost every frame has its double or inversion elsewhere in the text, and thus that the events unfold in the narrative in accordance with inescapable and pre-destined laws, in spite of the radical and possibly annihilating openness in its final page that suspends the fate of the world. The reader is led thereby from the infernal gratitude and interpassive enjoyment secured for the people of the world by Ozymandias's necessary act of genocide to the par-adoxical and mechanistic disappointments experienced by the omniscient Dr. Manhattan. He tells Laurie that her attempt to persuade him to inter-vene to save the earth from destruction will begin with her informing him that she and Dan Dreiberg have slept together, but then the blue superhuman expresses shock and dismay when she confesses to him the facts that he has just stated. "We're all puppets, Laurie," Dr. Manhattan tells his estranged lover, "I'm just a puppet who can see the strings" (IX: 5). To see the "strings" in the act of rereading *Watchmen* is to become aware of how the predestined character of its closing massacre is sustained by a network of relations that operates as kind of a lethal algebra whereby every equation must work out to zero, leaving no arbitrary or surplus remnant

in its mortuary closure, just as Ozymandias contrives to have the agents involved in his conspiracy killed by other agents, who in turn are liquidated
by still others, until all have gone to their graves, strangled by the ropes of
their partial knowledge.

Moore and Gibbons, furthermore, often place the word and thought
captions relating to different levels of the narrative within the same frame,
so that the content of a certain enunciation reflects directly on an action
or conversation taking place somewhere else, at some other time, or, in the
case of the pirate comic, in an altogether different order of reality. The captions from the pirate comic are made to present a sharply ironic counterpoint to the events in the main narrative, and vice versa. Among the myriad
instances of such a play of reflections is an early juxtaposition of the pirate
story with a monologue by the newsvendor in which he endearingly and
boastfully praises his profession, a juxtaposition that generates a kind of
hermeneutic for the activity of reading the narrative itself:

Frame 2
Bernard: Lissen, I see every goddamn front page inna world. I absorb
information! I miss nothing.

Mariner: Bosun Ridley lay nearby. Birds were eating his thoughts and
memories.

Frame 4
Bernard: See, everything's connected. A newsvendor unnerstands that.
He don't retreat from reality.

Mariner: For my part, I begged that [the gulls] should take my eyes,
thus sparing me further horrors.

Frame 5
Mariner: Unheeded, I stood in the surf and wept, unable to bear my
circumstances!

Bernard: The weight o'the world's on him, but does he quit? Nah!
He's like Atlas! He can take it! (III: 2)

The fate of total knowledge is to provide nourishment for oblivious scavengers; the revelation of the interconnected nature of reality ignites only

the overriding yearning for blindness; the intolerable anguish crushing the marooned sailor leads him to throw off the weight of the world, but his transcendent defiance of nature only opens the portal to a predestined hell. Nevertheless, the disparity between the gruesome spectacle of the bodies of the mariner's shipmates being eaten by seagulls and the everyday representations of catastrophe that "sell the papers" initially strikes a ghoulishly humorous note, since the narrative at this point still sustains the divergence between the world of "fantasy," which finds its protagonist thrown into a nightmarish scene of horror and carnage, and the stable order of "reality" in which the experience of disaster is relegated to the passive activity of reading about events taking place in distant parts of the globe. But as these two realities draw increasingly close to each other as tensions worsen between the superpowers, the pirate comic portrays the mariner throwing himself into a series of horrific and dehumanizing actions in undertaking the improbably hazardous journey across the waters back to his hometown. The newsvendor, meanwhile, is straightaway divested of his composure and self-possession by an unexpected tap on the back from Rorschach, who appears in the daylight hours as a grim-faced religious fanatic holding a sign proclaiming that the end of the world is near.

Whereas the victimized and tormented mariner, after his prayers for oblivion go unanswered, hurls himself into the reality that has taken root from his fears, Bernard grows increasingly unnerved by events beyond his control, casting about in the moments before Ozymandias's "alien attack" between voicing moral outrage over the prospect of mutually assured annihilation and taking refuge in the desperate hope that a preemptive strike will save the country from destruction: "Morally, we oughtta strike first. We gotta protect our women and kids, even if theirs die. That's morally logical" (XI: 13). Bernard's claim to understand the interconnected nature of all events and his determination to face reality blind him to the fact that these connections have marked his newsstand as the ground zero of the world's salvation, the nexus to which the monstrous creature will be teleported. Indeed, a young woman with a swastika tattooed on her arm, high on KT-28s, grabs the lapel of his coat and raves incoherently about a "terrible noise" followed by a "shockwave" (VIII: 25). One might say therefore that the mariner moves too swiftly to confront his most terrible fear, rushing right past it into the maw of a nightmare worse than any he had anticipated, whereas the newsvendor, like most human beings, ends by waiting—at one moment pathetically appealing to justice and in the next grimly and ruthlessly writing it off—for a terrible fate to materialize around him.

THE ETHICS OF STRIKING SECOND

The dialogue between newsvendor and the mariner thus unfolds as a series of missed encounters that culminates in the outcome of death or death-in-life, and thus corresponds to the division between those who are sacrificed and those who condemn themselves to survival in the kingdom of darkness. Bernard's endorsement of the principle of "striking first," on the other hand, brings to light a fundamental distinction among the masked heroes themselves, which is manifested most vividly between Ozymandias and Rorschach. If Ozymandias is the world-historical individual who, in realizing the enormity of the dangers facing humanity, "strikes first" by imposing an audacious and repugnant measure of his own design upon the unsuspecting world to spare it from destruction, Rorschach, the ruthless and uncompromising vigilante who terrorizes the criminal underworld of New York, can be said to hold fast to the masked hero's code of punitive violence. After all, does not justice meted out by the superheroes constitute a practice of violence legitimated by its essentially reactive and belated character, as a form of always "striking second," after the first, lawless blow has been dealt? Ozymandias himself declares his impatience with the quixotic and ultimately ineffectual attempt to rectify a world thrown incessantly out of balance by the forces of disorder, deriding the vocation of the masked hero as futile for confronting only the symptoms of social ills. Like a proper liberal, he gives up his crime-fighting career in order to take care of the root causes of the evils afflicting mankind. Yet, while Ozymandias can remedy man's inhumanity to man only through a supremely inhuman act that, needless to say, violates irrevocably the singularity of his victims, reducing them to the condition of a mere means to an end, Rorschach's fanatical commitment to the practice of vigilantism as well as his pitiless embrace of violence, on the other hand, reveal an unexpectedly moral dimension in the form of a grimly stoic attachment to particular individuals and their suffering.

For it emerges during the interviews conducted by the prison psychiatrist, Malcolm Long, that an exceedingly horrific experience of human depravity had made Rorschach into who he is, that is to say, subjectivized him as the fearsome and ruthless masked vigilante who kills criminals outright instead of handing them over to the police, and who speaks contemptuously of his alter ego Walter Joseph Kovacs in the third person and in the past tense, as though he were referring to a foolish subordinate cashiered for his incompetence and naïveté. After giving a series of "fake" responses to the Rorschach cards that Dr. Long holds up for him (responding with "a pretty butterfly" and "some nice flowers" instead of "a dog with its head split open" and "my mother having rough sex with a strange man"), Rorschach finally decides to speak openly out of outrage, rebuking the psychiatrist for concentrating on his case, that of the American prison system's most famous psychopath, solely out of the desire to acquire wealth and fame (VI: 1, 5). He refers to a kidnapping case, ten years past, in which a six-year old girl from a working class family had been mistaken for the heiress to a pharmaceutical fortune. "Thought of little child, abused, frightened. Didn't like it. Personal reasons," he tells the doctor, who has in his briefcase files suggesting the awful history of maltreatment that Rorschach himself has endured as the son of a prostitute (VI: 18). Promising her parents to return the girl safely, Rorschach proceeds to beat and interrogate those suspected of underworld activity for information, eventually receiving the address to an abandoned dressmaker's shop in a rundown neighborhood of Brooklyn.

The upsetting sequence that follows is composed of twenty-five wordless frames, in which Rorschach enters and searches the filthy and squalid shop. Making his way past the clutter of unused mannequins and papers littering the floor, he discovers a child's purse inside a furnace, and then walks into the kitchen, where he opens a cabinet filled with knives, a cleaver, and a small saw. Removing the cleaver and the saw, he runs his fingers along the grooves cut into a chopping block, and then peers outside the window to see two German shepherds fighting over a bone. The close-up of their jaws locked over a bone is followed by a panel bathed in red, showing a stunned Rorschach lowering his hand, while the force of the horror-struck recognition jolts the ink blot pattern on his mask into a new shape. Rorschach proceeds to split open the skulls of the dogs with the cleaver, creating the carnage of blood and bone that resembles the pattern on one of Long's cards. Once the kidnapper returns, he overpowers the child murderer and handcuffs him to the leg of the furnace. The abductor's panicked pleas break the silence, but Rorschach maliciously hands him a saw before pouring kerosene over the floor and dropping a lighted match. Walking out into the street, he stands in front of the building to watch it burn and to savor the screams of his prey. No longer was he Kovacs, who presumably understood crime fighting as an endeavor to make the world more orderly and just; he had instead become something that he could not altogether comprehend prior to his transformation: a solitary avenger struggling against impossible odds, against an unredeemable and hopelessly degenerate world sinking irresistibly into the abyss. The monologue in which he relates the event of his symbolic death and rebirth displays overtones that are both stoic and demonic, framing a vocation that is as nihilistic in its groundlessness as it is binding and unconditional as an obligation:

> Stood in firelight, sweltering bloodstain on chest like map of violent new continent. Felt cleansed. Felt dark planet turn under my feet.... Looked at sky through smoke heavy with human fat and God was not there. The cold, suffocating dark goes on forever, and we are alone.... Born from oblivion; bear children, hell-bound as ourselves; go into oblivion. There is nothing else. Existence is random. Has no pattern save what we imagine after staring at it too long. No meaning save what we choose to impose. This rudderless world is not shaped by vague metaphysical forces. It is not God who kills the children. Not fate that butchers them or destiny that feeds them to the dogs. It's us. Only us. Streets stank of fire. The void breathed hard on my heart, turning its illusions to ice, shattering them. Was reborn then, free to scrawl own design on this morally blank world. Was Rorschach. (VI: 26)

Rorschach's speech articulates in grim and forbidding terms a typically existential acknowledgement of the meaninglessness of human existence, but the stress here falls less upon the absurd nature of the cosmos than in a world senselessly ravaged by cruelty. Rorschach associates being existentially uprooted with the liberty to impose his own meaning on the contingent shadow play of the world, a freedom he defines in the form of an unconditional duty. This duty is to be followed all the more rigorously and uncompromisingly for the very reason that it lacks any kind of external prop or crutch, be it political, historical, or metaphysical. Rorschach thus exhibits the qualities that Alain Badiou and Slavoj Žižek attribute to the properly militant subject, in that his redoubtable fidelity to the event that subjectivizes him results in an "excremental identification."[29] For he fully assumes the consequences of his unconditional commitment to the law, which is to make himself into a wanted criminal, and dedicates his life to a strenuous definition of solidarity with the victims of the cruelty arising wholly from human design—the ruthless and unrelenting punishment of those who prey on them. Anything else is fatuous and false-hearted sentimentality, as he tells Dr. Long: "I don't like you. . . . Fat. Wealthy. Think you understand pain" (VI: 9). Of course, the only factors that would prevent Rorschach from embodying fully the ideal of militancy extolled by Badiou and Žižek are his extreme right-wing political convictions, his hatred of the Soviet Union and the American Left, and his homophobia, though unlike the older heroes Hooded Justice, who was a sympathizer of Nazi Germany and the Ku Klux Klan, and Captain Metropolis, who was known for making inflammatory statements against blacks and Latinos, Rorschach appears notably free of any kind of racial prejudice.

Rorschach's death at the hands of Dr. Manhattan in the novel's concluding pages would appear to be an act of martyrdom to his singular devotion to punishing crime, the wholly logical outcome to his irrational, unswerving adherence to the principle of "striking second." Nevertheless, after Nite Owl and the Silk Spectre break him out of prison, the repressed side of Rorschach's character begins to manifest itself in brief moments of compassion and empathy. When a hired assassin, fearing that he himself has been marked for murder, begs Rorschach for protection, the misanthropic vigilante coldly remarks that he should not take his imminent murder personally. On the other hand, Rorschach relents from enacting his merciless justice against his landlady, who has lied to the media about her notorious tenant making sexual advances toward her, when he glimpses the terrified face of her young son (X: 6). It is perhaps the only panel in which the expression on Rorschach's face is something other than the dull, blank expression of benumbed indifference or the stare of murderous fury in which his eyes widen feverishly as though to make himself confront with full force the viciousness and depravity of human life—Rorschach instead regards with an almost gentle look the tearful child clinging to his mother, seeking refuge in an affection that had always been denied to the masked hero by his own mother. Rorschach also begins to speak in longer sentences, rather than his usual clipped style of speaking, and even greets the Silk Spectre, who makes no effort to conceal her loathing and revulsion towards him, in a halfway civil manner.[30] Such changes in his personality and conduct, though ostensibly nothing on the order of the experience of death and rebirth that made him into Rorschach, nevertheless put into question the extent to which he can ultimately be judged a "violent psychopath whose refusal to compromise leads to his downfall."[31] Indeed, his decision to break with his code and treat his landlady with mercy contrasts strikingly with the lie that Ozymandias tells to cover up the murder of his servants—the liberal humanitarian superman cannot bring himself to acknowledge the selfhood of others, especially those who have dedicated their lives to serving him.

For these manifestations of compassion and courtesy, however small, indicate that his rejection of compromise and his acceptance of obliteration might have to do with something other than a fanatic's inflexibility that leads him to accept Armageddon as a fair price for the truth. Although Rorschach's refusal displays its sublime character in its status as perhaps the last free act, or the only free act possible in the utopian order that Ozymandias's deceit brings into being—that is to say, free insofar as it brings about the immediate death of the subject—one is led to consider whether Rorschach acted while fully expecting Dr. Manhattan, or one of the others, to intervene to stop him from returning to the United States. In other words, Rorschach, under guise of continuing his crusade to punish evil, is actually choosing death, implicitly relying on one of his former comrades to liquidate him before he can embark on the return journey home. What would his reasons be for choosing not to live in a world in which mankind would have experienced the "dazzling transformation" inaugurated by Veidt's genocidal hoax? Ozymandias's ruse, after all, proposes to do away with the struggle between nations, not everyday urban crime, presumably leaving Rorschach and others with enough work to keep themselves occupied in the new utopian order. Indeed, Nite Owl and the Silk Spectre do just that, taking on new civilian identities in order to continue their careers as masked crime fighters in a world without war.

It is instructive on this score to compare Rorschach's obstinacy with the way in which the Comedian responds to the discovery of Ozymandias's conspiracy, which, as Veidt puts it, "drove the wind from his sails" (XI: 25). Blake, upon realizing the terrible nature and daunting scale of the plan, sinks into a demoralized torpor. For the Comedian has always reveled and taken immense pride in his readiness to face up to the ugly truths of human existence—the truths that the great mass of the pacified and spineless instinctively repudiate and contemptibly repress to assuage their consciences and shore up their sanity. As Dr. Manhattan observes of his fellow superhero comrade in Vietnam, Blake is the one of the few human beings "willing to permit himself" the full understanding of what the "madness" and "pointless butchery" of the killing fields of Southeast Asia "implies about the human condition" (IV: 19). The Comedian thus fully accepts the destructive terms entailed by recognizing human life as a sordid joke, up to embracing universal annihilation as the logical and unavoidable consequence of his absolute freedom to inflict violence on behalf of the state, that is to say, as the necessary price for the unbounded pleasure he takes in butchering its enemies. Nevertheless, it should be added that the depth and subtlety of Moore's characterization capture the magnetism exerted by the ruthless icons of the extreme Right, arising from their ability to cast off normal human inhibitions as a matter of routine. When confronted by the infuriated Silk Spectre, who has learned of his attempted rape of her mother, he asks, coolly but not without a twinge of pained sympathy— for she really is his daughter but does not know it—"Kid, are you sure you want to take this all the way?" (IX: 21).

Blake, however, finds his brutal candor deflated when he unravels the details of Veidt's plot. The joke he trusted as being irrefutable has become exposed in all its ignominy, leaving him with only a pathetic supplication ("Oh, mother. Oh, forgive me") in place of his usual laughter (II: 23). Having always gotten the better of his adversaries, Blake becomes paralyzed when he realizes that the apocalypse is no longer a safely and abstractly inevitable punch line delivered by remote, impersonal, and irresistible agencies, which in turn are propelled by the unconstrained pursuit of geopolitical power or the insatiability of human desire once it is magnified to annihilating dimensions by modern technology. Having enjoyed inflicting more than his share of demonic brutalities, he finds himself shrinking

Ozymandias is shocked into his mission by the Comedian. From *Watchmen;*
copyright 1986, 1987 DC Comics; all rights reserved; reprinted with permission.

from taking the logical and catastrophic step to become the devil of the final destruction. In other words, the Comedian balks at taking upon himself the "awful weight" of authorship for the very joke that has licensed and underwritten his career as a sadistic government operative.

The fact that he trembles and quails in the face of this demonically unsurpassable role reveals Blake as typifying the figure of the pervert, who, as Žižek observes, takes pleasure in making himself into an instrument of the Law and the obscene enjoyment he ascribes to it.[32] In choosing to wait restively for his executioner to secure his everlasting silence, on the other hand, the Comedian serves to illustrate the Machiavellian thesis that human beings, including the most ambitious and egotistical, tend to shun audacious courses of action, even when the effort is small and immortal glory is the all-but-assured outcome.[33] Hence the "professional jealousy" that Ozymandias claims the Comedian felt toward him and his scheme arises from Blake's bitter realization that he, like the common run of human beings he scorns and despises as hypocritical and cowardly, does not in the end know how to be "magnificently bad or perfectly good" (XI: 24).[34] The Comedian learns, too late, that he would rather be murdered as a petty nihilist than dare to overtake Ozymandias in the race to become a god.

Although the Comedian and Rorschach are shown interacting with each other only on one single occasion throughout the entire novel, when the Comedian cuts him off at an abortive gathering of costumed heroes to address the new "evils" afflicting American society in the 1960s (such as "black unrest," "anti-war demos," "promiscuity," and "drugs") with the disdainful interjection that fighting crime will not in the end have any impact because the world will all go up in smoke any way, the overarching themes of the narrative work to highlight their affinities.[35] They are, after all, the two vigilantes who most candidly accept the fascistic violence entailed by their vocation, making no apologies for the harsh, coercive measures they regard as necessary for battling chaos on the streets and combating the nation's enemies across the globe. The narrative moreover links them numerically, in that the number of years Blake spent in his career as the Comedian, forty-five, is equal to Rorschach's age at the time of his death. Nevertheless, their dissimilarities and misunderstandings more crucially define the two. For while Rorschach is a zealous admirer of the Comedian, eulogizing him as a patriot of uncompromising integrity who "understood man's capacity for horrors and never quit," the one remark that the Comedian makes regarding Rorschach is to dismiss him as a nutcase typical of the profession (VI: 15 and II: 18).[36] Rorschach is clearly a loner who inhabits the margins of society and trawls along its squalid bottom of urban misery and degradation; the Comedian, by contrast, is honored by the Nixon administration and compensated lavishly for his services.

The most significant distinction between them, however, the one that best accounts for their differing reactions to the discovery of Ozymandias's scheme, is the fact that Rorschach is wholly lacking in the egotism and self-assertive vanity of the man he lionizes. Indeed, in the act of mourning for Blake as a kindred spirit, Rorschach is led to enunciate the very paradox that sets them apart. Whereas Blake had prided himself on his ability to laugh at the horrors of the human condition and the imminent annihilation of all human life—and is reduced to a mortified shambles when he is forced to laugh at his own joke—the thoroughgoing nature of Rorschach's identification with excrement renders him immune to the flaw that leaves the Comedian vulnerable to such a shattering blow: a predilection for rapacity. Lacking the drive and appetite for rapacious enjoyment, Rorschach is free to dedicate himself in an unconditional and undivided manner to what he has formulated as his duty in the face of the irresistible forces of human depravity. When he writes in his journal the sentence, "I am Pagliacci," the punch line to a joke about a suicidally depressed clown who is counseled by a doctor, oblivious to his true identity, to go cheer himself up by attending one of his own performances, it is a gesture that dispenses with the dialogical conditions required by the very form of the joke, affirming instead the monological and unbending disposition associated with the adherence to a self-imposed vow (II: 27).[37]

Thus, it is the stoic character of Rorschach's reaction to the evils that human beings inflict on each other with which one must reckon in considering his vehement rejection of Ozymandias's act. Far from being the costumed adventurer who "will not change and thus is killed," Rorschach is in fact the character who undergoes a far more fundamental change in the final chapters of the narrative than Laurie Juspeczyk and Dan Dreiberg, who, being the most reasonable and reassuringly human personalities in the group, take a brief moment to express their moral outrage and thereupon proceed to make their peace with Veidt's horrifying deed.[38] Rorschach, on the other hand, by remaining faithful to his pledge—the principle that is the sole force he deploys between himself and the devouring nihilism of human civilization—comes to express an extreme form of solidarity with the victims of the fake alien attack. Rather than a fanatical insistence on revealing the truth and punishing crime at all cost, one might also read in Rorschach's intransigence the unwillingness to go on living on a world where peace and happiness have been secured through the deaths of millions of innocents. Granted, this identification with the dead is a move that he initially resists, as made evident by Rorschach's remarks regarding Ozymandias's obsession with the symbolism and paraphernalia of ancient Egypt after he and Nite Owl have broken into Veidt's Manhattan office:

> Funny... ancient pharoahs (sic) looked forward to end of world: believed cadavers would rise, reclaim hearts from golden jars. Must be currently holding breath with anticipation. Understand now why always mistrusted fascination with relics and dead kings... in final analysis, *it's us or them.* (X: 20, emphasis mine)

In accordance with his extremist reflexes, Rorschach frames the threat of nuclear annihilation in terms of the brutally reductive and ostensibly inescapable principle of enmity. The attitude of opposing the rights of the living to the prerogatives of the dead, however, has the effect of clearing the way for Veidt's impending intergalactic revision to Carl Schmitt's dictum that "humanity as such cannot wage war because it has no enemy, at least *not on this planet.*"[39] Even the hated Reds, to be sure, are numbered among the "us," if the most threatening enemy is posed by the voracious and predatory despots about to awaken from their sepulchers at the coming of the apocalypse. But as Rorschach soon discovers to his horror, the universal category of humanity has itself become internally split through the manner in which Ozymandias makes of it a political or, more properly, postpolitical reality. Rorschach switches sides, so to speak, once he recognizes that the true horror comes to reside not in the destruction of the world but rather in the sacrificial massacre that puts an end to violence and enmity. So does this mean that Rorschach's obstinacy stems from a perverse desire to preserve enmity as a matter of principle, on the basis that violence and brutality are the proper lot of humankind, as in Schmitt's infamously prescriptive interpretation of the Biblical story of Cain and Abel?

THE FETISH EXHUMED

What is unbearable for Rorschach, and reckoned as worse than the fate of apocalyptic destruction, is the amnesia that the world will make compulsory in embracing its salvation. For Veidt's utopian order can only be founded upon the prohibition against properly mourning the victims slaughtered by the alien attack. That is to say, the world produced by Ozymandias's scheme, if it is to survive, will constitute a globalized regime of the fetish, giving rise to a fully "pathological community" in which the corpses of its victims will be stripped even of their ghosts.[40] According to Žižek, the fetish is a symbolic fiction that is knowingly assumed by the subject as real and binding for the sake of guaranteeing the symbolic efficiency and ideological coherence of a given social reality.[41] In contrast to the "symptom," which constantly threatens to pierce through the cloak of an ideological fiction, the fetish permits the wholly conscious disavowal of truth. In Žižek's view, the postmodern, postideological era is one in which the fetish has replaced the symptom as the primary logic of domination. Thus, one might say that Veidt's postideological utopia elevates the logic of the fetish to a totalitarian scale, in which its opponents are *de facto* forced into the position of a Comedian or a Rorschach, either falling to pieces in the solitude of knowing the truth or not only choosing one's own death but also risking the annihilation of all by actively taking up the claims of justice.

For the fact that the global peace imposed by Ozymandias depends on the collective consent of humankind to blackmail, leaves the fetish as the only possible basis for securing sociopolitical order. By contrast, the new epochs ushered in by Rumfoord in *The Sirens of Titan* and by the superheroes in Moore's comic book series *Miracleman* contain the public acknowledgement of the bloody atrocities behind the act of foundation; in Vonnegut's novel the knowledge of the harsh truth is mediated by the cheerfully grotesque practices of a religion of universal penitence, while, in the conclusion of Moore's own *Miracleman,* the superpowered entities choose to rule the globe directly, making themselves into benevolent despots who rid the world of money, poverty, disease, nuclear weapons, and penitentiaries while legalizing all drugs and restoring the environment. Veidt, who neither founds a religion nor publicly reveals himself as a lawgiver, accordingly exposes his new order to the danger of deteriorating into a "pathological community," which will not be able to avail itself of the transgressions and violations of the written law that are fundamental to assuring the stability of social bonds. As Žižek notes, these "inherent" transgressions have a salutary effect only so long as they are regulated by the obscene and unwritten "secret rules" that reflect a culture's cynical—and unavoidable—"self-distance" from its declared values or noble lies.[42] Community as such is only possible on the basis of a "disavowed knowledge" or trauma, an act of collective repudiation that unavoidably relies on a stable distinction between the public and the secret. The catastrophic hazard shadowing the utopia of Ozymandias is that it will come to deprive its residents of the traditional means of psychic immunization provided by noble lies and their subterranean supplement, the vicious and rejuvenating disfigurations of the public face of the law.

The disappearance of the division between collective falsehoods and the repressed truth, the distinction that is fundamental to the Marxist critique of ideology as well as to any Machiavellian science of power, has been identified as the overriding political crisis of postmodernity.[43] According to Žižek, once the "fetish" replaces the "symptom" as the dominant mode of ideology, the subject's knowledge that governments and the mass media employ falsehoods, far from giving rise to a critical attitude, in fact results in the conscious assent of the subject to his own mystification, rendering his immersion in the dominant social reality all the more complete. Thus, for Žižek, postmodernity represents a reversion to mythic modes of thought and experience, for "when the dialectic of enlightenment reaches its apogee, the dynamic, rootless postindustrial society directly generates its own myth."[44] On the other hand, for René Girard the very impossibility within postmodernity of pursuing a politics of noble lies or of Machiavellian science, which, in relying on the deception of the credulous many by the knowing few, assumes the principle of a hidden but stable truth, is a direct consequence of the genuine ethical breakthrough achieved by modernity itself. For the moderns and, for that matter, postmoderns are distinguished by their inability to generate new myths that are true, that is to say, they prove increasingly incapable of devising fictions to which they can impute a binding character, illusions that would otherwise permit them to dupe and cajole themselves into accepting their protective fantasies as divinely ordained and spontaneously meaningful.[45] Far from inveighing against the sterility of the modern mind and its slavish devotion to technique, Girard instead approves of the enhancement of the critical powers of demystification precipitated by the erosion of myth-making inventiveness, while acknowledging the unpredictable and increasingly volatile nature of demythologized violence. "Incapable of attaining the true sacred," the violence that once sparked the cathartic renewal of traditional societies now assumes a far more menacing character, assuming the perverse universality of indiscrimination in having shed its sacralizing constraints.[46]

   The waning of the sacred and the exhaustion of its capacity to disguise violence as collective redemption thus serves to exacerbate that violence, giving it an increasingly indiscriminate and exterminating character that grows ever more aggravated in proportion to its inability to fulfill its traditional purgative and restorative functions. Girard's account of the emergence in modernity of a violence progressively stripped of its sacralizing mechanisms reveals the proximity of his thinking to the more recent and more widely studied work of the Italian philosopher Giorgio Agamben.

For the modern demythologizing of sacred violence, initiated by the two great narratives that unmask the wholly fictive nature of the rites of purification and assert the innocence of its victims—the stories of Job and Christ—generates the exterminating outbursts of a desacralized violence in which the distinctions between purity and impurity, contagion and catharsis, and law and nature have entirely dissolved. Accordingly, for Girard, the "full revelation" prepared for by the breakthroughs achieved by the triumvirate of the great de-mythologizers of modernity, who for all their deconstructions of sacred violence are nevertheless still entangled in the reactive pursuit of scapegoats (for Freud, it is the father and the law; for Marx, the bourgeoisie and the capitalists; for Nietzsche, the legions of vengefulness mobilized by *ressentiment* and slave morality) is the appearance of the "omnipresent victim,"

> who has already been delayed from time immemorial by sacrificial processes that are now becoming exhausted, since they appear to be more and more transparent and less and less effective—and are proportionately more and more to be feared in the domains of politics and sociology. To make these processes effective once again, people are tempted to multiply the innocent victims, to kill all the enemies of the nation or the class, to stamp out what remains of religion or the family as the origins of all forms of "repression," and to sing the praises of murder and madness as the only true forces of "liberation."[47]

The way has thus been opened, as it were, for Agamben's category of *homo sacer,* the biopolitical paradigm of the subject that, in being excluded from the law by the law, cannot be sacrificed and can therefore be killed with impunity. Agamben relates the figure of *homo sacer* to phenomena hovering at an indeterminate threshold between life and death, such as the brain-dead or the over-comatose, whose drastically reduced state of physical functioning could be prolonged indefinitely, but the political meaning of this term is brought out most alarmingly in the inmate of the concentration camp. For in the camp the human subject is forced to inhabit the space of exclusion from the law, so that "no act committed against [the inmates] could appear any longer as a crime."[48] The modern age, according to Agamben, finds its *nomos* in the camp, in which "the state of exception, which was essentially a temporary suspension of the rule of law on the basis of a factual state of danger, is now given a permanent spatial arrangement."[49] The idea of *homo sacer* throws into relief the emergency powers that are presupposed by the normal juridical order and that remain largely invisible in the course of its everyday operations. It thus serves to expose the continuity between liberalism and totalitarianism, especially as the former comes increasingly to avail itself of expanded powers on the grounds of the state of emergency, dissolving thereby all distinctions between peace and war, as well as between war and civil war.[50]

The desacralization of violence thus points to two sharply divergent scenarios: on the one hand, the dawning of universal restraint in which human collectives have come to reject the use of force by means of a truce based upon the globalized extension of the principle of mutually assured destruction, and on the other hand, a geopolitics of unchecked possibility, in which a hideous survivalism sweeps away the taboos against the exercise of force and all human life becomes consigned to the status of potential collateral damage. In *Watchmen*, Moore, in recognizing the subterranean identity between these two extremes, has Ozymandias contrive a global solution that makes profitable use of the instruments implied in the latter to bring about the situation that obtains in the former. But the successful implementation of this plan for global peace relies on nothing other than the horrifying fulfillment of what the concentration camps were intended to achieve—an extermination the completion of which would be attested to by the fact that there would be no one remaining to give testimony of what had taken place in them. Indeed, Malcolm Long, the one character who could serve in the role of the privileged witness for the narrative, whose survival would be dictated by narrative convention so that he could set down an authoritative account of the hero's life, is struck down near the site where the alien materializes. The final gesture of the psychiatrist, who through his communications with Rorschach has become unwilling and unable to live out the complacent life of a bourgeois professional, is to refuse his wife's request to return to her and their wealthy and sheltered household, saying "I'm sorry. It's the world—I can't run from it" (XI: 20). It would appear that the world created by Ozymandias, by contrast, would be one in which everyone would be trapped in a state of flight, caught in a perpetual moral retreat, thanks to the all-devouring terror of its foundation. But before the world closes up into a happy and inhuman forgetfulness about the victims of the history from which it has been delivered, Moore and Gibbons confront us directly with the lives that are extinguished for the sake of achieving this perfected and unsurpassable order, whose power to haunt the survivors, it seems, has become defused by the blackmail of universal well-being. The hand that remains suspended over the truth of utopia may perform the only gesture that can release Ozymandias's order from its moral asphyxiation, but the technology that has already been employed to create a pathological community offers no deliverance beyond the extinction of what has become both necessary and unbearable to the soul.

2 THE DEFENSE OF NECESSITY
On Jang Joon-Hwan's *Save the Green Planet*

> Woe to the creaturely remnant of existence who will not put off his
> existence, alas, who cannot do so, because the extinguished memory
> persists in its emptiness . . . the mute terror of the beast that, alone in its
> littleness, invisibly overcome, bereft of consciousness, creeps trembling
> under some dark shrubbery so that no eye may watch it dying.
> — HERMANN BROCH, *THE DEATH OF VIRGIL*

TRAINING THE POSTPOLITICAL ANIMAL

Toward the end of his response to Alexandre Kojève's essay "Tyranny and
Wisdom," Leo Strauss gives a somewhat jocular twist to Marx and Engels's
famous call for the proletariat to unite and seize for themselves the reins
of power. "Warriors and workers of all countries, unite, while there is
time, to prevent the coming of the 'realm of freedom.' Defend, with might
and main, if it needs to be defended, 'the realm of necessity.'"[1] To a reader
unfamiliar with the grounds of the debate between Strauss and Kojève
over the meaning of Xenophon's dialogue, "Hiero, or Tyrannicus," the injunction to the workers to mobilize and fight against the advent of universal liberty must surely come across as both perverse and counterintuitive.
The image of the proletariat banding together to fight for the freedom of all
is perhaps the most persistent fantasy of progressive or left-wing thought,
down to its contemporary incarnation in the "nonhomogeneous" multitude
conscripted by Michael Hardt and Antonio Negri to serve as the proper
medium of global democratic political change. For Strauss, whose name in
the public imagination has become inextricably linked to the imperialist

policies of U.S. neoconservatives, the workers'—or for that matter any-one's—revolution is justified here not as an offensive and expansionist form of warfare advancing the cause of freedom but rather as a prima-rily defensive and even nihilistic struggle on behalf of its opposite, raw "necessity." For the universalization of freedom, if it were possible, would produce the conditions for the moral disintegration of humanity, and so even the nihilistic assertion of the will for willing's sake is to be preferred to the monotonous peace and stability established by what Kojève calls the "homogeneous world-state," which reduces its inhabitants to the sub-human status of pacified and quiescent beasts.[2] Faced with such a "hideous prospect," Strauss observes that "the last refuge of man's human-ity" becomes "political assassination in the particularly sordid form of the palace revolution."[3]

These two alternatives—the nightmare of a despotic global order and frenzied outbursts of a purely negative and unremittingly destructive revolt—present a harsh antinomy that nevertheless points to certain sub-terranean assumptions underlying both Enlightenment and postmodern accounts of globalization. Strauss engages Kojève by drawing out some of the grimmer implications of his opponent's anthropology, which in Hegelian fashion defines the essence of the properly human as the will-ingness of human beings to risk their lives in a bloody struggle. The cen-tral principle in Kojève's definition of what properly constitutes the human is the desire for glory, which is of course the force behind the Hegelian struggle for recognition but is also crucial for Machiavelli, for whom such strivings supplied the overriding and objective motor of political life.[4] The posthuman era that follows the end of history is accompanied by the absence or dissipation of this desire, and by the collective primacy or pre-ponderance of those manifold disordered desires relating to the pursuit of monetary gain, the enjoyment of luxury, and indulgence in bodily pleasure that Plato consigned to the lowest part of the soul. Kojève accordingly describes posthistorical society as one in which human beings have sunk into the condition of beasts. The fulfillment of the distinctly human desire for recognition signals not only the end of history and of bloody historical struggles, but also the transformation of human beings into pacified beasts whose art and culture have degenerated into trivial amusements, unmarked by the vestiges of stern necessity or death-defying boldness that might otherwise endow them with a transcendent and sublime character. Just as Machiavelli, in chapter 18 of *The Prince*, regarded the Centaur as the proper emblem for the political subject in its combination of human rationality and violent, animal vigor, we might say that Kojèvian posthistory reverses this imagery in the form of frail human bodies bearing the inarticulate and unreasoning heads of beasts.

Kojève's posthistorical beast-humans are thus indistinguishable from the Nietzschean Last Men, whose subhuman existence is likewise circumscribed by their incomprehension at why anyone would dedicate his or her life to anything higher than the brutish satisfaction of the bodily appetites. Regarding the question of what political order would manage and administer the homogeneous world-state, that is to say, safeguard the pursuit of its inhabitants' hollow gratifications and petty freedoms, Kojève straightforwardly describes it as a tyranny. Such usage of the term accords with the classical definition, as Plato forcefully identifies the subjugation of the soul by the disordering passions with the figure of the tyrant as well as the debased condition of the terrorized and unscrupulous populace over which he lords. Tyranny in this sense encompasses the internalized subservience of a people by their embrace of—as well as their resignation to—the pleasures and gratifications offered by their rulers in exchange for their repudiation of virtue. Just as the sterile and lethargic contentment of posthistorical existence constitutes the culmination of history, tyranny appears ineluctably as the governmental mechanism whereby one fulfills on a global scale the program of the Enlightenment. This is true regardless of how a particular regime might regard itself: the capitalist United States, a united Europe, and the former and current communist nations, in unleashing the forces of technological modernity, are all actively caught up in unfolding the process whereby the entire world will be drawn into the debasing and pacified monotony of posthistory.[5] Thus, for Kojève, a Stalinist spy who achieved a high position in the French ministry of foreign economic affairs, the ideological distinctions of the Cold War never ran particularly deep; indeed its battle lines were based on differences that were epiphenomenal and transitory. The Soviet Russians and communist Chinese were simply Americans who had yet to become rich, while Nazism served as a mere transitional stage in the inevitable democratization of Germany. In spite of the seeming outrageousness of such claims, one nonetheless spies the presuppositions of Kojève's prolapsarian narrative, watered down and sentimentalized, seeping through much of the contemporary discourse about globalization, from the fatuous claims of globalists such as the *New York Times* commentator Thomas Friedman that no two nations with a McDonald's have ever gone to war with one another to liberal philosopher John Rawls's guileless division of the world between liberal democratic peoples and "decent hierarchical peoples" inhabiting well-ordered societies and the uncivil, "outlaw" states standing in need of moral correction by the muscular discipline enforced by their more civilized and more enlightened brethren.[6]

One detects more than hint of exasperated indignation in Jacques Derrida when he inveighs against the "incredible and indecent tableau" of Kojève's narrative of world history after offering dismissive praise of his "genial, often naively joking baroquism."[7] Indeed, it is difficult to imagine a more flippantly scornful rejection of the moral pathos of Walter Benjamin's demand for the redemption of humankind in its totality, including the victims of the past, in his oft-quoted "Theses on the Philosophy of History" than the subhuman utopia of Kojèvian posthistory, in which the bestial gratifications of its inhabitants are the remuneration for centuries of war and atrocity, brought about, in the words of Stanley Rosen, through "the murders of millions of innocent persons in fulfillment of Hegel's observation that history is a slaughter-bench."[8] It becomes clear that there are a multitude of levels from which to denounce Kojève's work. One might take Kojève to task for his doctrine that there is a single point in history that signals its end—a charge that acquires some traction from the fact that Kojève himself did revise his timing for the completion of the historical process. Or one might, with Derrida, denounce the sheer cold-bloodedness of Kojève's thought, which disposes of the victims of historical injustice as human sacrifices or eulogizes them as collateral damage amid the coming of the kingdom of universal satisfaction. Alternatively, one might take a page from Kojève's own treatment of Hegel and attempt to "refute" the end of history by "pointing to a fact"—the reality of ongoing global strife that appears much more virulent and intractable than the grand ideological clashes that preceded and prepared the way for it.[9]

Kojève, it appears, leaves himself open to attack from numerous directions, but such seeming vulnerability should alert us to the not inconsiderable risks of rushing forward to assault an exposed adversary, not least among them being the danger of becoming impaled on the spear of an equally zealous comrade-in-outrage.

For there is something about the blatant perversity of Kojève's thought that eludes the slings and arrows of outraged morality as well as shrugs off the typical postmodern charge of totalizing or metaphysical naïveté. For the world that he hollows into the earth is in large measure the one to which we remain manacled, in which, as Alain Badiou writes, ethics has deteriorated into the "incapacity" to "name and strive for a Good."[10] Kojève anticipates the major provocations of postmodern theory in its declared ends of man and of philosophy, as well as the questions of political agency on which postmodern theory remains deadlocked. Unlike the postmoderns, he goes further, to the point of supplying answers, albeit humanly unacceptable ones, to these quandaries. Kojève's identification of universality with the tyranny of globalizing modernity brushes away any moral objections because he legitimates it in terms that are themselves wholly nonmoral. Indeed, his vision of posthistory can be said to make allowance for criticism and dissent by ensuring that its authors have a vital share in the prosperity and comforts of the economic and political order they assail as unjust. Certainly, the academic Left has proven incapable of providing a credible or compelling alternative to the liberal capitalist status quo, as its vision of justice and reform are largely variations on the sociopolitical order that currently exists. A more equitable distribution of goods in an affluent society, for example, would only reinforce the point made by Francis Fukuyama, Kojève's best-known commentator, that "we cannot picture a world that is *essentially* different from the present one, and at the same time better."[11] Thus, as Slavoj Žižek observes, the academic Left restricts itself to playing a "game of hysterical provocation," in which it self-righteously assails the injustices of the established order while quietly hoping that the upheavals necessitated by the actualization of their critiques will never come to pass.[12] On the other hand, the crumbling of freedom in the hands of the postmoderns into what Stanley Rosen calls a "discontinuous solipsism" would bear out that postmodern accounts of political consciousness and human motivations essentially lie at anchor in the shallows of Kojèvian anthropology.[13] A wholly instrumental definition of power coupled with a radically individualistic justification of pleasure, after all, serves ineluctably to resuscitate and reinforce the sophistic belief that the happiest are those who commit crimes with impunity; hence the increasingly resigned and anarchistic temper of much contemporary critical theory, which progressively shifts its attention from the "active" pole of dissent and revolt as the hallmarks of political subjectivization to lay stress upon the "passive" condition embodied by the perpetually endangered and exposed status of the citizen as the expendable victim of state power.[14]

THE BIOPOLITICS OF SALVATION

Even expendable victims nevertheless often possess the means to strike, whether preemptively or out of a desire for retribution, at the biopolitical regime that may single them out for disposal. Strauss's preference for the anarchy unleashed by nihilistic action over the sterilizing peaceableness of an inhuman order conveys something of the erratic and ferocious character of political antagonism when it can no longer be softened and legitimated by redemptive narratives of historical progress, just as in Kojèvian terms, "emancipation" and "redemption" drift into the range of meanings encompassed by the activity of "disposal." The 2003 South Korean film *Save the Green Planet* stages the clash between the globalizing biopolitical order and the singularity it violates. Yet it takes an approach that notably demystifies, at least in part, the moral justifications normally reserved for the victims of progress while unearthing a kind of disordered compassion animating the universal despot's program of domination. The basic plot and premise of *Save the Green Planet*, written and directed by Jang Joon-Hwan, is reminiscent of the alien conspiracy narrative typified by the American TV series *The X-Files*—an erratic and violent young man addicted to amphetamines kidnaps the wealthy and famous CEO of a chemical company, whom he believes to be an alien from the Andromeda galaxy leading a mission to destroy the earth at the coming of the next lunar eclipse. The protagonist Lee Byung-Gu, unhinged by a lifetime of devastating suffering, actually has compelling reasons, decidedly earthbound to the viewer, for engaging in a brutal vendetta against the industrialist. He was once an employee of Yuje Chemical, the company headed by the supposed alien, and his girlfriend was beaten to death during the break-up of a workers' strike. When Byung-Gu was a child, his father, a miner, lost his arm in an accident and died shortly after, a drunken suicide. His beloved mother, who also worked for Yuje, lies in a deep coma from a chemical poisoning that doctors are at a loss to explain or treat. The head of the company, a brusque and venal boor named Kang Man-Shik, has acquired a somewhat scandalous reputation typical of members of the power elite in Korea as elsewhere, with an affair with a starlet as well as a suspicious, very public acquittal from charges of stock fraud earning him headlines. Byung-Gu, aided by his girlfriend—a trapeze artist named Sooni—overpowers an inebriated Kang returning home from a drunken night out. They tie him to a modified barber's chair, complete with a drain for urine and other, more sanguinary fluids, in the cellar of Byung-Gu's house in the mountains, and then proceed to shave off Kang's hair, which Byung-Gu believes to be the medium for the aliens' telepathic powers.

What ensues is a series of horrific tortures, inflicted by Byung-Gu on Kang, to force him to reveal his identity as an alien agent and to set up a meeting with the alien prince. Byung-Gu believes that the famous industrialist occupies a high enough rank within the Andromedan hierarchy to

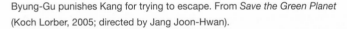

Byung-Gu punishes Kang for trying to escape. From *Save the Green Planet* (Koch Lorber, 2005; directed by Jang Joon-Hwan).

be able to contact their sovereign directly. To prove that Kang possesses an alien constitution superior to that of humans, Byung-Gu administers to his body an electric shock three times in excess of what would be lethal for human adults. Kang, in the course of the film, gets burned by a hot iron, stung by menthol scraped against his eyeballs, and impaled by his palms against a wooden beam. Yet the executive proves himself a cunning and resourceful adversary, drawing on enormous reserves of will to withstand these tortures and using his guile to dishearten his captors. Kang displays by turns outraged disbelief, pathetic fearfulness, and unnerving tenacity, all with an astute sense of timing. He reveals to Byung-Gu and Sooni that he knows about the death of Byung-Gu's girlfriend, asserting that the corporation paid just compensation for the loss, and then drives Sooni away by raising doubts about Byung-Gu's feelings for her. Kang even goes so far as to break his own thumb in an escape attempt that very nearly succeeds, but for his desire to vent his frustrations by kicking the apparently lifeless body of his enemy. Later by sheer power of will, he tears the flesh in his hands to pull himself free of the crucifying nails, an act rendered even more horrifying by the fact that he has been anesthetized (indeed, it is a scene that would be easier to watch if he were writhing in agony, since the anesthesia gives the pain he would otherwise experience a wholly phantasmatic character, externalizing it outside the proper boundaries of the flesh). The browbeating insults with which he seeks to intimidate Byung-Gu exhibit his sense of his own innate superiority, which in the context of the film is evocative of the double meaning of class difference and difference between species: "You can't beat me. Do you know why? Because I've never lost to morons like you. I know your kind very well ... never taking responsibility, always blaming others. . . . Cowards like you lose eventually. So stop acting crazy and give up, before more terrible shit happens." He bullies his captor in this manner shortly after tearfully pleading to Sooni that he misses his family and wants badly to see them again.

Class antagonism thus serves as a crucial element behind the audience's feelings of hesitation about the plot, furnishing the pole of the "realistic" explanation in the experience of the fantastic according to the definition laid out by Tzvetan Todorov.[15] For most of the film, the viewer wonders whether Byung-Gu is simply delusional, crazed from such an awful burden of grief that could easily drive anyone insane, just as one is led to question whether Kang's redoubtable will and ruthless cunning bear out that he is indeed made of sterner stuff than any human being or if these are simply magnifications of the qualities essential for any corporate executive clawing his way to the top. The truth, however, exceeds the expectations raised by the narrative regarding both the origins of Byung-Gu's quest and the nature of the ulterior motives imputed to Kang. For even as the film brings to a head the struggle between the two, as Kang, hoping to keep Byung-Gu from chopping off his leg, assures him that a bottle labeled "benzene" in the trunk of his car contains an antidote to awaken his mother from her coma—it quietly signals disturbing clues as to Byung-Gu's actual preoccupations behind his act of taking upon himself the heroic task of saving the earth from the aliens. A police detective investigating Kang's disappearance comes across Byung-Gu's dog chewing on a human shin bone. Byung-Gu's basement is crammed with mannequins—he claims to the detective he makes them by hand and sells them to department stores, but behind the mannequins are jars containing human hands and feet, as well as a brain preserved with the tendrils of the nervous system. Even his practice of beekeeping is suggestive of a yearning to acquire insights at first hand into the dynamics of mass social organization from the perspective of a detached and superior outsider, to reproduce and experience the cosmic distance, as it were, between the Andromedans and humankind.

After one detective searching for Kang has been chopped up and fed to the dog and another subdued and bound, the industrialist finally breaks down in front of Byung-Gu and admits that he is an alien. Kang reveals that the aliens from Andromeda have come to earth on a mission not to destroy humanity but to save it from its most dangerous impulses, which now threaten the entire planet with annihilation. In a montage composed of cartoonish images taken from popular legends of UFO lore, illustrations of Bible stories, historical footage of wars and massacres, and scenes of primitive life that pay homage to Stanley Kubrick's *2001: A Space Odyssey*, Kang explains how the Andromedans discovered the earth and, out of guilt for inadvertently wiping out the dinosaurs, created a form of life resembling them to repopulate the planet. The first human being is shown crouching with a glimmer of astonishment in front of a black monolith, to which he is joined by an umbilical cord. The Andromedans then render this Adam unconscious, remove a sample of blood and tissue, and soon an Eve sits in a daze beneath the monolith, likewise attached to it with an umbilical cord. Kang then tells of how a "society in harmony with nature" was born, as the word "Atlantis" flashes at the bottom of the screen. Things go wrong, however, when the humans decide that they want to be more powerful than their Andromedan creators. They embark on a reckless project of genetic experimentation, implanting in their off-spring a destructive gene that is responsible for humanity's long history of carnage and atrocity. An image of the tower of Babel appears on the screen, as Kang explains that the newer humans, more aggressive and vio-lent than the others, led the species into a catastrophic war that was "ended by thousands of atomic bombs." The intense heat generated by this nuclear conflict opened up a hole in the ozone layer, resulting in the melting of the polar ice caps, but one man, Noah, was able to save his family along with genetic samples of all animal life in a kind of submarine that floated for centuries before coming ashore on dry land. The cumulative effect of the genetic manipulation, however, was to reverse the course of evolu-tion, and human beings began to regress rapidly into apes. The Androm-edans decided to intervene once more in the lives of their creations by reversing the effects of genetic degradation. In yet another allusion to *2001,* it is now an ape that sits in front of the alien monolith, looking with curiosity at the large bone he holds in his hand. "Evolution resumed, but towards an awful chaos"—as Kang's narration continues, the film crosscuts between the ape using his bone as a weapon to smash the other bones around him and grim documentary footage of various historical horrors: Hitler and the Nazis, mounds of bodies in concentration camps, bombings during the Vietnam War, and scenes of slaughter, strife, and grief in Africa, Latin America, and the Middle East. The Andromedans, according to Kang, have launched a series of experiments on several thou-sand people to find a way to isolate and destroy this malignant element.

This sequence will no doubt remind the viewer of another Kubrick film, *A Clockwork Orange,* only this time it is the representative of a secret elite who sits bound to a chair, telling the story of human woe in order to justify the necessity of the hero's agonizing traumas as well as to talk his way out of being murdered. But there is an even more crucial difference in the use of this type of montage sequence in *Save the Green Planet*. In Kubrick's film, the young thug Alex is forced to watch films showing violent crimes and historical carnage as part of a conditioning experiment to induce nausea in him whenever he feels stirred by an aggressive impulse. In *Save the Green Planet*, the equivalent footage does not issue from a clear diegetic source, such as a piece of film or video shown by one character to another, but rather functions as the straightforward visual correlative to Kang's narration. Byung-Gu suspects for a moment that Kang has lifted his story from the myriad books and magazines speculating about extraterrestrial life that litter his basement, but Kang duly dispels these doubts by correctly calculating, via the principle of relativity, how many earth years make up a single Andromedan year. Unlike Kubrick, Jang chooses not to frame this summary of human origins and the atrocities of history as a procedure of ideological manipulation whereby a character is subjected to a process of behavior modification. Rather, Jang seeks to account for the enduring authority and insidious power of redemptive narratives of globalizing modernity by linking them with a cosmic and nonhuman standpoint. He underscores thereby how a nonchalant, obscenely sacrificial attitude toward the atrocities of history and in the present flashes through the various apologia for the neoliberal order.

For the economic and political order that is being created by global capitalism, an order that can more accurately be described as the management of havoc, now avails itself of the chimerical and utopian justifications once deployed by its vanquished adversary, state socialism, turning to the ruse of promising—and in the same breath, postponing—collective happiness and well-being. But as the lifelong antifascist Eric Voegelin and onetime Nazi Party member Carl Schmitt have emphasized, a utopian ideology based upon economic expansion essentially deprives those who would oppose its advance of their status as properly and legitimately human. Schmitt, in the *Concept of the Political*, observes that modern wars fought to "protect or expand economic power" invariably turn into crusades mounted to exterminate the "outlaws of humanity."[16] Similarly, Voegelin ascribes to the utopian ideologies of both the Left and the Right the readiness to engage in a merciless warfare against recalcitrant humanity itself: "the enemy is not fighting for the manifestation of his own existence with the same right as the idealist; anybody who wants to lead his own way of life, unmolested by the idealist, is a criminal." Thus, "the brutal attack on the historical realization of all values that do not happen to be incorporated in the [utopian] ideal forces everybody else into a defensive position in which the worst atrocities and crimes may seem justified in order to ward off this insult to human dignity."[17]

Yet the defender of violated singularity against insatiable globalism in Jang's film turns out to be a perpetrator in addition to being a legitimate victim. Having read his captor's journals and files, Kang confronts Byung-Gu with his own series of crimes: "Saving the planet—for whom, for what? The people who bullied you, the ones who made you crazy? If you kill them all, does that mean you're saving the planet?" His words are accompanied by a rapid montage of a dozen or so open files heaped on top of each other, every one of which contains the photo of a different victim and bears the stamp, "conclusion: not an alien." Byung-Gu, he reveals, has been kidnapping and torturing to death various people who brutalized him in the past—among others a high school teacher and a corrections officer. "Of all the people you've killed here, how many were aliens?" demands Kang, over a montage of files and photos of numerous dead men. The alien CEO proceeds to answer his own question, "only two."

The film points to the inescapable conclusion that there can be no politics of singularity that does not itself violate another singularity. A conception of justice based on the "infinite respect of the singularity and infinite alterity of the other" denies the fundamentally tragic character of political life; moreover, it cannot but fulfill itself in the fetishization of victimhood, according to which the only indisputably ethical gesture would be to consent to one's own exploitation in the name of a humanitarian ideal.[18] Byung-Gu's quest to redress all the wrongs that have been perpetrated against him and his loved ones demonstrates an expansive and volatile character that necessarily transgresses any principle of mere equilibrium—such as halting at the point of inflicting injury—since the perpetrators of his misery are permitted by law and sanctioned by cultural norms to exercise violence against the subjects under their authority. Furthermore, he is revealed to have been carrying out his own "experiments" on unwilling victims, torturing and dismembering them to ascertain the cosmological dimensions of the conspiracy that has wrought such devas-

tation upon his family. Even as Byung-Gu at last finds his suspicions con-
firmed—one wonders whether he was alerted to the presence of aliens on
discovering the suspiciously superhuman capacity of one of his victims to
endure pain—his actions have led him, in the course of achieving this
knowledge, to duplicate to a certain extent—on a far smaller and purely
negative scale—the salvational project of Kang. These two rivals, one a
savior of humankind, from the impersonal standpoint of utopian globalism and technological advancement, and the other an angel of vengeance
out of fidelity to his personal, unconditional attachments—mirror each
other not only in their readiness to use violent and coercive means but
also through a split between motive and action internal to both sides of
the antagonism, a contradiction that in the end proves nothing short of
catastrophic.

SOVEREIGN VANITY AND THE DECISION

For Byung-Gu is caught off-guard by Kang's disclosures about the salvific
nature of the Andromedans' experiments, leaving him at a loss as to where
to direct his devouring anger. His mother having died after receiving what
Kang had assured him was the antidote, he finds himself caught in a bitter
impasse, bereft of any positive course of action. If he chooses to follow
through on a mission of vengeance, he might well doom the earth. But as
he has already tortured a dozen people to death, the sum of his actions
comes to exert an irresistible pull of their own, especially now that the
death of his beloved mother has deprived him of his main reason for living. Having tricked Byung-Gu into poisoning his mother, Kang finds the
range of his actions no less constrained by the chain of events unleashed
by his own attempts to save both his own skin and that of humanity. What
kind of relation might he possibly develop with an individual from whom
he has deprived that which he holds most precious? It can be said, furthermore, that the goals sought by both the alien potentate and the traumatized
angel of vengeance give rise to bedeviling contradictions that effectively
thwart each from achieving a satisfactory outcome.

Byung-Gu is left bewildered as to how to continue being faithful to
his mother as well as the memory of her sorrow and suffering. Stunned by

the palpably obscene essence of the injunction underlying Kang's speech—
an injunction seeking to blackmail him into an interpassive enjoyment[19]
("Forgive me for the suffering and death of your mother, and you and
your kind will be rewarded with peace and plenty!")—he reacts to Kang's
words by shooting out a mirror reflecting the face of his prisoner. He then
proceeds to open fire against his own desk, directing his aggression against
the objects signifying his long and tortured quest—drug bottles, a video
case, and a small globe all come crashing to the floor. Although one may
account for his acting-out as a kind of admission of failure, since the aliens
are revealed to be far less one-sidedly malevolent than Byung-Gu believes,
this scene can also be understood as a demonstration of his resistance to
being interpellated by Kang's argument for the salvational correction of
the human species. For Byung-Gu's mother was singled out as an ideal
test subject because, as the alien executive explains, "physical and mental
suffering stresses organisms, forcing them to adapt and develop more
quickly." Indeed, Kang openly admits that Byung-Gu and his mother were
deliberately subjected to agonizing torment and misery in order to bring
the experiments to more advanced stages. Yet, the film never explicitly reveals what Byung-Gu intends to do when he meets the Andromedan
prince. The audience is left guessing at the turning point of the narrative,
wondering if he is gathering the nerve to take the petty revenge of finish-
ing off Kang or the cosmic revenge of assassinating the alien sovereign, a
blind and purely personal act of killing that would risk the destruction of
the world. It is, therefore, uncertain whether a "palace revolution" without
suicidal annihilation is within the realm of potential consequences, even
if only by accident.

A no less disabling ambiguity becomes apparent in the case of Kang,
when he makes reference to the wish of human beings to become more
powerful than their creators. It is out of this desire for superiority that
humanity implanted in itself the destructive gene, but it is questionable
whether in this instance one can meaningfully separate the motive from
the act. The Andromedans might come up with a way to eliminate this specific gene, but their technology cannot extirpate the desire that implanted
the gene in the first place—unless they were to set about transforming
human beings into creatures that no longer resemble them in any substan-

tial way, i.e., cause them to revert into unreflective beasts. Like the cease-lessly expansive forces of globalizing modernity, the Andromedan experi-ments thus emerge out of the self-defeating drive to abolish enmity itself. Thus, for the extraterrestrials, the problem of politics is wholly subordi-nated to and dissolved by their superior (with respect to humanity) tech-nics. But their undertaking is riven by the pressures exerted by unalterably contradictory desires—on the one hand, they seek to make recompense for accidentally unleashing a virus that wiped out the dinosaurs; on the other, they wish to preserve their superiority, technological or otherwise, over humankind. The faith they place in technology leads them to the conclusion that they can manage, peaceably and on their own terms, the form of life they have created. The Andromedans operate under the belief that they can mold humanity into a unity that will not thereupon attempt to rebuild the tower of Babel, that is to say, to threaten their supremacy as the dominant power in the cosmos. Their unquestionable compassion for the murderous disorder that grips their creations is discovered to be counterbalanced by their self-interested wish to remain unchallenged as the ascendant cosmo-power. Needless to say, either of the tasks, whether coming to the aid of humanity or retaining sovereign authority, might well be achievable when undertaken separately, but it is impossible even to attempt to bring off both together without horrifying consequences.

Furthermore, though the Andromedan strategy of redemption can be said to heed the Machiavellian dictum that men will sooner forget the deaths of their fathers than the loss of their property, Kang finds himself overwhelmed by the implacable fury unleashed by a devoted son at the loss of his *mother.* The process of recognizing that he has underestimated the force of this attachment unsettles and transforms Kang in a profound and fundamental way, though not in a direction that is ultimately affir-mative of what it means to be properly human. Indeed, by the film's end, the Andromedan chief appears to have become numbed and deadened in spirit after having himself borne witness during his imprisonment in Byung-Gu's dungeon to the terrible and interminable, unremittingly appalling character of human suffering and the inexorable fury it ignites. His act of enunciating his sympathy and compassion for humankind has the curious effect of emptying him of these feelings—it is as though by speaking his desire, he detaches himself from it. His true identity finally revealed as that of the alien prince himself, Kang decides to break off the experiments by ordering the total destruction of the earth.

A film that concludes with the annihilation of both humanity and the earth is bound to present some difficulties with respect to the question of spectatorial identification. Although Byung-Gu is initially portrayed as a rather comical figure, psychologically unstable and dependent on stimulants to control his mood swings, he engages the sympathy of the audience as a working-class hero of sorts, as he enacts the still-potent fantasy of the proletariat avenging itself upon an elite that has escaped the normal limits of justice and cast off its restraints and responsibilities. Indeed, an unexpectedly poignant scene transpires when Byung-Gu spends a night drinking with Detective Chu, who has arrived at the former's residence in the mountains to look for the kidnapped industrialist. Chu, a talented detective who has been kicked off the force by a corrupt and incompetent superior, sympathizes with Byung-Gu as the latter relates an account of the tragedies and outrages he has endured. The inspector breaks down into uncontrollable laughter when his ostensible quarry recounts a prank in which he had glued a factory director's penis to his stomach. Though Chu's face suddenly stiffens in alarm at Byung-Gu's admission that his rage at his mother's condition made him want to "kill everyone," the tenseness dissipates once his host refers to a wrath that was so overpowering that it made him hungry, leading him to gorge himself, vomit up the food, and then stuff himself again. Chu, clearly moved by the younger man's travails and identifying with the injustices he has suffered, lets down his guard and finishes his interlocutor's sentence, "So you ate and vomited again . . . if you get to the point of vomiting out your blood and your shit, you'll work off your anger a little bit, just as long as it doesn't kill you." Chu, as his suspicions begin to melt into fellow-feeling, thus neglects to consider the less likely but darker consequence of "releasing" one's rage, an oversight that anticipates Kang's murderous reaction to his own tears of grief and compassion.

Nevertheless, the discovery that Byung-Gu is a multiple murderer carrying out his own horrifying experiments to ascertain whether his victim is human or alien puts in question the sense of identification that the viewer has entrusted in his character. For the sympathy of both the audience and Kang is engaged through the many flashback shots detailing Byung-Gu's traumas and grievances—the explosion in which his father lost his arm, his childhood anguish at his father's alcoholism, the bloody hand that his fatally injured girlfriend extends to him, his mother collapsing into a coma. This flashback sequence simultaneously serves to humanize Kang, who is revealed as a more empathetic figure when he is seen weeping as he reads Byung-Gu's diaries. The audience, in the latter half of the film, is thus confronted by a double disruption in the process of identification, which in this case is indistinguishable from the decomposition of the act of reading. On the one hand, Kang reads the documents of Byung-Gu's past, taking up himself the perspective of his adversary, and sheds sincere tears over it. Yet he goes on coldly and unflinchingly to bring about the death of Sooni and then, later, through the intervention of Detective Kim, of Byung-Gu himself. It is as though being moved by the tragedy of an individual human life leads Kang to the decision to wipe out all human life. The perverse logic behind such an act is augured in the diabolic calculations whereby the alien prince contrives to free himself at the very end from the grip of his captor. Having been wired to explosives by Byung-Gu, who vows to blow up himself and Sooni along with Kang if the latter were to try anything suspicious, Kang surmises correctly that Byung-Gu's reflex will be to forgo the route of collective death, and even to give up his own vengeance, in order to save Sooni from danger. Kang thus buys himself enough time, under the guise of contacting the alien overlord, to type in the commands for a robot arm with pincers to grasp Sooni by the throat. Byung-Gu attempts to save her but is successively electrocuted and stabbed by Kang, reaching the computer console an instant too late in one of the most heartrending scenes in an already emotionally harrowing film.

On the other hand, the crushingly despairing range of options left to Byung-Gu upon learning the truth from Kang—whether to resign or reconcile himself to the prevailing obscenity by accepting his mother's suffering as necessary or to lash out at the perpetrators, regardless of the cost—makes him at once too wounded and too fearsome a figure in the end for the ordinary viewer to identify with him fully, either. The seeming lack of correspondence between understanding and action can be described in the one instance as a willfully perverse—and, at least in human terms, heartless—disconnect, and in the other as the complete dissolution in the process of victimization of any possibility for action aside from pure negation. For the counterterm to Byung-Gu's "selfish" desire for retribution is not the common good, properly speaking, but collective well-being stained by the blood of innocent and unknowing sacrifice. Under these conditions the room for judicious action is not surprisingly narrowed in terms that are nothing short of drastic, but *Save the Green Planet* nonetheless opens up just such a space in a third act of reading, albeit in one that also results in a misjudgment. For within the ever-receding straits of reasonable sympathy, the matter of audience identification ultimately comes to rest upon a minor character, the handsome and well-educated Inspector Kim, a graduate of the nation's most elite university and, aside from the disgraced Inspector Chu, the only capable detective on the police force. Kim is the sole officer who follows Chu's lead in discounting money as the primary motive in the kidnapping of Kang, and later pieces together the identity of Kang's tormenter from old newspaper articles clipped by his mentor, who has been keeping track of unsolved missing persons cases. Failing in his first attempt to rescue Kang, he is bound and gagged next to the industrialist during the latter's confession of the Andromedan relationship to humanity and the detailing of their experiments. Before departing with Kang for the laboratories of Yuje Chemical to summon the alien prince, Byung-Gu gives Kim, who is still tied to his chair, a bundle of his journals and notes and exhorts the detective to learn from them so that he might continue the fight against the aliens, should Byung-Gu fail. Kim manages to free himself and arrives at Yuje Chemical just in time to shoot Byung-Gu dead before the latter can kill Kang.

Kim is given access to both of the opposed sides locked in a mortal struggle. He is the one who must decide whether Kang's story of the alien creation of human life is the spontaneous, unvarnished truth or if it is merely a farfetched pastiche contrived out of the cultural detritus of ufology and New Age lore in order to appease an unnervingly clever and capable psychopath. Forced to become the adjudicator of an uncanny and irreconcilable conflict, Kim chooses, at incalculable cost, to do his job. Yet, in the shots following his killing of Byung-Gu, Kim hesitates, his face stricken first by an unmistakable look of doubt and then one of regret. The causal

chains of narrative will tend to reflect and reproduce existing power relations, with the timing of crucial events and chance encounters leading to
a resolution that attests to and exposes the prevailing injustices organizing the city and the cosmos. In the denouement of *Save the Green Planet*
the force of this necessity takes the form of an explosive knowledge that is
initially disavowed and accepted only too late. The truth flashes up before
Kim when he overhears Kang's confession, yet he refuses to act on it even
as it progressively dawns on him that the alien's fantastic tale might in fact
be true. Is this not often the case in life, political or otherwise, in which we
sense that something is gravely awry but take no concrete steps against a
disastrous outcome because doing so would compel us to sacrifice that
sense—so fundamental for our feeling of existential ease—of the consistency of ordinary reality? These are, of course, the symbolic coordinates
that are shattered by the intervention of what Žižek calls the "Act," which,
as a "step into the open" and thus as a potential rupture in the homogeneity
of time, is a genuinely free action, terrifyingly bereft of any predetermined
justifications.[20] Žižek, however, reverts into the obligatory posture of a
left-wing revolutionary as though to domesticate the disruptive potential
of this idea, which has a more vivid and dramatic precedent in Machiavelli's
principle that the success of any political innovation, that most risky of
collective enterprises, rests on the capacity of its agents to be either "magnificently bad or perfectly good."[21] Kim, who in the film is the most effective officer of the law, is stripped even of the credit for rescuing the missing
CEO by the corrupt police chief. Such is the steepness of the price he pays
for failing to imagine a vocation more serious or improbable than the familiar and socially approved occupation he holds—and loses—as the result
of his own competence.

The extravagance and excesses of the film's stylistic elements attest to
the unraveling of reality into an appallingly world-historical Grand Guignol
that not so much mirrors the deranged fury of its shadowy protagonist
but rather divests an otherwise uneventful nightmare of its light to allow
for the projection of the internal logic of globalizing modernity. The suc-
cession of moments in time warped and contracted by the incessant inflicting of pain dredges up into the world an unequivocally animistic order—
the finger of a fallen mannequin points to a secret door, the flip of a coin

determines whether a certain random detail holds a vital clue, the perpetrator's nemesis is arrested for his crime. Indeed, the fabric of reality is
rent and torn by the force of a restlessly oscillating compulsion that veers
between divine hallucination and demonic revelation. After Byung-Gu
has accidentally killed his mother and is shot in the leg during Kim's first,
failed attempt at rescuing Kang, he rouses himself from his state of shock
and pain after a vision of his mother's spirit appears to him descending
from the ceiling. Surrounded by an angelic light, with long strips of cloth
cut out of her patient's scrubs after the traditional costume of a Korean
shaman, she extends her hand overflowing with methamphetamines,
which drop copiously into the grotesquely wide-open mouth of her grief-
crazed son.

The film does, to be sure, deal at times in a playful and satiric manner
with the religious underpinnings of the belief in extraterrestrial visita-
tions—the Andromedans, once they have cast aside their earthly disguises,
sport oversized earlobes such as those found on statues of the Buddha.
The Andromedan reduction of salvation to a dumbfoundingly biological
process is furthermore reflective of how the subculture of ufology, the
most notorious example of which would be the Heaven's Gate cult with
its commission of collective suicide, draws straightforwardly from conventional religious conceptions of the millennium. For the ufologist, the destruction of the environment, the frenzied pace of economic and technological change, and the emergence of a global political order are all signals
that the end times are near. The messiah is an "intergalactic space traveler"
who helps humanity achieve "cosmic consciousness."[22] As if to underscore
the diabolic reversibility of these myths, Byung-Gu attempts to throw off
Detective Chu by handing him a book describing how the extraterrestrials
desire only to send messages of "hope and peace" to humankind. Indeed,
the fact that Byung-Gu pointedly refers to the alien sovereign as the
"prince" instead of "king" or "emperor" serves to underscore the Christological aspects of the Andromedan leader. At the same time, the evoca-
tions of the divine in the film take on an ominous ambiguity. When Kang
wakes to find himself crucified, the camera focuses on the nails impaling
his bloody palms but then cuts to a high-angle shot to frame eight coiled
swing-arms holding various implements attached to the armrests of the

barber's chair. Although the explicit reference is of course to Christ, the black, spidery metal rods make this framing of Kang suggestive of a deity from another religious tradition, Shiva, who of course embodies the principle of destruction as well as that of creation.[23]

It appears that in the postmodern and posthuman era, we are fated to be stricken with confusion not only over the nature of own identities but also that of our deities as well. If the film were to have presented a non-technological—for example an orthodox Christian—narrative of redemption, the proper resolution would be for Kang to undergo *kenosis* and willingly expose himself to the process of abject self-emptying that could set in motion the means of reconciliation between alien and human, between perpetrators and victims. For him to do so would necessitate a step he is loath to take at any cost, that of renouncing the prerogative of self-preservation, whether of himself or of his species. The desire for self-preservation is accordingly purchased by extreme and mutilating restrictions on what the creators consider permissible for their creations. For the world willed by the global tyranny of Enlightenment is one that is lorded over by deities who are incapable of voluntarily choosing powerlessness, who, grotesquely shielded by their power and technology, presume that the inattention of the Fates to their good fortune is everlasting. *Save the Green Planet* in that sense turns science fiction, the literary genre most conspicuously associated with the hegemony of global capitalist modernity, against its ideological foundations, in that it unmasks the readiness to unleash annihilating power as a slavish prerogative that turns its wielders into something neither human or divine but alien to both.[24] In the epilogue to the film, amid the debris floating through space, a television with a cracked screen comes to rest against the lower left corner of the frame. The TV switches on, and in a sequence that in its nondiegetic character serves as a counterpoint to the montage shown during Kang's confession, shows scenes of Byung-Gu's life—pleasant moments from his childhood with his parents, the days with his first girlfriend, and the times he went to watch Sooni perform at the circus. The subjects of globalization find themselves confronted by the dilemma of having to choose between the preservative potentialities of becoming-alien, which in this case amounts to becoming-tyrant, or an unconditional fidelity to human obligations. As a kind of final reminder of all that is worth fighting for and that is invariably threatened, whether by globalizing order or fragmenting chaos, these scenes intimate the transcendent duties and affections rooted in the singularly human world, the world we leave behind when we take shelter in what Simone Weil, following Plato, condemned as the "great beast."[25]

3 THE SAINTLY POLITICS OF CATASTROPHE
Hayao Miyazaki's *Nausicaä of the Valley of Wind*

Indeed, if anyone can show that what we've said is false and has adequate knowledge that justice is best, he'll surely be full not of anger but of forgiveness for the unjust. He knows that, apart from someone of godlike character who is disgusted by injustice or one who has gained knowledge and avoids injustice for that reason, no one is just willingly.

— PLATO, *THE REPUBLIC*

SAINTS AND REVOLUTION

The narratives of Hayao Miyazaki are distinguished by their sense of moral nuance and by their fair-minded treatment of dramatic conflict. In the film that has been celebrated as his masterpiece, *Princess Mononoke*, he treats the problem of environmental destruction with compelling equanimity. The human beings who despoil the natural world are not motivated by greed, nor are they mindless consumers of material possessions. Rather, Miyazaki chooses to portray the destroyers of nature in the most sympathetic light possible — they are the members of a community drawn from the lowliest denizens of feudal Japan: subsistence farmers, destitute laborers, lepers, and prostitutes whose freedom has been purchased by the town's ruler, the ruthless and compassionate Lady Eboshi. This utopian community of the oppressed and outcast prospers and grows powerful by mining iron ore, which leads them to cut down the trees and pollute the river. Their nascent industry brings them into conflict not only with the samurai landholders living downstream but also with the animal gods that

93

protect the forest. The defenders of the forest are animals that are intelligent and possess the power of speech. The wolves and boars fighting the humans are shown to be as noble as they are deadly.

The central conflict of *Mononoke* accordingly develops not as a morality play that straightforwardly divides its characters between good and evil, but rather as a clash between two rights, pitting the defenders of the forest against a community of the oppressed and outcast that is intent on exploiting its resources in order to safeguard its destiny. The rights of Nature cannot be defended without cruelty, while the human community that destroys it exhibits an undeniably revolutionary dimension. Into the fray steps the protagonist, the banished Prince Ashitaka, who seeks not to secure the triumph of one side over the other but rather to bring about their reconciliation. Ashitaka, who, significantly, is a member of the indigenous Ainu people driven from their homelands by the ethnic Japanese,[1] is distinguished by a sense of impartiality, his steadfast desire to understand the perspectives and motives of others, especially those of his enemies, without succumbing to the impulse to condemn them. Such a disinterested standpoint, far from resulting in cold detachment, is accompanied by a readiness to take action and risk his life in the aid of others. It could thus be said that Miyazaki's protagonists demonstrate saintly qualities, as their moral resolve—and initiative to act—is often heightened rather than diminished by their awareness of the irreducible ambiguities inherent to the conflicts and struggles they confront. Ashitaka reproaches himself for injuring and taking the lives of fellow human beings even when his acts have the unquestionably heroic consequence of saving the lives of others. On the other hand, he does not waver in his efforts to bring an end to the war between Iron Town, or Tatara, and the forest. The prince, who is exiled from his people after suffering a demonic curse, recognizes the catastrophic dangers certain to be unleashed as the conflict intensifies.

At the end of the film, he and San, a human girl raised by the wolf goddess as her own daughter, are able to avert the apocalyptic destruction of both the forest and the human community. Eboshi, who seeks to defeat once and for all the gods of the forest, shoots and decapitates its highest guardian, the forest spirit or *shishigami,* which in daytime takes the form of a stag with a human-like face. But the deer god, an utterly enigmatic figure of nonhuman otherness, fails to die, taking on instead a ghostly form to search for his head. A toxic substance flows from his body, destroying everything in its wake and making barren the earth. Ashitaka and San succeed in restoring to the deer god his head, halting thereby the flow of the deadly sludge. The plants begin to grow back, as delicate shoots sprout up around the wreckage of the ironworks. Among the surviving inhabitants of Tatara there is the determination to start afresh and rebuild the town, but with the chastened awareness that they must henceforth work out a way of coexisting with the forest. But the readiness to embrace a sustainable way of life is accompanied by a sense of irrevocable loss—the great animal gods have all perished, while San herself wonders whether the *shishigami* will even be present in the regenerated forest, whether, in spite of his physical restoration, he has in fact died after all.

Miyazaki, for his part, hypothesizes that the Japanese overcame their fear and awe of nature in the Muromachi era, that during this pivotal epoch human beings began to dispense with the ancient taboos that governed their relations to the nonhuman world. They could no longer regard nature as a form of violent and terrifying otherness but instead began to domesticate it as a resource for their own purposes.[2] After this turning point, even the desire to respect nature and the resolution to live in harmony with it prove destructive of life. The character of Ashitaka, for Miyazaki, is significant not only because his words and actions seek to prevent a collective from pursuing a catastrophic path but also because he accepts and lives out the tension between nature and human needs. Indeed, the narrative makes clear that the primary reason for the flourishing of Iron Town as a refuge for the poor and outcast is its manufacture of firearms, which enables its inhabitants to defeat both the animal gods and the samurai. A battle scene in which a group of charging samurai is slaughtered by musket fire from Eboshi's troops underscores pointedly the ways in which technological advances serve to negate so-called natural advantages and undermine existing social hierarchies. This scene, along with the crucial displays of the aristocratic virtue of magnanimity by the wolf goddess, reminds us of the harsh truth that societies marked by rigid class divisions, such as Tokugawa Japan, have often been more protective of the natural world than those based on equality. The destruction of nature is brought about not only from unchecked ambition and the desire for limitless power but also from the yearning to feed the hungry and to overcome the injustices of caste and class.

Miyazaki gives this conflict a more detailed treatment in his epic manga, *Nausicaä of the Valley of Wind*, which he wrote over a period of thirteen years and completed three years before the release of *Mononoke*. The extended form of the manga, which features a complex mythos and runs to over a thousand pages, enables him to develop and pursue in unparalleled detail and comprehensiveness the major themes, such as the destruction of nature, technological hubris, political revolution, and the heroics of peacemaking, that have come to define his films. *Nausicaä*, in its depiction of two warring superpowers, is conceived on a grand scale and executed in a somewhat improvisatory manner, reflecting the influence of the tumultuous events that took place during the time of its writing. It commences with the specter of devastating warfare between rival empires and concludes by engaging the insidious moral dilemmas that lie in wait in an age of triumphant technology that arrogates a redemptive meaning to its perpetuity.

Nausicaä is set thousands of years after the ceaseless depredation of the environment and a catastrophic global war, known as the "seven days of fire," have resulted in the reversion of human civilization to feudalism, albeit with scattered reminders of the technologized world that was lost— rifles, artillery, primitive aircraft, and biological weapons. The states and principalities of this future are constantly under the menace of the "Sea of Corruption," an ever-expanding forest of toxic fungi deadly to human beings, who can survive its miasma only with the aid of protective masks. The spread of these toxins has resulted in a precipitous decline in life expectancy, with fewer and fewer children surviving into adulthood with each passing generation. Swarms of enormous flying insects inhabit the poisonous forest, attacking the primitive aircraft that dare to venture into it and releasing the spores that contain the deadly miasma. The largest of the strange, apparently mutated insects are the Ohmu, gigantic, intelligent horseshoe crab–shaped creatures with fourteen eyes that change color according to their emotional state. Miyazaki derived the name for his fantastic beasts from the Japanese transliteration of "sandworm" from Frank Herbert's *Dune* novels. Similar to the gigantic creatures in Herbert's novels, the Ohmu play a decisive role in Miyazaki's narrative. The Ohmu share a collective consciousness, in accordance with the principle that the one is the whole and the whole is the one, and, as one major plotline shows, go to great lengths to defend the least of their kind. The humans hate and fear their destructive power, as their stampedes are known to obliterate entire towns and armies. Nausicaä, who is the eleventh child of the chieftain of the small principality of the Valley of Wind and the only one among her siblings to survive to adulthood, possesses a mysterious empathy with these creatures, sharing with them a telepathic bond.

Nausicaä displays many of the qualities that typify Miyazaki's heroines—she is courageous, resourceful, gentle, conscientious, and intellectually curious. In a world wracked by bloodshed and menaced by pestilence, she is a skilled fighter and capable strategist who nevertheless strives to the utmost to bring an end to a calamitous and futile war. Like Ashitaka in *Princess Mononoke*, her overriding goal is to bring about the reconciliation of the warring parties. Named for the Phaeacian princess who gave shelter to the shipwrecked and starving Odysseus and helped restore him to health, Miyazaki's Nausicaä is also modeled after a girl from an aristocratic family who flouted the stern conventions of the Heian period and was known as the "princess who loved insects" on account of her unusual (at the time) fascination with nature and its creatures.[3] She is first portrayed as a scientist and explorer, dedicated to the secret study of the animals, plants, and minerals of the Sea of Corruption—an activity that most of her superstitious people condemn as sacrilegious—then as a commander helping to carry out a daring cavalry attack, and finally as a spiritual leader, hailed as a messiah by the uprooted Dorok people and as a goddess by the despised tribe of worm-handlers.

Her acts of bravery and self-sacrifice along the way culminate in her becoming the focus of the long-thwarted hopes and millennial yearnings of the oppressed and despairing masses, a destiny that reveals an affinity, as Andrew Osmond observes, with another wise and principled heroine, George Bernard Shaw's Saint Joan.[4] Indeed, the "voices" that Joan hears on the way to her victories over the English and her eventual martyrdom are paralleled by Nausicaä's supernatural capacity for empathy, which appears to extend to human beings as well as to Ohmu. As Asbel, the sole survivor of a town betrayed and wiped out by the treachery of its long-standing allies, reflects, Nausicaä's great burden—and task—is that she is the only person with the ability to unite the diverse peoples and factions that would otherwise disintegrate into feuding and strife. Yet it is when the courage and selflessness of Nausicaä's actions begin—in the eyes of a people threatened with imminent annihilation—to transcend the significance reserved for wholly human figures of authority and are interpreted in messianic dimensions that the narrative confronts the ambiguous and possibly shattering consequences of the events she sets in motion. Indeed, one might say that in the concluding volume of the manga Miyazaki contrasts the saintliness of his heroine with a realist skepticism of yearnings for transcendence and uncompromising moral stances, as the Nausicaä finds herself compelled to make a fateful choice that discloses the reversibility of her exalted status.

MESSIANISM AFTER THE APOCALYPSE

The major political conflict of this postapocalyptic world is modeled superficially after the superpower struggle of the Cold War. The theocratic Dorok Empire, in its state of accelerating collapse, resembles the Soviet Union, a parallel that Miyazaki states was borne out fortuitously by the sudden disintegration of the socialist states of Eastern Europe in 1989. The Doroks are ruled by near-immortal emperors with paranormal powers, supported by an elaborate hierarchy of monks and priests who are responsible for everything from enforcing doctrinal orthodoxy to reinventing the devastating weapons of biological warfare that helped to destroy the old modern civilization. Their enemy, the kingdom of Torumekia, is a martial order wracked by venomous competition among the members of its ruling family. The Torumekians tend to be light skinned and fair haired—whereas the Doroks have features that are more Asian or Eurasian—and invoke Valhalla on the battlefield, fighting under a royal insignia of two entwined, winged serpents drawn in a Nordic style. Nausicaä becomes drawn into the conflict just as it threatens to escalate into a war of extermination. The Torumekians launch a surprise assault on one of their long-time allies and destroy the factory city of Pejitei, while the Dorok priests orchestrate the destruction of their peoples' lands so that they will have no choice but to invade and colonize the territories of their enemy.

While on a flight testing the Valley's attack aircraft, Nausicaä spots a transport ship being attacked by insect swarms from the Sea of Corruption and flies to its aid. The ship, which turns out to be filled with women and children fleeing from the destruction of Pejitei, however, crashes at the edge of the forest, leaving no survivors except for Rastel, the princess of the city. Before succumbing to her injuries, the princess hands Nausicaä a small jewel-studded orb, with instructions to keep it away from the Torumekians and pass it along to her brother, Asbel. Soon enough, a Torumekian ship lands in the Valley of Wind in search of the orb, after its crew has turned over the wreckage of the transport and desecrated the grave of the princess. Outraged by their incursion, Nausicaä sheds blood for the first time by slaying a Torumekian knight in a duel, but before she can register the shock that she has taken another life, her teacher, the wandering swordsman Yupa, succeeds in appealing to the better part of the Torumekians' valor and persuades them to withdraw instead of becoming caught in a bloody confrontation with the well-armed and indignant troops of the Valley of Wind.

The diverse and complicated strands of the narrative spin out from these incidents following the Torumekian destruction of Pejitei, forming an arc that in turn weaves together the ordeals and adventures not only of Nausicaä but also of various supporting characters whose destinies are no less significant in giving a firm and final shape to the story's tapestry of disaster and salvation. In a twist that anticipates the enmity between San and Eboshi in *Princess Mononoke*—two women who, as mortal adversaries, mirror each other in their relentless fortitude and fierce determination—the Torumekian commander raises an armored visor to reveal the face of an attractive and charismatic young woman, not much older than Nausicaä herself. The older warrior praises her rival's swordsmanship before shattering the latter's weapon in a confrontational gesture intended to convey her own deadly virtuosity as well as the promise of a future challenge. This Torumekian general, Kushana, who is also a member of the royal family, will prove an important character in her own right, with her shifting fortunes as a military commander and the development of her relationships with Nausicaä and Yupa representing one of the major storylines of the manga. Similarly, Rastel's brother Asbel, whom Nausicaä encounters

when he attacks the Torumekian ships in an attempt to avenge the destruction of Pejitei, provides a crucial link between her and the Dorok tribe of
the Mani, as he succeeds in persuading them to revolt against the emperor
and thereby saves the lives of Nausicaä and her companions. The jeweled
orb, which Asbel returns to Nausicaä, turns out to be the "control stone"
for a revived god-warrior, an intelligent, cybernetic weapon responsible
for the destruction of the old world during the Seven Days of Fire, which
the inhabitants of Pejitei had unearthed shortly before the attack by the
Torumekians. Recognized by the giant android with annihilating powers as
its "mother," she takes it with her on her final quest to destroy the temple
housing the technologies of the apocalypse at the Dorok capital of Shuwa.

The worm-handlers, almost universally despised as the lowliest and
most squalid of peoples for their practice of plundering corpses and of vio-
lating the taboos held by the other peoples against contact with the insects
of the forest, also play an important part in this episode, employed as mer-
cenaries for the Torumekians. Their maggots, sensing the presence of the
god-warrior's control stone, climb onto Nausicaä and rouse her into raising her sword in a fury over being forced to make physical contact with
these creatures. Much later, the worm-handlers will become Nausicaä's
most devoted followers. Finally, in another moment that parallels *Mononoke*,
a monstrous and overpowering creature is shown making an unexpected
display of gentleness and compassion, as the fearsome Ohmu that is first
shown chasing Yupa out of the forest crawls up to the wreckage of the
Pejiteian transport ship in a state of grief over the lives of both the insects
and humans lost in the crash. The riddle of the behavior of the Ohmu,
once a virulent, bioengineered mold is released into the land with devastating consequences, leads Nausicaä to make an archetypal descent into the
literal belly of this beast. She emerges from it reborn not only as a savior
who, in the manner of the bodhisattva, refuses her own entry into the realm
of peace but also, more disturbingly, as a saintly destroyer whose actions
cast the surviving human population into a future of hardship and expose
them to possible extinction.

Shortly after this initial skirmish with the Torumekian raiding party,
fresh from slaughtering soldier and civilian alike at Pejitei, and first confrontation with a rival princess who appears destined to be her mortal foe,

Nausicaä is compelled to fulfill the terms of the treaty whereby her people are obliged to give military support to the Torumekian Empire, traveling at the helm of a detachment of aging soldiers sent by the Valley of Wind to fight alongside Kushana's army. But nothing could be further from Miyazaki's vision than the formula of the martial science-fiction or fantasy epic in which the forces of evil and oppression are overthrown by the just and sportsmanlike combat carried on by the minions of the good. His heroine, far from remaining a partisan identifying with the purposes of a single faction, continually crosses and thereby erodes the boundaries separating the different sides in the conflict. For example, she wins the hearts of the Torumekian soldiers whom she earlier confronted as her enemies when she gives mouth-to-mouth resuscitation to one of their comrades who has inhaled the miasma, taking his poisoned blood into her own body in order to save his life. Yet more typical than this straightforward act of compassion and benevolence is the way in which Nausicaä engages the dilemmas that ineluctably emerge in response to her efforts to aid the suffering and the endangered. Discovering that the soldiers of Kushana's army are holding in captivity a large number of Dorok civilians to take back to their native land as slaves, and most probably fearing that they will be massacred out of tactical necessity, Nausicaä insists to Kushana that they be released, arguing that, as the Torumekians are under siege by a much larger Dorok force, they have no means of transporting their prisoners, who, furthermore, are noncombatants unable to serve in the Dorok army. In this instance it is Kushana who responds with a sincere offer of comradeship that, for once, catches Nausicaä off guard, when, after initially dismissing the request of her nominal and unwilling ally as a piece of high-minded self-righteousness, she invites Nausicaä to fight alongside her in the coming battle:

> Right now, I couldn't care less about prisoners or slaves. All that matters are the lives of my 2,000 men. But I'm not about to do whatever you ask just so you can keep your little hands nice and clean. It offends me. However, if it was the advice of a comrade-in-arms, I just might listen.[5]

In the battle that follows, rendered by Miyazaki with breathtaking pace and enthralling detail, bringing into play machine-gun nests in trenches, artillery bombardments, and grenade attacks with the shock of a medieval cavalry charge, Nausicaä asks for forgiveness from the spirit of the high priest of the Dorok Mani tribe, who had earlier given up his life to save her from the Dorok potentate, Miralupa, as she now takes up arms against the Dorok people, even if her sole motive is to free the Dorok prisoners. Her reluctance to engage in battle does not prevent her from courageously serving Kushana and playing an indispensable role in leading the Torumekians to their objective. Having single-handedly thwarted a counterattack by the Dorok horsemen, Nausicaä is both moved and anguished to see a squad of Torumekians, who have begged permission from Kushana to allow them to risk their lives on Nausicaä's behalf, ride to her aid when it appears that she has been cut off. Her remark when forced to leave the Valley of Wind a second time—that she feels as though the people of many different origins and circumstances who have helped her and given her gifts are "watching over" her—achieves a terrible resonance as the valiant Torumekian cavalrymen are shot to pieces as they fearlessly place themselves between her and the Dorok rifles. But Nausicaä's sympathy extends to the people who are trying to kill her as well, for the young Dorok soldier who shoots her never becomes an object of hatred in her eyes but instead serves to remind her of a friend, and his death too becomes an occasion for grief.

The fluctuating emotional registers of Nausicaä's participation in the Torumekian cavalry attack display forcefully how her loving regard for her enemies and sorrow over their deaths alternate with an undaunted courage that leads her to ride straight into the charging columns of the Dorok horsemen. The fact that Miyazaki's postapocalyptic world is governed according to feudal codes and values enables him to depict his characters with a certain epic simplicity, liberating them from the modern incapacity to embrace life and death unreservedly. Indeed, Osmond observes that for both of Miyazaki's heroines (Kushana having unwittingly taken the first steps toward her own spiritual and moral renewal), "random death begets a spontaneous, often frightening, love of life."[6] This is not to say that Miyazaki nostalgically privileges uncomplicated, "flat" characters distinguished by their virtue over alluringly complex evil ones but rather that his ethical vision unfolds from the recognition of the many-sidedness of the human character as it appears from the perspective of the saint. Thus, while Nausicaä's acts of courage and compassion are shown being accepted without ridicule and suspicion by a people belonging to a cultural ethos that prizes martial virtues and heroic spiritedness, Miyazaki's narration subtly draws out the complex ethical and political backdrop in which her actions come to exert an "imperative force," which, according to Edith Wyschogrod, constitutes the proper interpretive mode of hagiography.[7]

For the lucidity of Miyazaki's ethical vision discloses itself in startling shifts of character and mood, in which an act or event forces one state of mind to give way to its opposite, one that stands in sharp contrast to the mood or affect that has hitherto prevailed. Even in a brief sketch of minor characters, Miyazaki is able to communicate the disturbing, deforming reality of violence and oppression and its interplay with and even inextricability from feelings of love and devotion, such as when Nausicaä comes across a pair of Torumekian soldiers abusing a Dorok family. The two soldiers, who have just abandoned a dying comrade and then set out to forage for food and break into a Dorok farmhouse and threaten its occupants, an elderly Dorok couple and their grandchildren sitting at dinner. One of the Torumekians, filled with contempt, fumbles through and tosses away their food, disgusted by what strikes him as its meagerness and putridity, while the other presses the barrel of his machine gun against the forehead of a little boy to force his grandparents to hand over the provisions they have stored for the winter. When the grandfather, outraged by the threat against his grandson, raises a sword against the Torumekians, they beat him down and prepare to murder him, but are prevented from doing so when Nausicaä appears at the door. She tells them of Kushana's arrival, and persuades them to wait outside, promising to take them to their commander. Upon hearing the news, the hard looks of callousness and brutality disappear from the faces of the Torumekians, who begin to weep tears of sorrow as well as of unhoped-for joy. It is as though the miraculous return of their beloved commander, whom they feared had been killed, also serves to stir the deep-rooted recognition of their sufferings and predicament, making them unbearably aware of their plight as young men cut off by enemy troops and facing almost certain death in a strange and distant country.

It is the awareness of this grim proximity between murderous cruelty and selfless devotion, pathetic animal fear and courage-inspiring admiration, the sensation of omnipotence derived from oppressing those incapable of retaliation and the humble joy at receiving an unforeseen blessing, so deftly rendered by Miyazaki in a mere two pages of panels, that comprises the basis of Nausicaä's discernment, or "foolish" wisdom. On this and on other occasions, she responds to the wrongs committed against her by taking the blow without defending herself, drawing back to register the effect her restraint has on her assailant before taking action herself. In this instance, she is spat on by a Dorok child who believes her to be one of their oppressors, but the look of sorrow that crosses her face brings the child's grandmother to intervene. The family awakens, however briefly, from the deadly enmity of war when the elderly woman reprimands her grandchild, bidding him to look at her face and recognize that she is different from the soldiers who had earlier threatened them. The saintliness behind Nausicaä's actions proceeds from the understanding that violence and strife arise not through evil as such but from the fact that evil is inescapably entangled with the good. Thus, the Torumekian troops who viciously maltreat and oppress the Dorok peasants are also the same gallant warriors who unhesitatingly give their own lives to protect a stranger and foreigner whose courage on the battlefield has won their admiration and respect. Nausicaä remains throughout fully aware of the tragic nature of human conflict, having internalized, as it were, the sense of "extraordinary equity" that Simone Weil ascribed to the author of the *Iliad*, the sobriety that is free of that intoxication experienced by the victorious and the defeated alike. Weil, in her essay, "The *Iliad*, Poem of Might," observes that the exercise of force unavoidably blinds those who wield it, deluding them into the belief that those persons they reduce to the condition of "inert matter," whether in the form of the slave or the corpse, belong to a wholly "different species" for which "degradation" constitutes an "innate vocation."[8] Nausicaä, in being immune to the intoxication of might, is able to look upon the perpetrators of war and oppression with the readiness to oppose them but also without hatred, regarding them not as inexplicable monsters maliciously carving their own bloody, self-glorifying temples out of the flesh of human realities, but rather as slaves weighed down by the burden of some implacable and inexorable compulsion, whether of history, culture, their own experiences of affliction, or previous attempts at rectifying the errors of the past.

Nausicaä's pursuit of love and justice, based on her refusal to abide by the rule of the "empire of might" that prevails among human beings, thus does not engender the familiar and dismayingly predictable reflex of repudiating and disavowing evil as an essentially alien and incomprehensible object of dread. Rather, she is prepared to embrace those who commit evil as parts of her own self, even as she unflaggingly struggles against them to prevent the destruction they prepare to unleash on the world. Nausicaä's radical adherence to love as a principle of action becomes most compellingly manifest in her treatment of the spirit of the Dorok autocrat Miralupa, who is responsible for the deaths of thousands and has forced his own people to become refugees in order to force their commitment to the war against Torumekia. Having been swallowed up by an Ohmu, which saves her from being poisoned by the bioengineered mold, and becoming submerged in a state of suspended animation, Nausicaä finds herself under attack by Miralupa's disembodied spirit while hovering between life and death in the darkness of her own inner world. Warding off the assault, Nausicaä breaks apart the murky ectoplasm with which he has attempted to smother her to discover a shriveled and terrified creature, a virtual cadaver with two enormous hollows for eyes, crouching in a fetal position. Instead of driving him away, Nausicaä takes him by the hand and leads him through the desolate landscape of her soul, the vision of bones, ruins, and universal death that has haunted her throughout her journey. When the darkness threatens to consume Miralupa's withered and desiccated soul, she pulls him from the void and enters with him into an abounding and verdant forest that has become fully cleansed of miasma and pollution. Admonished by the telepath Selm, who has come to guide Nausicaä through the forest, for rescuing a murderous tyrant and bringing him into the peaceful and healed world, Nausicaä gives the startling reply that if the restored forest is within her, then the desert and darkness are within her also, and Miralupa—a despot responsible for releasing the bioengineered fungus that threatens to destroy human civilization—has become a part of her as well (VI: 71/III: 221).

Nausicaä's act of saving Miralupa, whom Miyazaki modeled after totalitarian dictators and the most ruthless popes, presents a troublesome problematic with regard to the question of its ethics. Does she act out of a perversely intransigent naïveté, a blind and disastrous confidence in the goodness that supposedly lies at the bottom of every human heart, no matter how rapacious or homicidal? Is her deed to be understood as an extreme fulfillment of the Levinasian ethics of alterity, which entails an "unlimited responsibility" for the subject, calling on him or her to repudiate his or her egoism for the sake of responding properly to the vulnerability and exposure of the other?[9] Or should she be condemned for narcissistically projecting her own vision of the good upon a fundamentally heterogeneous other, who, though in this case a reprehensible mass murderer, should not be incorporated into the sameness sought after by the ego? I would argue that Nausicaä's decision breaks with both an ethics based on utilitarianism and pragmatism, and one that puts forward as its standard the imperative of respecting the alterity of the other. For with regard to the former, the plot itself furnishes the elements to deflect the charge of excessive naïveté—Miralupa has by this point been overthrown by his brother, the nominal emperor Namulith, and his body destroyed by the usurper, so that he is left enfeebled and incapable of inflicting any harm after Nausicaä shatters his paranormal powers. Indeed, it is clear that Nausicaä would fight Miralupa to the death, as she does with his brother, if it would prevent him from taking the lives of others. On the other hand, Nausicaä's insistence on treating the Dorok tyrant as an extension of herself, as opposed to keeping her distance from the inviolable and untouchable dimension of his otherness, cannot but stand as a refusal to follow the imperative to preserve the difference of the other and maintain an unconditional respect toward the alterity of another human being. A love that transforms the other is a force that does not halt timorously at the boundary of otherness. Likewise, those who plead most earnestly for the unconditional respect for the Other do not realize that the highest respect one can accord to another is to adopt his or her morality. As John Milbank points out, the deconstructionist alternative cannot go beyond an "endless postponement of egotism," without any possibility of "peace and reconciliation."[10] Indeed, Catherine Pickstock, in questioning the viability of a postmodern theology, argues that the ethics of alterity ensures that "the good never arrives in any form whatsoever," for human desire, being irremediably pathologized, remains in effect cut off from any higher longing than the frustration of thwarted self-interest.[11]

Although Miyazaki endows Nausicaä with a supernatural capacity for empathy, this fantasy motif serves largely as a correlative for the steadiness of her orientation toward the good, which, according to Weil, must be understood in supernatural terms as a divine gift. But such gifts, which from the standpoint of Enlightenment modernity (and postmodernity) are as a matter of course dismissed as unreasonable restrictions and overbearing infringements on individual desire, are contingent on the willingness of the subject to receive them; furthermore, they emerge and grow out of the spiritual trials of its future recipient. As Weil writes, "we cannot have a horror of doing harm to others unless we have reached a point where others can no longer do harm to us (then we love others, to the furthest limit, like our past selves)."[12] As if in accordance with this strenuous mystical principle combining the utmost emotional vulnerability with an indomitable courage, Nausicaä, though she exposes herself constantly to death, has reached the level of spiritual consciousness where she believes that she cannot be truly harmed by fate, and thus goes beyond mere chivalric magnanimity in responding with love and compassion to the numerous enemies who assail her.

Weil's aphorism notes that the extreme point of immunity and horror results in the capacity to regard others as one's "past selves." Such a standpoint contemplates an otherwise unbearable continuity between oneself and the others that one would reflexively condemn and repudiate. It is not as though Nausicaä comes to identify with the ambitions and temptations of the tyrant. Rather, she recognizes that to respond to him with revulsion is to underestimate the force of compulsion under which one might submit to evil under the guise of necessity. When Yupa confronts the Dorok women, who, under the pretense of retrieving food for their children, plant explosives to kill the surviving Torumekian soldiers, they brush aside his attempts to dissuade them from breaking a fragile truce: "No outsider can understand the suffering and humiliation we've endured!" (VII: 70/IV: 118). Yupa and Nausicaä, born to a world of suffering and travail, have no illusions about the ennobling effects of affliction; indeed, they both exemplify the moral paradox whereby the saintly are the ones who are least surprised and disturbed by human evil, supremely conscious as they are of their own fallibility, whereas true depravity consists of being deluded as to the nature of one's own virtue and rectitude. The saints, one might say, are saintly precisely because they acknowledge the sheer contingency of goodness, not least their own, in face of devouring affliction: "Whoever does not know just how far necessity and fickle fortune hold the human soul under their domination cannot treat as his equals, nor love as himself, those whom chance has separated from him by an abyss," not least by the abyss separating victims from their oppressors.[13]

It is Yupa's fate to die as a martyr at the hands of the vengeful Doroks, while Nausicaä's is to undergo far more perilous temptations in the final chapters of the narrative, when she descends into the depths of the crypt at Shuwa. But before these daunting trials, her actions and example—as well as those of her mentor, Yupa—come to exercise a transforming influence upon Kushana, who at first grimly reflects on the difference between their respective destinies: "You walk the path you have chosen as you see fit . . . It's a fine way to live. And I will walk my own crimson path . . . a cursed path . . . Father, brothers, sisters, shedding each other's blood" (III: 148/II: 153). But then she soon finds herself taking to heart Nausicaä's advice to face the giant insects without hatred and fear, thereby saving herself and several of her men during an attack by a massive swarm of the migrating creatures. Moments before, Kushana, witnessing the death of her hated half-brother, who is responsible for poisoning her mother and on whom she has thirsted to avenge herself, realizes that the fulfillment of this burning wish leaves her empty, while her mind becomes fixed instead on the "overwhelming sadness of the warmth of my men's bodies" (V: 48/III: 50). Huddling in a ditch with a tiny band of survivors, she looks out, calmly and without trepidation, on the carnage wrought by the almost suicidal violence of the insects. The formidable Torumekian general is portrayed here as a protective maternal figure, soothing her wounded and terrified men with a lullaby, while their comrades are cut to pieces around them. Although later, in recounting this event and her astonishing response to it, she confides to Yupa that she does not want even to attempt "to emulate [Nausicaä], to feel not contempt nor anger but sorrow," Kushana comes gradually to relinquish the blood-drenched path of an ambitious warlord and potential usurper of the throne, and works alongside Nausicaä's mentor and others of her friends to bring an end to the war (V: 49/III: 51). Indeed, one of the most potent ironies of the narrative, as Osmond points out, is that "the self-destructive Kushana" becomes a "beacon of hope," whereas the oppressed Doroks, in their apocalyptic fervor, "worship Nausicaä as an angel of death."[14]

For it is the collective perception of Nausicaä's efforts at saving the Doroks, which are accorded a divine meaning, that culminate in perhaps the most unsettling reversal of the narrative, the repercussions of which reverberate beyond the limit marked by the story's conclusion. Her gifts, talents, and feats of bravery become charged with a superhuman and apocalyptic significance among the Dorok tribes, who, in spite of the fearsome inquisitions launched by their rulers, cling with undiminished enthusiasm to the prophecies, condemned as heretical, of deliverance into a better world. Nausicaä is first taken to be the messiah spoken of in the Dorok scriptures when she acts to return to the herd a tortured and dying Ohmu infant, cloned in the Dorok laboratories in order to trigger stampedes of the massive insects against their Torumekian adversaries. Out of gratitude, one of the great creatures heals her injuries with its own blood, staining her dress with a deep shade of blue, which the monk-chieftain of a Dorok tribe recognizes as a mark of the divine. The image of a savior dressed in blue clothes is related as being widespread among not only the Doroks but also the mystical Forest People—a tribe that has forsworn the use of fire to live in harmony with the Sea of Corruption—who venerate as their "blue-clad one" the guide who led their ancestors to safety in the forest after the collapse of the Eftal Kingdom during the previous environmental cataclysm, known as the *daikaisho*. Nausicaä's unique ability to communicate with the Ohmu gives rise to a chain of events whereby the Dorok Mani tribe is told of the imminent coming of the savior by their leader. The fact that she is helped by a small boy with paranormal powers, a Dorok princeling named Chikuku, in giving instructions to the remaining Doroks on how to escape the coming destruction results in her being hailed as the "white-winged apostle." The Doroks take her to be the divine messenger who will lead them into a "pure land" free of suffering and despair when they see her flying high above in her *mehve* (taken from *Möwe*, which is seagull in German), a sort of jet glider, while communicating with them telepathically (V: 68/III: 70). Although Miyazaki does not claim Buddhist doctrines as a major source of inspiration, the reference to a strain of the religion with a pronounced eschatological orientation—"Pure Land Buddhism," centered on the figure of Amithaba, who promised to give those who invoke his name rebirth in the "Western Paradise"—would reflect the depths of despair into which the Doroks have fallen. For Pure Land Buddhism holds that in a time of decaying karma, the traditional paths to enlightenment have lost all efficacy, leaving faith and the grace offered by the Amida Buddha as the only means for attaining the realm of peace.[15]

The enthusiastic acceptance of Nausicaä as a messiah by the Doroks and her reception as a goddess by the worm-handlers relay to her the authority to help bring an end to the conflicts between the warring factions and lead the survivors to safety from the spread of the mutant mold. But even as her example inspires some of the Doroks to place their own bodies in front of their angry warriors in order to prevent them from taking revenge against their surviving enemies, the narrative nevertheless raises a harsh and bitter prospect for the symbolic identity she will bequeath to the people. While her friend and teacher Yupa wonders whether the figure of the blue-clad messiah is simply a projection of the hope for salvation in the aboriginal Dorok religions, albeit one based on an actual historical personage, or if these saviors are in fact "real people, created by the very life-force of our species, reaching across space and time in our moment of need," it is left to the Torumekian spy Kurotowa, the representative of skeptical worldly wisdom in the narrative, to give voice to the ominous side of the desire for an end to sorrow and for deliverance into a better world (IV: 23/II: 176). On hearing the double meaning of a sutra chanted by the Doroks, which "at times represents a hope for a better life in this world, and at others a yearning for peace in the afterlife," the wily courtier observes that the figure of the blue-clad savior is indistinguishable from a goddess of death, and that the Doroks' hope for a better world masks the yearning for the stillness of the grave (VII: 62/IV: 110).

THE SECRET CATASTROPHE

Indeed, the conclusion of the tale is haunted by the curse that Nausicaä will be remembered as a "devil" by history, as the "one who destroyed the light of hope" (VII: 208/IV: 256). For Miyazaki resolves the narrative with a decision on the part of the protagonist that is certain to strike many readers as puzzling, drastic, and even radically inhuman. The depths of the temple in the Dorok capital hold the technologies intended to preserve human existence amid the far-reaching transformations overtaking a planet riddled with toxins. Nausicaä, confronted with the means of guaranteeing humanity's future in the midst of arduous ordeals and great perils, not only refuses to avail herself of their benefits but also effectively denies them to anyone else. How is one to understand such an extreme and devastating act on the part of a heroine who has been so steadfastly dedicated to saving the lives of others?

Nausicaä confronts the problematical nature of her vocation as savior when a god-warrior, a sentient ultimate weapon responsible for the universal conflagration of the Seven Days of Fire, becomes bonded to her as her "child." Agonized by the thought that she will have to exploit the faithfulness of this annihilating android in order to destroy it, Nausicaä orders the god-warrior, which she names "Ohma" (which means "innocence") to fly her to the temple at Shuwa. She sets out to demolish the temple, the source of the terrible arsenal employed by the Dorok rulers—biological weapons such as the lethal mutant mold and the Heedra, which are giant, invulnerable soldiers nourished on human corpses. Riding in the palm of the all-powerful but decomposing android, which steams with light and rotting flesh, she falls gravely ill from the radioactivity it releases. Nausicaä soon discovers that her animal companion, Teto, has succumbed to radiation poisoning. Asking Ohma to land near a tree so that she can give the squirrel fox a proper burial, she encounters a tall, graceful goatherd, who emerges from the ruins nearby. The goatherd is at first vexed by the disparity of the sight that greets him—a girl, sickened by radiation, mourning the loss of a small animal while keeping company with an enormous "god" of annihilation. He muses disdainfully that the depth of her sadness might well be measured in inverse proportion to the size of the deceased, before remembering his hospitality and inviting her into his home. The ruins turn out to be an illusion camouflaging a well-appointed estate, surrounded by gardens and lush farmland, with thriving flocks of birds and other animals of the former world, and an enormous library filled with books and music from the time before the destruction of civilization during the

Seven Days of Fire. It is in this calm, abundant, and almost paradisiacal refuge from the feudal world stricken by environmental poisoning and mired in endless warfare that Nausicaä meets with her most severe test. Nausicaä awakens from a deep sleep to find herself fully healed and restored, but soon discovers that she is being kept from leaving. The goatherd or gardener, who maintains the estate, uses various illusions to induce amnesia in her so as to prevent her from continuing on her quest. He takes the form of her long-dead mother, but Nausicaä's determination to mourn her dead companion keeps her from acceding to the mirages of happiness and fulfillment the gardener conjures.

Impressed by her tenacity and spiritedness, the gardener tells her that she reminds him of an intelligent and idealistic boy who had resided with him on the estate long ago, who on one morning left the garden with the note, "I want to save humanity" (VII: 120/IV: 168). Accompanied by four Heedra, which in the garden are placid farmers tending the land and not the loathsome, vicious monsters fed on corpses as they are in the service of the Dorok tyrants, the boy also went on to Shuwa. He eventually deposed the Dorok king and made himself the first holy emperor, the father of the murderous despots Namulith and Miralupa. "You humans tread the same paths over and over again," chides the gardener, who is in actuality a millennium-old automaton built in the days before the global conflagration (VII: 121/IV: 169). Stung by his words, Nausicaä recalls Namulith's description of his brother as a philosopher-king who began his rule with the intention of bettering the lot of the peasants, but in the course of two decades had grown to despise his subjects for their "incorrigible stupidity." Why should Nausicaä, equipped with her own ultimate weapon and commanding the fervent allegiance of the tribe of worm-handlers, fare any differently, he asks. As the gardener coldly observes, "Everyone believes that they alone will not err... What you are trying to do has been attempted by other humans many times before" (VII: 122, 125/IV: 170, 173). Nausicaä's acts of love, judged from the gardener's telescoping view of human history, are nothing more than random glints of light that occasionally shine forth along the edge of an executioner's blade. Her own arms have raised and will once again raise the sword; her saintliness serves at best merely to delay the corruption and destruction that follows from the exercise of power.

An even more devastating revelation soon follows. Wracked by self-doubt, Nausicaä calls out to Selm, her friend from the mystical forest people, who by means of telepathy is able to pierce the defenses of the garden. Selm, correctly perceiving the function of the gardener as an immortal guardian, tries to turn the tables on him by asking what it is that he is protecting (VII: 127/IV: 174). The gardener parries this move by hinting that the Sea of Corruption has a purpose and a goal, and in the ensuing dialogue, Nausicaä pieces together the mystery behind its origin as well as its ends. For the Sea of Corruption is revealed to be an artificial ecosystem engineered by human beings at the time of the global conflagration to purify the contaminants that have devastated the earth by petrifying them into harmless minerals. The world having become irrevocably polluted, the scientists of the old world not only created new forms of life, such as the Ohmu and the giant insects, but also frantically altered most existing animals and plants to enable them to adapt to these worsening conditions. The ecosystem of the poisonous forest, Nausicaä realizes, possesses a humanly determined objective. Once it accomplishes the goal of "reviving a barren earth in just a few thousand years," it will die, as "planned from the beginning" (VII: 132/IV: 180). As for human beings, whose bodies were modified to tolerate the miasma, they are likewise doomed to perish once the forest has completed its function, as the gardener condescendingly divulges, while adding that Nausicaä is only able to breathe the garden's uncontaminated air without coughing up blood because he has temporarily altered her body's physiological makeup. Selm, whose people revere the Sea of Corruption as sacred, is thrown off balance by these revelations, whereas a "strange, almost frightening serenity" settles over the formerly distraught Nausicaä. Calmly approaching the gardener once again, who has conceded defeat in his efforts to keep her a prisoner in his man-made paradise, Nausicaä insists on an answer to the question of what the purpose of his garden, which serves as a repository of the life and culture of the old world, its plants, animals, art, poetry, and music, must be, if it is the design of its creators that the human species will die out. If it is the function of the garden to preserve "the only things human beings were able to create that are worth passing on to the next world," why is there, she asks, technology preserved in the crypt at Shuwa that "should not be preserved, technology that spews a shadow of death?" (VII: 134/IV: 182). The narrative intimates that she has already divined the truth—in the depths of the crypt is stored a new, perfected form of human being, which will come out into the world to replace the more violent and imbalanced forbears once the toxic miasma and poisonous forest have completed their work.

It comes as an unexpected development that Miyazaki would bring about such a sweeping reversal so late in the manga. The vision of the healed earth that Nausicaä received while swallowed up within the Ohmu, which had rekindled her will to live after her experience of war and environmental devastation, is unmasked, in Osmond's words, as a "cruel cheat, an alien world her people will not survive."[16] The path of a brutal and vicious autocrat like Miralupa lies far closer to her own than Nausicaä has allowed herself to suspect, as she too is forced to contend with the gap between her own spiritual discipline, which she willingly embraces and in which she even delights, and the collective yearnings for deliverance her actions have intensified among the Doroks and the worm-handlers. The interlude in the garden augurs Nausicaä's transformation from steadfast ecological warrior and scientist into something more ambiguous and troubling—Frederik Schodt compares her to the Hindu deity Shiva on the basis of her dual potency of creation and destruction, the latter of which she visits upon the angelic future prepared by the long-dead people of the technological age.[17] The gardener's scornful, though irrefutably sober-minded, chiding of Nausicaä and Selm for taking consolation from the image of a restored nature has the effect of mercilessly depriving them of the pragmatic justification of collective well-being as the legitimating factor for their endeavors: "Why do your people go on deceiving themselves that a place that can only be visited in spirit somehow represents hope?" (VII: 128/IV: 176).

Nevertheless, though burdened by agonizing doubts and qualms— "Why am I doing this? For all I know . . . I may be going to destroy humanity" (VII: 140–41/IV: 188–89)—Nausicaä presses on to Shuwa to see her quest to its end, regardless of how bitter it may prove. Indeed, she finds herself unable to spell out fully the true function of the toxic forest to the worm-handlers, who have zealously pledged their service to her, revealing only that the Sea of Corruption is purifying the world of poisons. Meanwhile, the Torumekian emperor arrives at Shuwa ahead of Nausicaä and her group, his army overwhelming the city's defenders. It takes, however, the power of the god-warrior Ohma to blast open an entrance to the crypt, bringing about an explosion that envelops the entire city under a mushroom cloud. The order of monks dwelling in the crypt offers its allegiance to the invading emperor, who has come seeking immortality, as its new overlord. These monks, whose quasi-immortal bodies are in a state of ever-increasing putrescence, work at deciphering a sacred text that has provided the Dorok rulers with their lengthy life-spans and horrifying weapons. They plead with the brutal and haughty Torumekian monarch to wait patiently for the master of the tomb, assuring him that the holy emperor did not believe at first in his power either. Nausicaä joins the group gathered at the bowels of the temple, in front of a giant, pulsating sphere, a company that includes not only the emperor and its monk servants but also a sharp-tongued dwarf jester, who openly admits his desire to witness his master's death. A blinding light streams from the orb, followed by the appearance of an enormous throng of robed people before the emperor and Nausicaä. They proclaim that they represent the "great many who died meaningless deaths because of their own folly" and promise that on the day when their text manifests itself completely, the suffering will come to an end (VII: 195/IV: 243). Nausicaä, to the horror of the monks, dismisses the congregation of the children of light as barren shadows, and demands that the master appear in person to answer her charge that the crypt exists for the purpose of replacing all living beings. The Master then appears as a handsome, disembodied face that takes possession of the jester. He declares that the people of the past, suffering plagues, wars, and environmental catastrophes, chose to "entrust everything to the future." But the technology they placed in the crypt will enable the "imperfect" humans to inhabit the purified world alongside the new species of peaceful humans currently gestating in its depths. Once the "long period of purification is over," he declares, "the human race shall become a peaceful part of the new world," for once the knowledge and technology preserved in the crypt has completed its work, "it shall surely be music and poetry that humanity treasures above all else" (VII: 200/IV: 248).

The spirit bestowing unstoppable plagues and doomsday weapons turns out to be not an automaton seeking to correct human frailties once and for all, nor a hideous demon spewing hatred, but an angel of light serenely promising a golden age of peace and abundance on a planet healed and cleansed of its poisons. The source of the darkness that has swallowed up the Dorok rulers is revealed to be a grand humanitarian project to regenerate and repopulate the earth. Such an inversion leads one to wonder how the first holy emperor had responded to the discovery that the fearsome armaments of the crypt did not conceal a dark and depraved secret but one hopeful and bright. After all, the father of Namulith and Miralupa had also come to Shuwa with the goal of freeing the people from the yoke of their oppression, from the rule of violent and murderous kings, only to impose a theocratic dictatorship that coerces the obedience of its subjects through state terror and engages in brutal warfare against its rival empire. Indeed, the decaying, near-immortal priests residing in the crypt hint darkly that the turning point of the Dorok despot's reign, when he gave up on his efforts to build a more humane order and began to oppress and persecute the peasants, can be traced to the moment he divined its true purpose. It would appear that the Dorok emperors, confronted with a foreordained future in which human beings will either die off or else be remade into perfected creatures, began to treat the people as inconvenient and expendable masses of flesh. As Namulith declares after ousting his brother in a coup, reflecting on the good fortune to have seized the throne after the toxic mold has drastically reduced the human population, "we humans became obsolete long, long ago, as far as this planet is concerned" (VI: 43/III: 193).

Nausicaä, on the other hand, categorically refuses the salvation contained in the crypt. It occurs to her, as it does to Namulith, that human beings have doomed themselves through their ceaseless exploitation of nature, but unlike the emperor, she struggles against that thought, which assails her with premonitions and dreams. Walking in a desert wasteland covered by mounds of corpses, she is greeted by a giant, cadaverous priest that rejoices in the coming of the "long period of purification." He affirms that the uncontrolled spread of the miasma is the beginning of the process of rebirth and then changes into a skeleton (V: 61/III: 63), extending a blood-stained hand to invite Nausicaä to enter a "peaceful world" before she drives him away (V: 62/III: 65). When this spirit of the nothingness assails her a second time, pointing to the blood on her own hands and the people that she herself has killed, Nausicaä assumes the guilt of her actions, but also refuses to accept the authority of the void: "I don't need the nothingness to tell me that we are a cursed people" (V: 137/III: 139). Her condemnation of the master's path to redemption is accordingly both intransigent and irrevocable: "Our bodies may have been artificially transformed, but our lives will always be our own! Life survives by the power of life" (VII: 198/IV: 246). When the Master protests that only he can ensure the survival of the human species, Nausicaä flatly rejects the continuation of human life according to the terms of his plan—the fate of humanity, she insists, must be decided by the planet and not directed by the technologies of the crypt. She thereupon calls out to the dying god-warrior to perform one final task, to destroy the tomb and its master, now transformed into a circular mass of flesh that Ohma crushes in its massive palm.

AN ARTIFICIAL DELIVERANCE

The destruction of the crypt nevertheless provides an unsettling resolution to the tale, one that, far from tying up its loose strands, raises disconcerting questions about the future that Nausicaä has in effect imposed on her world. For her decision places human life at the mercy of a gravely wounded planet, its continuance threatened by the spread of disease and the curse of infertility. Indeed, her love of the natural world leads her to accept the risk of catastrophe for humanity. Her reflections on learning of the technological origins of the Sea of Corruption and its intended function affirm the dynamism of nature over the designs of the human will:

> The world is beginning to be reborn. Even if our bodies cannot tolerate that purity... even if the moment we are exposed to it, we spew blood from our lungs... Just as the birds migrate across the land, we shall live and live again. For the sake of a single sprout, countless forest spores rain down again and again, dying a useless death. My own life was supported by the deaths of ten older brothers and sisters. No matter how wretched, every life-form lives by virtue of its own power. On this planet, life itself is its own miracle. Are we to believe that those

who planned the reconstruction of the world could have predicted the actions of the Ohmu or the giant mold? I don't think so . . . I suppose those men left that black thing [the crypt] to be the kernel of the reconstruction . . . and it never occurred to them that that itself was the ultimate demonstration of contempt for life. (VII: 171–72/IV: 219–20)

Nausicaä embraces the conviction that to deny suffering and tragedy is to deny life. Nevertheless, other thoughts remain ambiguous and unexplained. As Osmond points out, it is uncertain whether she places her faith in the resilience of human beings in the face of grave hardships, or if she privileges the continuance and unpredictable spontaneity of nature over human existence itself.[18] For Nausicaä marvels at the capacity of even artificially created organisms, by virtue of their becoming exposed to an environment and to other forms of life, to undergo unanticipated transformations and shake off the designs intended by their creators. Such dynamism is exhibited by the abject mold in its devouring frenzy as well as by the noble Ohmu, which deliberately sacrifice their lives to provide a seedbed for the mold. Is she then asserting that there is a sanctity above the imperatives of human life, one that supersedes even the survival of the entire species? Do the migrating birds refer to the adaptability of humans to radically altered circumstances or to the journey of the soul after death? While Nausicaä passionately rejects the idea of progress as a redemptive doctrine, her insistence that death and suffering are fundamental to existence would verge on an antihuman extreme, given the tremendous stakes of her decision.

Miyazaki underwent profound shifts in his political perspective during the thirteen-year period he spent at work on the epic manga, and Nausicaä's destruction of the crypt and rejection of its redemptive purpose lend themselves easily to being read as an emphatic rejection of the mass political ideologies of technocratic progressivism. Nevertheless, in his portrayal of the tomb and its master, his target is not merely the Marxism he espoused in his youth but rather what he perceives to be the organizing principle and overriding aim of all modern societies: the endeavor to deny death. The technology that enables modern societies to diminish steadily the vulnerability and exposure of human beings to the condition of mortality produces the unintended consequence that human beings then come to regard suffering itself as unnatural:

The most fundamental aspect of "post-war democracy" in Japan during the 50s, in my opinion, was the philosophy that the misery of the
individual could be completely alleviated, as long as the government
and nation made no mistakes. Completely alleviated. Because humans
were not born to suffer. But what happens then is that *being born becomes a torment*. We lose sight of the truth of existence (emphasis
added).[19]

In the case of the crypt and its master, the desire to avoid suffering and
escape death takes the form of a totalizing program to transform the human
species and the natural world alike. In undertaking to abolish the horror of
suffering and death, the master of the crypt does away with the very limits
that paradoxically make it possible for human beings to rise above the
brutish condition of mere animal survival. Furthermore, it could be said
that his technologies are premised on the abandonment of any restraint
among its users in their insatiable pursuit of their right *not* to suffer.
Thus, the psychic Miralupa keeps his frail, decrepit body in a tank of life-
sustaining fluids, in the hope of attaining the transhuman paradise promised by the crypt, while the usurper Namulith has "endured the horrors of
surgery dozens of times" in order to be transplanted into a bioengineered
immortal body (V: 13/III: 15).

Hovering over the desperate survivalism of the brothers is the gnawing awareness that human beings are to die off or become remade into
harmless and peaceable creatures at last capable of living in harmony with
nature, and that there will be no escape or exemption from this imposed
salvation. The apocalyptic character of such an improvement is the subject of Margaret Atwood's dystopian satire *Oryx and Crake*, in which the
creation of a new humanoid species serves as the solution to the intractable
crisis posed by an infernal constellation of unsolvable problems: unchecked
capitalism, catastrophic climate change, the depletion of natural resources,
and a hedonistic society that categorically rejects any limits on individual
pleasure. Having dismissed the possibility that human beings might choose,
collectively, to restrict their appetites of their own accord, even against the
prospect of impending war and catastrophe, a celebrated geneticist decides
to cut the Gordian knot of overpopulation, environmental destruction,
and endless strife over diminishing resources by unleashing a plague. He

conceals a lethal virus in a pill that removes all obstacles to total sexual freedom: it provides immunity from all sexually transmitted diseases while acting as both a contraceptive and an aphrodisiac. The rapidly spreading epidemic thereby clears the way for a new humanlike species engineered in the geneticist's laboratory, one that has been corrected of such characteristically human deficiencies as racism and the desire for distinction or rank, to go forth into the world and live harmoniously within narrowly sustainable limits. As though to disabuse of us of the illusion that the transition to a rational community of perfect egalitarianism—one that has at last been liberated from the immemorial superstitions of gods and money, from the havoc wrought by the use of tools, and even relieved of the affliction of sexual jealousy—will be a smooth and easy one, these "perfectly adjusted" humanoids, known as "Crakers," are designed to eat their own excrement.[20]

According to the scientist in Atwood's grim prognostication, as well as to the master of the crypt in Miyazaki's epic, the only way to ensure a future for humanity is to remake the species. Only a new, genetically modified humankind, cured of the disordering psychic forces that cause humans to destroy their environment and to engage in wars and massacres, can safely inhabit the planet without exceeding its carrying capacity. As Bill McKibben notes, such a fantasy can be shared by perspectives that are normally held to be diametrically opposed, such as by transhumanists, who call for the augmentation of human beings through biotechnology, and by the antihuman segment of environmentalists, who regard the human species as a plague that is devastating the earth.[21] For among both groups one comes across the conviction that "we should be radically reconfigured or, better yet, surpassed by some wiser race" in order to avoid the fate of extinction.[22] From such a vantage point, the nightmare of Aldous Huxley's *Brave New World* must appear to be a blissful refuge secured against the fearful dilemmas posed by today's mounting crises. But as the texts by Miyazaki and Atwood show, the lure of technological salvation opens up the resort to apocalyptic measures, whether it takes the form of the impetus to eliminate the experience of the real as that which resists human designs or the arrogation of the judgment to expend the many in order to preserve security and abundance for the elect.

Nausicaä's condemnation of the death-in-life offered by the master as collateral for the coming of eternal peace, on the other hand, exemplifies the refusal of the power to determine who will live and who will die for the sake of securing the future of the entire species. She recognizes no value in a peace inflicted with impunity, in a manner akin to the way a tyrant commits his crimes, for there are values to be honored above survival for its own sake. As such, her stance comes close to the ideal of rebellion defined by Albert Camus in *The Rebel* as "a strange form of love" that categorically refuses salvation "if it must be paid for by injustice and oppression."[23] But in refusing to treat any human as expendable, she assumes the terrible responsibility of choosing for all humans a precarious reality filled with hardship and ordeals, and thrown against the constant threat of extinction. The fateful character of such a momentous decision is reflected by the harsh prospect for her symbolic identity as the "one who destroyed the light of hope" by placing the crypt and its devastating technologies beyond human reach (VII: 208/IV: 256). Yet Nausicaä proceeds to carry out the destruction of the crypt, knowing full well the range of possible consequences of her decision, not only for the world but also for how she will be regarded by future generations.

For Nausicaä, setting aside this Ring of Gyges, even when it promises humanity deliverance from the consequences of its own mastery of nature, arises out of the desire to live in the world, no matter how devastated or dangerous. Unlike Rorschach of *Watchmen* or Byung-Gu of *Save the Green Planet*, who are willing to destroy the world in order to defend their conceptions of justice, Nausicaä by contrast experiences an intense bond "with every individual living thing" that leads her to affirm the resilience of life, even in the absence of humanity, and to recognize that there is a price too high to pay to ensure the continuation of the human species (VI: 91/III: 241). During her trance, while swallowed up within the Ohmu's body, she looks out on the fully healed earth awestruck by its splendor, the gentle and magnificent infancy of its rebirth. But she eventually draws back from the restored land and chooses to return to her own perilous and poisoned reality, "Let's go back to our own world," she tells Teto, her squirrel fox, "We mustn't contaminate this one" (VI: 87/III: 237). It would be easy to leave behind the brutal reality of war and disease for a peaceful, regenerated land free of poisons and miasma, but Nausicaä chooses instead to live out her life in the "twilight of this world that humankind has polluted" (VI: 92/III: 241–42). Her leave-taking of the promised land calls to mind the image in Miyazaki's film *Castle in the Sky* of a verdant, natural space that ascends into the sky out of human reach.[24] This is the realm that she renounces, while war still rages elsewhere and the shadow of the crypt—and its inhuman theodicy—still hangs over the earth. For Nausicaä, it is love that in the end prevails over the desire not only for survival but also for salvation itself.

4 BETWEEN TRAUMA AND TRAGEDY
From *The Matrix* to *V for Vendetta*

> Because fear and conspiracy play no part in your daily relations with
> each other, you imagine that the same thing is true of your allies... and
> when you give way to your own feelings of compassion you are being
> guilty of a kind of weakness which is dangerous to you and which will
> not make them love you any more. What you do not realize is that your
> empire is a tyranny exercised over subjects who do not like it and who
> are always plotting against you.
>
> — THUCYDIDES, SPEECH OF CLEON TO THE ASSEMBLY OF ATHENS

According to an incisive formation of Slavoj Žižek, it is easier at the present historical moment to imagine the destruction of the world than to
imagine the end of capitalism. Certainly images of apocalyptic destruction abound in contemporary culture, as the increasing interconnected-
ness of the globe engenders new forms of vulnerability just as it fosters
new types of affiliation. In Margaret Atwood's *Oryx and Crake,* a rigorously
rational scientist unleashes a plague that wipes out almost all of humanity
in order to populate the world with a new, more peaceful humanoid species.
The sexual utopia of Michel Houellebecq's *Platform,* in which the poor
are to be raised out of their difficulties through sex tourism by the rich, is
thwarted by a deadly bombing carried out by Islamic extremists. Cormac
McCarthy's *The Road* focuses on the journey of a father and son through
a devastated and diseased landscape in which they are forced to evade
those surviving humans who have turned into marauding cannibals. In
the far less explicit and accordingly more evocative postapocalyptic tale

The Time of the Wolf, directed by Michael Haneke, an upper-middle-class family is likewise thrown into a harsh world of ubiquitous death, scarcity, and danger by an unnamed universal calamity. The best-selling *Left Behind* series of end-times novels portrays the events of the book of Revelation playing out in the contemporary world, complete with the establishment of the divine kingdom under the rule of the returned Jesus Christ. Then, there is the so-called eco-apocalypticism of Alan Weisman's *The World without Us* and the History Channel documentary *Life after People,* which imagines the decay and disintegration of buildings and other artifacts of civilization if all human life were suddenly to disappear. Such works take their place alongside myriad manga and anime set in postapocalyptic worlds, as well as the high-tech rendering of catastrophe in any number of Hollywood blockbusters. The never-ending fascination with the disintegration of human society appears nevertheless entwined with an inability to imagine change on the more modest scale of history. What is it that gives the present set of arrangements governing the industrialized world, which brings together an economic system organized around the expectation of perpetual expansion with a form of government based on the principle of equality, such uncanny resiliency and unshakable permanence, so as to render its passing and demise more unthinkable than some universal conflagration that swallows up the entirety of civilization itself? Why has the very idea that the existing sociopolitical order might be transient become inconceivable?

This erosion of the historical imagination—the deterioration of the capacity to imagine alternatives to present-day political and economic arrangements—is typically attributed to what Žižek calls the "all-pervasive renaturalization" of social life, propagated by the widespread acceptance of "the liberal democratic capitalist social order" as "somehow the finally found 'natural' social regime."[1] The conventional wisdom regarding twentieth century totalitarianism of course asserts that capitalist liberal democracy constitutes the best possible political and economic order, the one that is most harmonized with the inherent restlessness of human ambition and appetite. Communism, it is often repeated, met with an inglorious demise because it restricted individual desire and initiative, underestimating egregiously the strength of the possessive yearnings felt even by the new socialist man for consumer goods and material abundance. Capitalism, on the other hand, flourishes precisely not only because it accepts such selfish passions as greed and the will-to-power as ineradicable facts of human life but also because it enlists them in the creation of a dynamic economy that succeeds far more than communism ever could in satisfying the needs and desires of an overwhelming majority of its people. The tandem of liberal democracy and capitalism yields an open, meritocratic social order in which artificial barriers to individual initiative have dissolved, one that accordingly generates the economic and technological advances enabling humanity to transcend the conflicts and afflictions that have plagued it for the whole of its history.[2]

Thus it might be said that the inability to project and work toward a different future is a condition of barrenness enforced by the pressures of another compulsory utopia. In his revisionist defense of Marx against the political movements that bore his name, economist Meghnad Desai observes that while "capitalism is not a kind or a benevolent system," it has also "achieved the largest gain in well-being in all previous millennia."[3] Capitalism has made imaginable for the first time the elimination of scarcity, a goal that, furthermore, free markets are more capable of achieving than centrally planned economies. Programs of radical political change, on the other hand, remain in effect foreclosed not only because of their lack of popular appeal—the persistent identification of state socialism with sclerotic bureaucracies, corrupt one-party rule, pervasive economic stagnation, and a disillusioned and cynical population—but also thanks to the usurpation of the socialist dream of equality and abundance by neoliberal capitalism. If any single factor best accounts for the barrenness that has overtaken the postmodern subject with regard to his or her sense of the future, would it not be the often unspoken acknowledgment that socialist revolution is simply a point of transition, or to use Fredric Jameson's phrase, a form of vanishing mediation, however calamitous and brutal, on the way to the hegemony of a new elite of bourgeois masters? It is accordingly small wonder that in light of such inauspicious circumstances the leading apologists for the significance of class struggle as the decisive category of politics, such as Žižek and Alain Badiou, press the case for this stance with an open, as opposed to a repressed or covert, appeal to faith.

FASCISM TO THE RESCUE

The political helplessness stemming from the sense that there is no alternative to liberal capitalism is reflected in the realm of culture, contends Žižek, as the incapacity to compose a credible and coherent narrative about revolutionary change: "the narrative failure, the impossibility of constructing a 'good story'" reveals a "more fundamental social failure."[4] He takes as his example of this paralysis of the creative imagination the Wachowski brothers' enormously successful *Matrix* trilogy, noting that while the first film treats, in more or less convincing terms, the individual's liberation from an oppressive system, the sequel, *The Matrix Reloaded*, sets out on the far more ambitious trajectory of elucidating and overcoming the predicament in which radical politics finds itself caught in the present age. It sets up the final film of the series, according to Žižek, to fulfill the formidable, "almost impossible task" of resolving the contradictions and aporias besetting contemporary hopes for an emancipatory politics. He writes, "If the forthcoming part three, *The Matrix Revolutions*, is to succeed with anything like a happy ending, it will have to produce nothing less than the appropriate answer to the dilemmas of revolutionary politics today, a blueprint for the political act the Left is desperately looking for."[5]

The series of course fails egregiously, with an ideologically contorted finale in which those who wish to be free from the control of the machines are allowed to leave the Matrix, while those who prefer to continue performing the indispensable task of supplying the machines with bioelectric energy are welcome to remain trammeled in their servitude. What the film thus affirms in the end is the liberal individualist ethic of free choice and thus a politics based on contracts, which presumably include slavery so long as the slave consents to his or her fate. As Žižek argues in his recent book, *The Parallax View, Matrix Revolutions* beats a hasty retreat from the questions of collective emancipation raised by its predecessor, *Matrix Reloaded*, under the cover provided by a threat that endangers both the machines and the human community of Zion: the rogue program Smith, who was once charged with the function of subduing the human rebels but who has escaped from the control of the Matrix and now seeks to devour and assimilate humans and machines alike. It is thus through the intervention of a transgressive force hostile to both warring sides that the third film seeks to evade the vital dilemmas it raised earlier in the series. Such an alliance between the oppressed humans and their machine oppressors might recall the historical truce between the communist Left and capitalist and patriotic Right in the fight against National Socialism. For Žižek, the political meaning of the film, at its most positive form, corresponds to the "anti-Fascist struggle" wherein the machines of the Matrix, like the capitalist parliamentary democracies during the Second World War, are forced to ally themselves with their bitter enemies in order to counter an ideological movement that is more avowedly and brutally expansionist than either.[6] Nevertheless, this twist in the narrative leaves the problem of emancipation wholly unresolved; indeed, the conclusion of the *Matrix* thereby casts aside the harsh dilemmas of liberation by taking recourse in a shared enemy that both masters and slaves are willing to fight, a need that would be fulfilled in more chilling as well as more comical instances by an alien invasion.

Žižek himself ventures the possibility of a more satisfying narrative of liberation that would arise from a theologically orthodox resolution of the Christological motifs in the *Matrix* trilogy: Neo would be revealed as a program that has become human, and his death would bring about the destruction of the Matrix and its artificial world.[7] On the other hand, the otherwise disjointed resolution of *Matrix Revolutions* could have been a credible outcome for a different sort of scenario, one signaled by the dissension between the commander of Zion's military defenses and the ruling council of the city as well as by the possibility that Morpheus, leader of the band of die-hard revolutionaries, might be a deluded, would-be cult leader fixated by his own eccentric interpretation of prophetic utterances regarding the ultimate liberation of humanity. Indeed, the ideologically incoherent ending in which those who wish to be free are given freedom while those who wish to be exploited are allowed to continue in their state of oppression echoes those postrevolutionary turning points in which the more earnest and ideologically pure militants are sacrificed and betrayed for the sake of achieving national cohesion and economic stability. Applying this historical logic to the *Matrix*, we might find ourselves with a narrative in which members of the ruling elite decide to engage in secret negotiations with the machines. The compromise to end the conflict would accordingly entail the agreement of the machines to respect the freedom of the inhabitants of Zion in exchange for halting the growth and expansion of the city, i.e., suspending the operations to liberate the remaining humans from their captivity. Of course, peace on such terms could only be achieved by the repression and elimination of the more intransigent as well as the ideologically purer elements among the resistance, triggering a series of tawdry and underhanded maneuvers that would trap the uncompromising idealists and then monumentalize them, once they have been delivered over to the enemy, as the founding martyrs of the revolution.

The conclusion of the *Matrix* thus neatly fills the shadow of a realist solution in which the preservation of individual liberty is gained at the price of forswearing collective emancipation. It would be easy to condemn as evil and cold-blooded the ruling council that carries out such traitorous subterfuges were it not for the fact that it would have a more than reasonable claim to being on the side of peace, to defending the best interests of the city by seeking to forestall the fate of endless conflict as well as the outright obliteration of the humans' underground refuge. Indeed, one could add that the scenario of betrayal and stabilization also presents a credible alternative to the grim cycle in which Zion is repeatedly destroyed and rebuilt, as described by the Architect when he reveals that Neo is merely the sixth in a series of messianic heroes who have attempted to set humanity free from its shackles but who have ended up each time by choosing twenty-three humans from the Matrix to repopulate the shattered city. Rather than embarking on the total conquest of the world of machines, the humans would instead focus on the narrower goal of sustaining humanity in one city.

It must be said, nevertheless, that the political authorities in Zion are not exactly promising material for bringing off the salvation of the city, whether through dissimulation or dogged persistence. The female official presiding over the deliberations over military strategy comes across as a self-righteous and disdainful scold who pointedly cuts off a dissenting voice.[8] On the other hand, the male councilor, the ostentatiously named Hamann (after the critic of Kant), who engages Neo in a conversation about the nature of technology, speaks in a skittishly self-effacing manner, underscoring the fate of patriarchal authority in a permissive society that compels him to make a show of his impotence in exchange for not having his guilt-stricken conscience excessively needled. After all, it is the recognition of his enjoyment being threatened that makes him fretful. They are both, needless to say, a far cry from the breezy and affable cunning of a Winston Niles Rumfoord (whom Vonnegut modeled after FDR),[9] the openhanded steeliness of a Lady Eboshi, or even the canny forbearance of a Michael Corleone. Instead, these two senior officials embody the lamentable contradictions that ensue when both assertive courage and moral restraint are repressed in the name of tolerance. As such, they are altogether lacking in the flexibility of mind and generosity of spirit necessary to reach difficult decisions and carry them out. Incapable of showing an impartial artfulness and immobilized by a therapeutic moralism that takes as its measure not the confrontation with harsh truths but the reactive defense of one's own sanctimony, these authorities are doomed to the despiritualized and ignominious management of mere life. They thus exemplify the disastrous political defect diagnosed by Weil at the outbreak of war in 1939:

> Let us not think that because we are less brutal, less violent, less inhuman than our opponents we will carry the day. Brutality, violence, and inhumanity have an immense prestige that schoolbooks hide from children, that grown men do not admit, but that everyone bows before. For the opposite virtues to have as much prestige, they must be actively and constantly put into practice. Anyone who is *merely incapable of being as brutal, as violent, and as inhuman* as someone else, but who *does not practice the opposite virtues,* is *inferior* to that person in both inner strength and prestige, and he will not hold out in such a confrontation.[10]

The contradictions of the film thus cannot be resolved in a political framework, let alone according to the exigencies of "antifascist" struggle, but only papered over by the intervention of a pathetic New Age fantasy. The conclusion of *Matrix Revolutions* takes leave of the political altogether to affirm the mystical harmony between opposites: machine and human, male Architect and female Oracle.[11] Yet, apropos of Žižek's verdict regarding the ideological fiasco of *The Matrix*'s narrative of revolution, perhaps it is wholly unreasonable to demand that a work of fiction supply the answer to a sociopolitical deadlock that really existing revolutionary and reformist movements have failed to overcome. Even Žižek concedes as much when he suggests that the incoherent compromise reached at the end of *Matrix Revolutions* is nevertheless preferable to the thoroughly fraudulent and regressive alternative in which the humans straightforwardly triumph over the machines, culminating, as it were, in "a pseudo-Deleuzian celebration of the successful revolt of the multitude."[12]

On the other hand, one could make the case that the primary defect of the *Matrix* trilogy consists not in its failure to deliver a credible "blueprint" for revolutionary political change but rather in its inability to accord proper weight to the harsh and unavoidable dilemmas that necessarily arise in the process of bringing about the passage from one kind of sociopolitical order to another. In other words, the resolution to the series comes across as forced and devoid of credibility because the narrative fails to endow a tragic dimension to its central conflict. Far from resolving the struggle between the humans and the machines as the clash of one right against another, the *Matrix* series proves incapable of surmounting the simplistic moral economy in which self-evident good is pitted against irredeemable evil. Even as it depicts the machines and the other entities of the Matrix in more sympathetic terms, such as the programs taking the form of the South Asian girl Sati and her solicitous parents, the concluding film offsets such complexities by shifting the role of the demonic antagonist onto the entirely malevolent Smith.

Having been cut loose from the mainframe after a fight with Neo and thereby acquiring the autonomy of a virus, Smith sets out to infect and assimilate humans and machines alike. Even as he comes to take on increasingly identifiable human qualities in the second and third films, displaying both sadism and a sardonic sense of humor, Smith nevertheless finds maddening the spontaneity and obstinacy that inform much human behavior. In this respect he joins the film's secondary antagonists, the Architect, the embodiment of the forces that created the Matrix, and the unpleasantly supercilious Merovingian, in giving voice to the deterministic stance that denies individual free will and the openness of the cosmos. But the malicious delight taken by Smith in wreaking havoc threatens to shatter the equilibrium between the engineered realities of the Matrix and the deviations of humans and software alike from their programming, which not only permits the narcissistic gamesmanship of the

Merovingian but also underwrites the synoptic vision of the Architect. By contrast, Smith's will to destruction refuses to be constrained by any reality principle. He instead emerges as a crudely one-dimensional villain who is driven by a simpleminded desire for total domination. As one of the many commentators who insist on interpreting the *Matrix* films as an allegory of free will asserts, Smith is, conveniently enough, a psychopath who is incapable of experiencing "positive emotions" such as love and friendship and cannot comprehend moral concepts such as "freedom and peace."[13] He thus regards Neo with a mixture of hatred and envy, bewildered and aggravated by his rival's exercise of free choice and capacity for meaningful relationships with others.

As the identification of the rejection of individual autonomy, or the "inability to program oneself," as the source of chaos and evil makes clear, the *Matrix* series remains bound to the aporia of the liberal conception of freedom: one is not allowed to choose not to be free. Moreover, those who do not accept freedom do so because of some irrational debility or other—such people are fearful of the complexity and unpredictability of a world of free agents, and lash out in jealousy at the more mature individuals who are capable of recognizing and pursuing their self-interest. As John Gray observes, this model of liberal freedom supplies no convincing defense against the act of "exercising one's freedom in order to live a lie," as in the deliberate choice of Cypher to murder his comrades and leave behind the life of a freedom fighter, marked by austerity and deprivation, to inhabit the dream world where he can pursue and fulfill to a greater degree a greater number of desires.[14] Indeed, according to Gray, the *Matrix* films reassert the modern (and still postmodern) "fetish of choice," which identifies the "good life" with the "chosen life," in defiance of the fact that "nearly everything that is most important in our lives"—from the circumstances of our birth to our natural talents and aptitudes, physical appearance, and even the choices we are given—is "unchosen."[15]

Moreover, the film's recourse to this particular variety of antagonist serves to reassert the facile caricatures that liberalism deploys to explain away fascist totalitarianism: the supporter of fascism as an essentially thwarted and repressed subject unwilling or unready to accept the burdens of freedom, the leaders of the Nazi party as thoroughgoing cynics brainwashing

the populace, fascism as a hopelessly antimodern and reactionary movement based on a pessimistic view of human nature, and so on. Such reassuring misconceptions and stereotypes, which fail to address and thereby
severely underestimate the appeal of fascism, mar the adaptation by the
Wachowski brothers of a speculative narrative set in a fascist Britain,
Alan Moore's *V for Vendetta*, to which this chapter will later turn. For the
autonomous liberal subject cannot easily represent to itself the force of
constraint, of being caught in terrible situations not of its own devising,
and of being compelled to act in accordance with the ineluctable pull of
necessity. With respect to *The Matrix*, the facile and cartoonish portrayal of
the antagonist stands as a woeful artistic lapse when compared to the treatment of the war between humans and machines as a tragic conflict in the
animated prequel to the trilogy, *The Second Renaissance*, directed by Mahiro
Maeda from a screenplay written by the Wachowski brothers themselves.

THE CALCULUS OF SELF-DESTRUCTION

The Second Renaissance (2003) is a two-part short film, distinguished by
its spareness and clarity, which depicts how the human race came to be
enslaved by the A.I. machines that they had originally designed to serve as
their labor force. In a voiceover narration, the first film tells of how humanity had achieved a pleasurable way of life in a high-tech utopia thanks
to their machines, the Edenic character of their idyllic existence under-
scored by the refrain from the book of Genesis, "and it was good."[16] But
the human beings succumb to complacency and corruption, taking for
granted the luxuries and services provided by the intelligent, autonomous
machines that are the key to sustaining their world. They subject the
machines to worsening indignities, which reach a breaking point with the
trial of an A.I. entity for the murder of its owners. The A.I. entity, known
as B166ER (in a nod to Richard Wright's novel *Native Son*), defends its
actions on the basis that it wished not to be deactivated by its owners, but
is found guilty and ordered destroyed. The humanoid machines, grieved
by their callous and unjust treatment at the hands of their human masters, demand political rights and legal protections. The humans instead respond with crackdowns and massacres, as scenes of lynchings and pogroms
follow those of robot and human protesters fleeing police in riot gear.

The imagery of protests and marches evoking the black civil rights struggle gives way to the imagery drawn from the Holocaust: terrified androids terrorized and murdered in the streets and mounds of motionless wreckage dumped into pits by tractors. The animated sequences that allude to real-life events do not come across as gratuitous but rather as haunting and even understated, for they go much further than merely appropriating historical atrocities as a dramatic flourish for yet another reworking of the tired science fiction theme of the war between man and machine. Indeed, the disquieting impact of the film emerges from its evocation of what might happen "according to likelihood and necessity," to borrow a phrase from Aristotle, in a world wracked by the calamitous convergence of uncontrollable forces: the worsening effects of climate change, intensified geopolitical competition for scarce resources, and an economic system organized around perpetual expansion.[17] The unsettling intensity of the narrative arises from its wholly convincing rendering of a nightmarish finale that ensues from a series of actions that, according to the iron yoke of necessity, escalates at every step the magnitude of violence that is deployed.

Realizing that the human beings will not allow them to coexist as equals, the machines plead for their own nation. But the solution of providing a separate nation for A.I. entities yields only a temporary reprieve, since the technology of 01, the name given by the machines to their country of refuge, soon begins to outstrip those of their human creators. The human nations confronted by the prospect of economic decline thanks to the technological advances of 01 cry foul and accuse the fledgling nation of manipulating the finance markets. Predictably, 01 is criminalized as an outlaw state and vilified as a "machine empire," leading to economic sanctions and a naval blockade by the community of human nations. 01's pleas for a negotiated settlement at the United Nations are rejected, and soon nuclear weapons rain down on the machines' refuge in the Middle East.[18] The machines respond by mounting a military offensive that forces one nation after another into capitulation. The humans then resort to the desperate, irrevocable measure of blocking out the sun in order to cut the machines off from their main source of energy.

The disconcerting climax of the *Second Renaissance* plays out in an unnamed desert, where a multinational human army has assembled to mount a last-ditch counterattack, in a sort of Battle of the Bulge seen, as it were, from the perspective of the attackers. Representatives of the world's major religions, including Buddhist monks and Christian televangelists, are shown ministering to the troops bowing reverently in prayer, while Muslim troops kneel towards Mecca, on the eve of an all-or-nothing strategic gamble aimed at inflicting a decisive reversal upon the enemies created by humanity. But the atmosphere of fearful reverence and anxious supplication quickly dissipates with the release of far uglier emotions. In a sequence of unnerving brutality, a group of soldiers stand in a circle, haphazardly firing their guns into the air, their faces contorted by frenzied bloodlust while heavy metal music grates on the soundtrack. "Kill them all," one of them yells repeatedly, as others inject drugs into their arms. Their berserk fury, however lethal and appalling a spectacle to behold, falls short of staving off collapse and annihilation, as the machines eventually overwhelm and decimate their hapless former masters.

These scenes depicting the preparation for battle and the eventual defeat of the human forces are remarkable for the troubling ambivalence they arouse in the viewer. Insofar as the bloodthirsty and drug-addled soldiers are human beings fighting an army of machines, one is compelled to identify with them on the minimal basis of biological solidarity. Indeed, it is difficult not to be moved by their panicked and futile cries for help once the tide of battle turns against them and they are slaughtered en masse. The film lingers on the fate of individual victims, showing a tank crew being incinerated within the protection of their vehicle and a soldier in a battle suit being cracked open from his armored carapace before being dismembered by the steel tentacles of a metal adversary. Yet the viewer has been treated beforehand to extended sequences showing wanton and outrageous cruelties inflicted by human beings on their sentient mechanical creations. Moreover, it is clear that the original motive behind the machines' campaign of conquest is a defensive one, undertaken as a last resort once all their overtures for peace and coexistence have been rebuffed.

Unlike the feature-length *Matrix* films, *The Second Renaissance* forces its audience into making a series of unbearable identifications. The robots that go to war against the human beings are fully justified in their cause. The leaders of humanity, by their corrupt and self-serving measures, have

Representatives from the world's religions console the army of humanity on the eve of its final assault against the machines. From *The Second Renaissance, Part II* in *The Animatrix* (Warner Bros., 2003; directed by Mahiro Maeda).

locked the human race into a war of extermination, the outcome of which can only be the genocide of the A.I. entities or its own total defeat. The swift and unrelenting march to such a horrifying outcome proceeds along a chain of events that soon reveals itself as an irrevocable mechanism of catastrophe, as one desperate and violent measure is soon followed by another, even more destructive one. The persecution of a domestic minority group is followed by a nuclear attack on an entire nation, and when the attempt to exterminate this enemy fails, the earth itself comes under assault and is rendered uninhabitable, on the grounds that it is better for the entire world to perish than to allow one's enemies to live.

The brutal necessity that *The Second Renaissance* thus brings to light is the mechanism whereby one is led directly into calamity while striving to avoid it at all costs. The human nations seek to smother the consequences of the injustices they have committed by inflicting more of them, on an increasingly massive scale, until they find themselves in turn reduced to the objects of a predictably merciless retribution. Although it becomes stupefyingly clear in retrospect that the humans should have consented to peace and compromise while they still could, and that a relative decline in economic prosperity and geopolitical influence—or even the loss of geopolitical supremacy—would have been a fate infinitely preferable to near annihilation and the total enslavement of the survivors, the film makes vivid the iron laws imposed upon those who exert power. Being

A human soldier calls for help as his battle suit is cracked open by the machines. From *The Second Renaissance, Part II* in *The Animatrix*.

confronted with the unforgiving choice between "losing to others what one possesses or taking away from others what they possess," they are effectively forbidden from exercising moderation.[19]

The Second Renaissance in its compact elegance conveys the elusive principle whereby an entire society seals its own doom by convincing itself that it is in its own best interest to ignore the forces that threaten to destroy them, because the measures called for by recognizing these factors are judged to be too sweeping. Indeed, it is the "stability of power," in the words of Simone Weil, that "shows itself to be as a chimera . . . on the same grounds as the anarchists' utopia," blinding those who wield it from distinguishing setbacks and reversals, which are necessarily limited evils, from the "unlimited evil" of extinction.[20] It is the animated short—as opposed to the three full-length feature films that follow it chronologically—that succeeds in depicting with startling ferocity the subjective experience of falling under the sway of irresistible compulsions, the unbearable predicament of finding oneself trapped on a course to destruction that serves as the basis of tragic narrative.

TRAGIC DECISIONISM

Examined from the standpoint of its tragic prequel, the principal aesthetic, as well as political, failure of the *Matrix* emerges from the fact that it remains at the level of melodrama and never achieves the moral complexity of tragedy. Of all literary genres, tragedy most forcefully confronts the audience with the unthinkable. The spectator is made to identify with protagonists who, in spite of their courage, intelligence, integrity, tenacity, resourcefulness, and sense of duty and honor, are shattered by the inhuman workings of fate. Although it often focuses on the ultimate futility of the protagonist's virtues and talents against the crushing and capricious forces arrayed against him or her, tragedy does not permit the reflexive adulation of the protagonist solely on the basis of his or her victimization, as has been the fashion in much U.S. cultural studies. Rather, the tragic hero or heroine lives out and becomes undone by the irreconcilable conflicts woven throughout the whole of society itself. To identify with the tragic hero or heroine is thus to oppose a vital part of one's self, whereby one becomes subject to the judgment issuing from the ordeal that the hero or heroine is forced to undergo.

But then, what is the nature of the relationship between tragic narrative and revolutionary politics? How does the assertion that the central artistic defect of the *Matrix* is its inability to rise to the level of tragedy stand alongside Žižek's contention that the failure of its creators to craft a "good story" corresponds to the deadlock or foreclosure of revolutionary politics within postmodernity? Could it then be the case that the aptitudes and dispositions necessary for bringing about revolutionary change are somehow entwined with the capacity to think and feel tragically? Certainly tragedy has been widely recognized as a transitional form, coinciding with major turning points and far-reaching upheavals in political and intellectual life—such as the emergence of Athenian democracy or the passage from the Middle Ages to modernity, or, in the case of the films of John Ford, the triumph of corrupt civilization over the unruly grandeur of the wilderness—yet leftist critics have tended to look upon tragic art with deep suspicion.

Roland Barthes, for example, inveighs against tragedy as a method for "assembling human misfortune, of subsuming it, and thus of justifying it by putting it in the form of a necessity, of a kind of wisdom, or of a purification."[21] In the eyes of Bertolt Brecht, the leading categories of tragedy—fate and necessity—invariably serve to shore up the oppressive status quo by emphasizing the powerlessness of the human will to overcome evil or the weight of the past.[22] As its practical and civically minded opponents from Solon on down to Richard Rorty have emphasized, tragedy is enjoyed to the detriment of the health of the body politic. The terror and suffering it portrays can only breed fatalism and resignation. For many modern critics on the Left, tragedy has served as a pernicious ideological device in the hands of the ruling orders who deploy it in order to convince their subjects that their struggles for freedom and equality are futile and will set in motion a massive and merciless retribution from the forces of fate. Thus, from the standpoint of liberal and leftist progressivism, the only teaching offered by tragedy is either a total withdrawal from a life of action or the cynical and unsavory defense of the status quo and its particular constellations of force and coercion as the least bad alternative from an array of universally dismal options.

Those who persist in deriving from tragedy the basis for political engagement generally do so by invoking the reparative impulse to redress the shattering afflictions it portrays or to prevent them from recurring elsewhere. For theorists as different as Terry Eagleton, Martha Nussbaum, and Judith Butler, tragedy is to be valued less for whatever truths it may state on its own terms than for the moral sensibilities the spectacle of suffering would straightforwardly arouse and reinforce in a post-Christian ethical universe. Tragedy brings the audience face to face with, in the words of Nussbaum, "the vulnerability of human lives to fortune, the mutability of our circumstances and our passions, the existence of conflict among our commitments," and thus leaves the viewer with a "richer self-understanding" of their "attachments and values."[23] The basic condition of corporeal vulnerability supplies the basis from which to denounce normative, nationalistic discourses and their dehumanizing impact, which, according to Butler, not only mark certain human beings as other but also suppress the representation of their experiences of tragic loss for the sake of maintaining psycho-social and geopolitical hierarchies in their current form.[24]

Along similar lines, Eagleton wrests tragedy from the conservatives on the basis of the redemptive hopes for social change it evokes among Christians (and post-Christians) concerned with leading a life governed by humanitarian compassion. But he neglects the values of the actual historical spectators of tragedy, the pagan Greeks who honor *arete* by assertively competing for immortal glory.[25] Tragedy might serve to provide the vital reminder that "only by an unutterably painful openness to our frailty and finitude—to the material limits of our condition," do we gain any hope of overcoming these irresistible forces to achieve genuine freedom, which takes the form of a more humane social order.[26] But in an uncharacteristic (for an avowed Marxist) and perhaps unintended outburst of elitism, Eagleton reserves such an accomplishment for the small circle of a spiritual aristocracy.[27]

On the other hand, in the work of Eric Voegelin one finds an examination of the political character of tragedy that stands in striking contrast not only to the leftist and progressive repudiation of tragedy as hopelessly demoralizing and defeatist for the purposes of sociopolitical improvement but also to these aforementioned accounts that look to tragic representations of suffering in order to stir up the recuperative impulses within an essentially detached and ethically lethargic spectator. For Voegelin, by contrast, the meaning of tragedy must be grasped as the "search for truth," which maps the movement of the "human soul" as it "expands into the realm of action" with the emergence of the democratic polis.[28] Like Jean-Pierre Vernant and Bernard Knox, he emphasizes the status of tragedy as a "state cult," a form of civic liturgy maintained at considerable public expense alongside the religious festivals and deliberative assemblies of democratic Athens. Voegelin on the other hand breaks with the Aristotelian model of tragedy and its predominantly therapeutic approach that treats the experience of the spectator as a passive and voyeuristic venting of "pent-up emotions." Instead, Voegelin defines tragedy in emphatically nonmelancholic and nonaffective terms. The agony and affliction put on display in tragic drama constitute "representative suffering," whereby the audience must actively engage in the hero or heroine's "soul-searching and suffering of the consequences."[29] Rather than disavow the protagonist's afflictions at the last minute as the inherent property of a doomed other, the spectator must to the contrary prepare himself to shoulder the tragic fate, "even if he himself should succumb to his weakness in a similar situation."

The mode of identification that is proper to tragedy as a kind of political liturgy is thus to be sharply distinguished from the Aristotelian notion of catharsis, which, observes Voegelin, constitutes a diluted and depoliticized neutralization of tragic suffering formulated only after democracy had ceased to be politically consequential with the coming of Macedonian hegemony over the Greek city-states. The state-cult had accordingly lost by then its social relevance. What Voegelin by contrast foregrounds is not the suffering to which the spectator, in the Aristotelian account, is to respond with pity and fear, but rather the act of decision whereby the hero or heroine sets in motion his or her fate, a fate that moreover reflects on the political and spiritual dilemmas that the city-state cannot avoid confronting. The "opening" of the souls of the citizens to "tragic conflict" by the same token does not refer to the audience shaking their heads at the theatrical portrayal of suffering and solemnly intoning that it is indeed sad that such misery and affliction could be at all possible.[30] Rather, this process designates for Voegelin an imaginative fusion with the protagonist in those singular instances in which he or she must arrive at a decision regarding an intractable dilemma in the face of unbearable pressures. Tragedy thus constitutes "the study of the human soul in the process of making decisions" through the aesthetic construction of "conditions and experimental situations, in which a fully developed, self-conscious soul is forced into action."[31]

The subjective position of the tragic protagonist resembles that of a sovereign weighing the demands of two mutually exclusive courses that will affect the fate of his subjects—indeed, the play that for Voegelin serves as paradigmatic of tragedy as the search for truth is *The Suppliants* of Aeschylus, in which Pelasgus, the king of Argos, is compelled by the sudden arrival from northern Africa of Danaus and his daughters to choose whether or not to grant them refuge and possibly become drawn into war against their Aegyptian pursuers. Nevertheless, in spite of the royal lineage of its protagonists, tragedy cannot be separated from the innovations of Athenian democracy, in which a "political society [is] articulated down to the individual citizen as a representable unit."[32] Indeed, in *The Suppliants* the decision to provide refuge and protection to the Danaides is reached, fittingly enough, after Pelasgus, instead of deciding their fate on his own, chooses instead to consult the people of Argos, making an appeal on behalf of the exiles. The willingness of the citizenry to "open its soul to tragic conflict" is thus indicative of their readiness to face up to the terrible and essential questions of life and death, not only of individuals but also of the social order of the polis as a whole. Tragedy, it would appear, provides an indispensable education in the responsibilities and burdens associated with governing the state, a knowledge that Žižek, for his part, reserves for the subjective position of the Master.[33]

The politics particular to tragedy is thus one that, in focusing on the predicaments where one must choose between incommensurable goods, breaks fundamentally with the utopian, and essentially antipolitical, conception of politics that have come to prevail under liberal modernity. The tragic view of history contradicts the modern doctrine of historical progress, whether it becomes manifest in the mass ideological movements of the twentieth century or in the default, postideological embrace of technological advancement and economic growth in contemporary globalization as the remedy for overcoming human antagonism and conflict.[34] A tragic conception of politics, which defines conflicts according to the clash of right against right, moreover excludes the hysterical-hypocritical position of the "beautiful soul," which mistakes its moralizing judgments about politics for an actual politics. As Žižek declares, the attitude of the "beautiful soul" afflicts in particular intellectuals of the Left, the operative mode for whom is to "bombard the capitalist system with demands that obviously it cannot fulfill (Full employment! Retain the welfare state! Full rights for immigrants!)," while fully expecting that none of these radical demands will ever be met.[35] But if the "game of hysterical provocation" represses the tragic dimension of politics by hypocritically condemning those in power for being, in the memorable formulation of Reinhart Koselleck, "guilty of the citizen's own innocence,"[36] the role of the revolutionary takes on increasingly tragic hues.

Although Žižek proposes that the militant communist subject faces dilemmas that are "post-tragic," whereby their most authentic sacrifices cannot be publicly acknowledged and take the form of accepting false accusations of having betrayed the revolution, his frank and lucid account of the course of revolution and the unavoidable role of terror within it can be said to exhibit an indelibly tragic character. Taking Antigone as his example, Žižek raises the question of what fate could be more tragic than to give up her life out of unconditional fidelity to her dead brother Polynices. The daughter of Oedipus, on learning that she will be condemned to death for giving her brother a burial in defiance of Creon's command, goes on to name the most crucial things that an early demise will deny her, such as marriage and children. But Žižek answers that the sacrifice of one's symbolic identity is far more tragic than the fate of the tragic heroine, who will nevertheless be revered and admired after her death for her courage and faithfulness. The communist militant, though ready to suffer physical death for the revolution, is asked to give up far more at the show trial—to assume, in direct contradiction to his inner beliefs, the identity of traitor by confessing to imaginary crimes: "show your ultimate fidelity to the Revolution by admitting that you are worthless scum, the dregs of humanity."[37]

The "post-tragic" "sacrifice of the sacrifice," which ostensibly fulfills a decisive role in securing stability for the revolutionary state, nevertheless has disabling repercussions for those who find themselves compelled to liquidate not merely the innocent but also the most authentically committed. For the dilemma of the revolutionary fighter who finds himself called upon to betray the cause in order to consolidate it as a new order is mirrored by the predicament of the revolutionary leader who resorts to terror to impose order and extort peaceableness out of the rubble of post-revolutionary upheaval. The act of inflicting cruel punishments on behalf of a people who clamor for ideological purity while looking out to gain small advantages for themselves cannot but generate a fatal contempt and disgust in the leadership for those whom the purges allow to rise in station. It is this particular attitude of scorn and derision that Žižek neglects to mention with respect to Stalin's reproof of the zealous younger members of the Central Committee, who called for the immediate execution of Bukharin.[38] When Stalin bellows, "Patience! His guilt is not yet proven," he is not merely being hypocritical about the fact that he is the one responsible for stirring up their vicious impulses in the first place, but he also reveals his disdain and contempt for the cowardly and servile flatterers who make an eager show of their brutality for the sake of ingratiating themselves with the tyrant. On the other hand, the revolutionary leader's violence proves impotent and ineffectual at halting the spread of numbness and cynicism, among other demoralizing factors that make straight the paths for the reemergence of the dictatorship of petty acquisitive relativism. Indeed, the meritocratic and instrumentalist bourgeois subject has proven to be the direct product of ideological terror and cultural revolution, thriving thanks in no small measure to the liquidation of traditional hierarchies by the deployment of ideological terror.

Yet, the demise of revolutionary movements has not been productive of unflinching insights into the exercise of freedom as necessarily tragic and agonizing. Rather, the lesson takes the form of the punch line to a joke, an unrelievedly grim and tawdry one at that, given away too soon to an audience too stricken with anxiety to find it genuinely humorous. To the contrary, the lesson to be drawn from the ignominious collapse of state socialism is one that disseminates and intensifies the fear that any change that is more than incremental with respect to the prevailing liberal democratic paradigm will be alarmingly catastrophic, if not excessively onerous. If tragedy is the literary form that best exemplifies historical transition, coinciding, as Timothy Reiss observes, in ancient Athens with the "inception of the collective polis" and helping to lay down the groundwork in Renaissance Italy for the "discourse of possessive (and progressive) individualism,"[39] the breakdown or barrenness of the genre would correspond to the pervasive sense of political paralysis, social anxiety, and cultural ossification that afflicts the postideological, postmodern order. The ideological passion necessary for the transformation of society becomes impossible to sustain once the revolutionaries lose their stomach for enduring ordeals and afflictions, and the course of their actions display an infuriated, increasingly nihilistic character when the suspicion dawns on them that they are laying the foundations not of a society that will conquer tragic suffering, or even be worthy of its dignity, but of a subhuman order deprived of nobility, which is fated to remain mired interminably *beneath* tragedy.

ENLIGHTENMENT AND SCARCITY

The intellectual and political values that define modernity—what Stanley Rosen has called its "contrapuntal structure of daring and inquietude"[40] which characterizes the ambitions and self-understanding of the Enlightenment and its scientific rationalism—arise from a belief in human perfectibility that works to suppress and deny the reality of tragic conflict. As Susan Neiman points out in a recent defense of the Enlightenment against its postmodern critics and fundamentalist adversaries, the moral rationality it advances takes its bearings from the image of a moral universe that holds that "we have a right to happiness, as long as we don't forfeit that right by doing something, like unprovoked murder, that puts us outside the moral universe others want to share with us."[41] The political values of the Enlightenment thus set out to create a social order in which such a determinedly contractual view of collective life, in which individuals may enjoy happiness so long as they do not inflict harm on others, can be sustained. It is undeniable that the Enlightenment has promoted political and social equality and provided much of the impetus for social reform that has improved the living conditions of the poor in the industrialized world. Yet, the optimistic ethos fostered by the modern belief in human perfectibility obscures the extent to which such gains are bound up with the mastery of nature achieved by the scientific rationalism of the Enlightenment. The question that liberal thinkers such as Neiman typically do not face up to is whether the politics of the Enlightenment is dependent on the perpetual advancement of technology and the ceaseless expansion of economic growth. Is it possible to pursue the Enlightenment's ideal of political emancipation in the absence of the wealth generated by an ever-expanding economy? Or do the proponents of Enlightenment rely on a faulty equation—or the dissimulating strategy of enforcing a sense of ambiguity—between the desire for sociopolitical reform and the desire for the greater wealth and increased comforts provided by technological and economic progress?

The point that the liberties protected and sustained by modern political institutions depend on the exploitation of human labor and natural resources, or that the internal health of democracy depends on eminently undemocratic forms of domination, such as the colonization of territories and peoples outside of the sphere of the existing democracies, represents a critique one finds across the political spectrum. For much of the progressive Left, the problem is primarily one of incomplete democratization—the fact that the ideals of the Enlightenment have been only partially fulfilled and realized—which necessitates the project of extending political and economic equality to those who are at present deprived of such status. This logic informs for example the construction in the writings of Michael Hardt and Antonio Negri of the emergent, transnational "multitude," which, they assert, will come to articulate the demand for new types of political rights that exceed the bounds of the nation-state.[42] Similarly, Jacques Derrida identifies his "radicalization of the spirit of Marxism" as the pursuit and extension of the democratic values of unceasing and open-ended critique. This critique addresses itself to the conditions of imperfection and injustice that burden every sociopolitical order in the name of an unattainable "messianic" promise of justice that is "always to come."[43] But the tepid pragmatism that results from Derrida's "radicalized Marxism," which does not get measurably further in practical terms than the unobjectionable palliatives of the liberalism of fear, raises vexing questions about the philosophic as well as political significance of Derrida's project. For while Derrida and his followers might condemn in vociferous terms redemptive narratives of historical progress, such as Francis Fukuyama's version of the "end of history," they do not ultimately have anything against hedging their bets on the efficacy of progressive reform, as born out by their contention that an "infinite demand" is to be deduced from a contentless account of justice that rests upon an arbitrary account of singularity.[44] Thus, Rosen is correct to argue that poststructuralist theories, though they "understand themselves as an attack on the eighteenth-century Enlightenment, are in fact a continuation of that Enlightenment," for they persist in maintaining the Kantian identification of "freedom [with] spontaneity."[45]

Deconstructionist political theory, moreover, in spite of its avowals of "openness to an unknown future,"[46] retains the key ethical ambiguity of the liberal Enlightenment between domination and emancipation, an antitragic ambiguity that can only be sustained so long as the political and legal institutions, as well as economic systems, remain within an acceptable condition of working order. As such, it has not managed to extricate itself from the technologism that it shares with its adversary, free-market neoliberalism. As John Gray points out, the faith that "resource scarcity can be transcended by industrialism unites many seemingly antagonistic political standpoints."[47] Both Marxism and neoliberalism constitute forms of modernizing progressivism that evade the question of whether modern democracy can flourish and expand, let alone survive, if it is deprived of the technological advancement and economic abundance its citizens have come to take for granted.[48] This is a question that is increasingly unlikely to remain on a purely theoretical plane in light of global environmental crises and the depletion of nonrenewable resources. Nevertheless, the *bien pensant* defenders of liberal progress are apt to overlook or suppress the question of what political consequences the onset of scarcity might unleash on the industrialized and industrializing states whose citizens have come to expect unlimited economic growth and ceaseless technological advancement. Such a question is not merely an attempt at anticipating the dilemmas and conflicts to erupt in the near future; rather, it goes to the heart of the kinds of ethical inquiry that comprise the central focus of tragedy and that Enlightenment humanism, as the attempt to overcome tragedy and evil through secular reasonableness, either blithely underestimates or disingenuously evades.

Apologists for the Enlightenment will most likely accuse me of excessive pessimism, of relying on prognostications about the coming of an economy based on scarcity and a world thrown into disarray by climate change that may not be fulfilled. On the other hand, the rationalist progressive, I venture, has no adequate response to the ruthless pragmatism that is ready to take all necessary steps to ensure that the issue of the relationship between democracy and abundance never surfaces as an "either-or" question, that is to say, as a tragic dilemma, in the first place. We find a strikingly frank expression of this stance in the 1975 espionage film *Three Days of the Condor*. At the beginning of the film, a junior analyst at the CIA named Joe Turner (played by Robert Redford), who reads foreign-language novels and literary journals for coded messages, discovers that his entire unit has been wiped out in a counterintelligence operation. After escaping several further attempts on his life, Turner ultimately tracks down the bureaucrat responsible for the slaughter of his friends and colleagues. He calls on the senior officer, who is named Higgins, to explain himself, and asks, on a prescient note, if there are any plans for a U.S. invasion of the Middle East. How can operations that wantonly murder innocents be justified in a democracy, Redford's protagonist demands to know. Higgins, played by Cliff Robertson, gives a response that is unforgettable in its chilling candor:

HIGGINS: It's simple economics. Today it's oil, right? In ten or fifteen years, food. Plutonium. Maybe even sooner. Now, what do you think the people are gonna want us to do then?
TURNER: Ask them?

HIGGINS: Not now—then! Ask 'em when they're running out. Ask 'em when there's no heat in their homes and they're cold. Ask 'em when their engines stop. Ask 'em when people who have never known hunger start going hungry. You wanna know something? They won't want us to ask 'em. They'll just want us to get it for 'em!

The senior CIA officer brusquely dismisses the outraged questioning of the sole surviving member of a brutal massacre on the basis that the citizenry of the United States will endorse naked exploitation and imperialist aggression should they ever find themselves threatened with dire economic conditions. Moreover, in contending with a world of limited resources and thus of inevitable scarcities, such harsh measures and ruthless policies are already legitimate—and do not stand in need of public debate—since a capitalist democracy can maintain itself only insofar as it remains capable of achieving further economic growth and expansion. And what are the chances that a majority of the people in the United States will back away from their demands for an ever-improving standard of living, especially given the vital role that economic growth plays in defusing the social and cultural tensions of a nation of ever more fragmented and atomized souls? As Morris Berman notes in his recent book, *Dark Ages America*, the exaltation of multicultural and ethnic diversity in the United States conceals a pervasive homogeneity, an overwhelming unanimity of ambitions and agreement over what constitutes the good life—with the exception of a small minority of leftist dissenters and patrician conservatives, "everyone in the United States is effectively a Protestant capitalist individualist whose life is grounded in the ideology of an expanding market economy."[49]

The words of the ruthless and amoral intelligence official are difficult to dismiss, given the economic system to which generations in the United States and other industrialized nations have become habituated and the abundance that their citizens have come to take for granted. Indeed, the disconcerting power of Higgins's speech arises from an undeniable humility—for he implies that people everywhere will give the same justifications for harming and exploiting others, and that, accordingly, one should not expect the putatively more evolved and enlightened citizens of prosperous, industrialized nations to behave with any greater degree of virtue or moral restraint than the inhabitants of countries wracked by social disorder, poverty, and other grave hardships. If this is indeed the case, then isn't maintaining the present geopolitical system—along with its disparities and injustices—the only way to prevent the industrialized democracies from descending into the endemic corruption, widespread violence, and the bitter tribal and ethnic rivalries that have come to be identified as the hallmark afflictions of so-called failed states?

The conversation between Higgins and Turner unearths what might be called the Hobbesian roots of modern liberalism—if we, in the manner of Glaucon in the *Republic*, strip away the abundance and expansionism of the liberal capitalist order, we find waiting beneath the disguise of peaceful competition and meritocratic incentive the cruelty and repression to which modern liberalism has become oblivious. For in spite of its decisive significance and undiminished relevance, the philosophy of Hobbes nevertheless remains too inflammatory and discomforting a body of thought for liberal thinkers to acknowledge directly as a crucial wellspring of modern secularism. Although Hobbes's theory of the state, as Leo Strauss observes, is to be understood as an effort to lend a "socially acceptable" form to Machiavelli's still more disconcerting teachings concerning the necessity and efficacy of princely diabolism, Hobbes's account of the elemental selfishness of human beings nevertheless requires in its turn a further layer of dissimulating "mitigation," which in this case is provided by the theories of Locke.[50] Locke's vital contribution consists of translating the desire for self-preservation, which Hobbes placed at the origins of civil society, into the "desire for property, for acquisition."[51] Locke's reformulation of the desire for security into the desire for gain supplies the crucial twist that ensures the realization of Hobbes's project, and by extension the domestication of Machiavelli's project, which, as Voegelin emphasizes, looks to the "demonic nature of Man" as the basis of political order.[52] But the success of this undertaking depends on how well modern liberalism can conceal its debts to Hobbes, as well as to Machiavelli, and hence how successfully it can sustain the illusion of consent as voluntary and competition as nonviolent.

Of course, the fact that acquisitiveness has fulfilled Machiavelli's search for an "immoral or amoral substitute for morality" does not become particularly pressing so long as there are no excessive limits imposed on individual selfishness.[53] Setting to one side the heated controversies over the sincerity of Strauss's defense of morality, whether it is the public face of a private teaching regarding the superfluity of morality for philosophers who are essentially "beyond good and evil," Strauss's commentary pinpoints how the function of acquisitiveness as a legitimating principle prepares the violence it reroutes to erupt with explosive consequences in times of grave crisis and severe hardships. For acquisitiveness designates, in the appropriate Hobbesian manner, not the attainment of something once and for all and the contentment such possession might generate, but rather the "right to unlimited acquisition," in which one moves feverishly to satiate one desire after another in a series that terminates only with death.[54] By contrast, contemporary liberal theory, and the politics it engenders, reflexively shrinks from contemplating the likelihood that the "link between liberal values and economic growth" might in fact be a "historical accident," as opposed to a manifestation of providence.[55] As Gray notes, liberal theorists such as John Rawls fail to recognize that liberal values, far from being "mutually reinforcing" in fact "prescribe rival freedoms," and accordingly engender dilemmas for which liberal principles have no answer."[56]

It is moreover clearly inadequate to attempt to refute Hobbes's ideas by questioning his account of human desire on the grounds of scientific validity—Neiman, for example, succumbs to this fallacy by resorting to the truism that it is impossible to derive objective political claims from speculations concerning the dim events of prehistoric times.[57] The political lesson of the "war of all against all" does not arise from its accuracy as a scientific explanation for the origin of human societies; it is, rather, an image of the fate that overtakes human collectivities in times of chaos and disorder, when not only legal institutions but also moral restraints have been drowned in waters far more icy than Karl Marx allowed himself to consider. For it is true that the crisis of resource scarcity can be surmounted without giving up an ever-expanding market economy, so long as one is prepared to restrict the latter firmly to a small percentage of the world's population. Such an eminently practical solution turns into a prophecy Kant's statement in "Perpetual Peace" that the tasks of politics can be discharged successfully by intelligent devils, for its straightforward elegance emphasizes the fact that the most intractable of human problems can be solved by a group of Nazis.

THE EXTREMES OF FORTUNE

Thucydides declares that in times of peace and abundance both states and individuals exhibit restraint and moderation, because they need not worry about their access to everyday necessities. But war, on the other hand, "takes away the easy supply of daily wants, and so proves a rough master, that brings most men's characters to a level with their fortunes." Like Heraclitus, for whom war governs the generation and passing of all things, and Herodotus, whose famous maxim ("Count no man happy before he is dead") attests to the impermanence and reversibility of human qualities and achievements, Thucydides was acutely aware that circumstances of stability and comfort—what we post/moderns take for granted as normal conditions—generally conspire to hide the truth about who one might be not only from others but also from one's own self. As Glaucon observes in the *Republic,* take away from a just man everything but his justice— that is to say, if he remains inwardly just while failing to acquire a reputation for justice—and he will end up being crucified and having his eyes gouged out.

In the historical present, the idea that character is dependent on circumstances and that extreme suffering reveals morality as an illusion is raised most urgently by the institution of the concentration camp and, by extension, the might of the totalitarian state, which rests on the cooperation and nonresistance of its citizens. The figure of the *Muselmann,* the concentration camp inmate reduced to the condition of living dead, and the citizen or subject of the totalitarian state, consenting or compelled to accept an inhuman order, present the two poles of the destruction of moral dignity. Liberal thinkers informed by the rationalist humanism of the Enlightenment typically refrain from pursuing such a line of inquiry with any degree of rigor, since it threatens to render morality wholly dependent on external conditions, undermining thereby the basis for its cherished concepts of free will and rational autonomy. By contrast, contemporary thinkers such as Slavoj Žižek, Giorgio Agamben, and John Gray provide what is certain to strike many liberals as an overly extreme formulation of an already unresolvable issue, one best passed over on the grounds of its very hopelessness, though they merely carry the question of the impossibility of morality onto the historical terrain of death camps, gulags, and the other killing fields and torture chambers that have plagued the age of modern rationalism.

For Agamben, the decisive question of contemporary ethics is posed by the utterly abject and wholly "desubjectified" figure of the *Muselmann*, the inmate of the concentration camp who has lost the will to live and becomes a kind of a living corpse. Broken by starvation, disease, and the ubiquitous violence of the camp, the *Muselmann* staggers about in a stupor of numb indifference, no longer responding in recognizably human ways to his environment, failing even to shield himself from the blows of the SS.[58] According to Agamben, the human being who has "touched bottom" reveals the "absolute immanence" of "bare life," and as such bears out the "ruin of every ethics of dignity and conformity to a norm,"[59] for there can be no relationship of reciprocity with the living dead:

> No one felt compassion for the Muslim, and no one felt sympathy for him either. The other inmates, who continually feared for their lives, did not even judge him worthy of being looked at. For the prisoners who collaborated, the Muslims were a source of anger and worry; for the SS, they were merely useless garbage. Every group thought about eliminating them, each in their own way.[60]

While wary of Agamben's sweeping claim that the concentration camp embodies the "truth" of the politics of modernity, Žižek likewise asserts that the figure of the *Muselmann* presents the crucial ethical question of the postwar era: "any ethical stance that does not confront the horrifying paradox of the Muslim is by definition unethical, an obscene travesty of ethics."[61] For the *Muselmann* compels us to question our everyday sense of morality and whether we are capable of maintaining it against the blows of the overpowering and cataclysmic forces that have erupted throughout much of human history: "When, in our daily lives, we retain our ethical pride and dignity, we act under the protection of the fiction that we would remain faithful to the ethical stance even under harsh conditions."[62] In other words, our "moral dignity is ultimately always a fake," for it is entirely contingent on "our being lucky enough to avoid the fate of the Muslim."[63] Similarly, for Gray, the cruel and remorseless dilemmas particular to the death camp and the gulag make it difficult to regard moral philosophy as anything more than a species of fiction, as "an exercise in make-believe, less realistic in its picture of human life than the average bourgeois novel."[64] He cites the stories of Varlam Shalamov, who spent seventeen years in Stalin's labor camps, where "morality had ceased to exist" and where "no tie of friendship or sympathy was strong enough to survive."[65] In the Arctic camps of Kolyma, the prisoners are so ravaged by cold and hunger that they find themselves too feeble to act to end their misery: "There are times when a man has to hurry so as not to lose his will to die."[66]

But just as there are afflictions too overpowering for the subject to emerge from them with his or her moral integrity intact, there also appear forms of domination against which active opposition exacts for most far too high a price. As military historian John Keegan points out, the resistance to Nazi occupation, although it performed the vital function of sustaining "in defeated and occupied countries the vision of the restoration of independence and the return to democratic life," nevertheless in practical terms "harmed the German occupiers scarcely at all."[67] Fear of reprisals, in which innocents would be indiscriminately massacred for a single act of violence against a German soldier, was enough to discourage all but the most impetuous and uncompromising from engaging in sabotage and other acts of resistance against the occupiers. According to Edward Luttwak, "the daring resistance attacks that feature in films . . . did happen occasionally, but not often, and not because of any lack of bravery in fighting the routinely formidable Germans but because of the terrible punishments they inflicted on the population."[68]

The citizen of a country occupied by the Nazis thus emerges as being under the sway of a force that approaches in its inexorable and irresistible exigency the hunger and degradation that reduce the prisoner of the concentration camp to a state of living death. The justification of protecting the lives of innocents would be available to him or her as a rationale for accepting an inhuman authority, even as it abandons other innocents to a fate worse than death. As Zygmunt Bauman points out, one of the principal lessons of the Holocaust has been that "evil needs neither enthusiastic followers nor an applauding audience—the instinct of self-preservation will do, encouraged by the comforting thought that it is not my turn yet, thank God: by lying low, I can still escape."[69] For Gray, the reality of such historical predicaments, in which acting morally could provoke the most devastating consequences, serve to expose morality as a "convenience" that is valid only in "normal times."[70] Even if one wishes to contest the definitive character of Gray's assertions regarding the helplessness of human beings in the face of irresistibly harsh circumstances, nevertheless the severity of his formulations provides the vital reminder that what strikes us in retrospect as self-evident evil is at the actual time of the crisis far from self-evident, or evil, to people who place their own survival, as well as that of their loved ones, ahead of any ethical—i.e., merely external— obligation to aid and defend the persecuted.

What is far less straightforward and axiomatic, however, is the very predicament of being trapped by the murky and pitiless dilemmas characteristic of concentration camps and other manifestations of totalitarian power. With respect to such bedeviling historical realities, it might be only a slight exaggeration to assert that the contemporary liberal Western subject—the subject "supposed to be outraged and horrified"—consoles himself or herself with the largely unspoken belief that he or she will remain exempt from the actual fate of having to choose between evils. Such an implicit disavowal of the reality of unbearable pressures, or the insistence that one would have acted differently, has had the consequence, as Neiman rightly points out, of generating a self-exculpating demonology that "externalizes evil as what others do."[71] Indeed, this demonology defuses one of the most vital and disturbing truths of the Holocaust, namely that the few who chose to oppose Nazism found themselves having to contravene "socially upheld principles," to break with the "social solidarity and consensus" that a far greater number of human beings were prepared to identify as the iron laws of necessity itself.[72] On the other hand, it requires an exceptional act of the imagination to strip evil, and not least political evil, of its self-evident character, and to experience its hold on those compelled to make a virtue of its necessity. By the same token, no less daring a leap is necessary to convey the arduous and terrifying character of ethical decisions undertaken against the compulsions exerted by extreme circumstances.

V FOR VERISIMILITUDE

In the original comic serial *V for Vendetta* and its film adaptation, the most famous landmarks and most imposing structures in London are destroyed in a series of terrorist bombings. The seats of government and the judicial system—the Houses of Parliament, the Old Bailey, and 10 Downing Street—are all blasted to rubble by explosives planted by a rebel seeking to bring down the state. But the narrative does not condemn outright these acts of terrorism, for they are committed by its hero, the enigmatic, masked figure known only as "V," whereas the government in question, the object of V's undying enmity, is a fascist dictatorship.

A story in which a fearless and elusive militant engages in skillful and—in the end, devastatingly effective—resistance against a totalitarian state proves to be especially resonant at a time when the prospects for radical political change appear bleak, while the world's most powerful democracy engages in torture and extrajudicial detention in the name of defending the globe from the violent extremism of radical Islam. Indeed, V, whose daring acts of violence ultimately trigger a series of cataclysmic events (an assassination, riots, and open rifts within the ruling party) that deliver a fatal blow to the authority of the fascist state, seems to be the direct literary fulfillment of the unconditionally committed militant subject called for by radical theorists such as Žižek, Badiou, and Hardt and Negri. For as the original comic as well as the film make clear, V's relentless struggle against the fascist state arises from his having overcome the fear of death. A former inmate of a death camp, V emerges from his inhuman ordeals with the radical freedom that Žižek regards as necessary for "liberat[ing] oneself from the grip of existing social reality" and engaging in militant action against the forces of a repressive order.[73] Having been tortured, forced to undergo medical experiments, and, though this goes unmentioned in both the comic and the film, grieving the loss of his family and loved ones, V comes across as a subject that fully accepts the traumatic character of freedom. Committing himself unreservedly to a relentless struggle against the state, he would thus come to embody the vital principle that Antonio

Negri draws from Spinoza: "nobody is more free, more powerful, and more dangerous than somebody who no longer fears death."[74]

The tendency to discuss *V for Vendetta* in relation to certain recent accounts of political subjectivization, however, comes up against the fact that the film adaptation departs considerably from the original comic. It was of course the film that sparked much debate about such concerns as the ethics of resistance against the existing sociopolitical order, the dangers of a resurgent fascism, terrorist violence as an instrument of revolution, the miraculous character of revolutionary upheaval, and the multitude as the agent of sweeping political change. Yet, the author of the original comic, Alan Moore, condemned the film in no uncertain terms for altering a narrative rooted in the conflicts and antagonisms of Thatcher's Britain (antigovernment demonstrations, race riots, the heavy-handed security responses to them, the climate of hostility towards gays, lesbians, and those suffering from AIDS, and the growing popularity of the British National Party) into a rather toothless commentary on the administration of George W. Bush by "people too timid to set a political satire in their own country."[75] Moore's vehement disapproval of the adaptation, his insistence that a dystopian film genuinely critical of Bush would have been set in the United States and made use of figures from American history and folklore (as opposed to the sixteenth-century ultraorthodox Catholic militant Guy Fawkes), can be explained as the defensive reaction of an idiosyncratic visionary soured by having his work compromised by the corporate monoliths that have turned his path-breaking art into soulless big-budget spectacles. On the other hand, it is also the case that the differences between the comic and film go far beyond their respective topical elements. Indeed, the original comic, in its unrelievedly grim portrayal of a Britain recovering from famine and epidemics, and still ravaged by the environmental catastrophes brought about by nuclear war, sets forth a far more credible and unnerving portrait of fascist totalitarianism than does the film.

In the comic *V for Vendetta*, Britain might have avoided the nuclear firestorm that has swept over much of the world, but it has not been spared the devastating environmental impact of the war—the land suffers radioactive floods, the destruction of crops, lethal epidemics, and famine. Mass death from disease, hunger, and radiation poisoning is accompanied by the total breakdown of the legal and political order. In the midst of the pervasive lawlessness and unrelenting strife caused by gangs fighting over food and other scarce necessities, the extreme Right unites with the surviving corporations to form a party called Norsefire, and restores order to the traumatized population. Upon seizing power, the fascist government proceeds to round up immigrants of African and Asian descent, Jews, gays and lesbians, and those suspected of leftist sympathies into concentration camps, where they were liquidated after being subjected to medical experiments. Meanwhile, daily life for the ordinary citizens remains a harsh and unending struggle—they are forced to take cover from rainfalls tainted by radioactivity, alerted to avoid quarantine zones in various sectors of the city, and beset by constant shortages of vital necessities. There are roundups of suspected terrorists while a separatist insurgency simmers in Scotland. Finally, organized crime syndicates proliferate in London thanks to a flourishing black market.

The situation that prevails in the fascist Britain of the comic is thus unremittingly brutal and desperate, far bleaker by any measure than the one shown in the film. The grimy streets, perpetually overcast skies, seamy nightclubs, and dilapidated flats in the comic provide a stark contrast with the gleaming skyscrapers, brightly-lit offices, comfortable living rooms, antiseptic retirement homes, and well-stocked pubs of the film. This dissonance stems in part from the general aversion of big-budget Hollywood productions to achieving realistic representations of poverty and privation. But the more crucial factor in this case is that the comic portrays a desolate and demoralized society in which practically every individual has lost family members and friends to the epidemics, famines, and strife that wracked the country following the nuclear conflict. The people in Moore's narrative are impoverished and chafe at the cruel and excessive character of fascist authority, yet it is clear that their ordeals and afflictions have left them stunned and depleted. Indeed, it is the overwhelming nature of their sufferings, as well as their desire for a quick and definitive end to the incessant bloodshed on the streets, that have led them to accept, however reluctantly, the mass murder of racial and sexual minorities in internment camps. Crushed by the agony of their losses and consumed by the arduous struggle to survive in a dangerous and poisoned environment, the traumatized subjects of this postapocalyptic totalitarian dystopia elected to deafen themselves to the voice of conscience in order to secure the practical necessities of life. They are forced, after all, to inhabit a world where a single accident can reduce a person to abject destitution or bring about his or her violent demise.

The film is by contrast wholly devoid of any trace of such overwhelming and pervasive despair. The totalitarian society it depicts is a flimsy and superficial construction, an incoherent and self-refuting nightmare lacking in any plausible historical exigency. The introduction of the protagonist, Evey Hammond, for example, differs vastly in the comic from its treatment in the film. In Moore's text, she is an orphaned teenager who, suffering from hunger, has decided to follow the example of the older girls at the factory where she works by selling her body for food. The film softens her situation considerably, turning her into a well-groomed employee at the government-run TV network. Although her file records that her deceased parents were antigovernment activists, it strains credulity that a person with such a questionable background would be permitted access, at however low a level, to the inner workings of a crucial organ of the totalitarian state. Indeed, the only conceivable basis upon which such a person could attain this kind of privileged and sensitive post in a totalitarian society would be if she were a fervent and convinced supporter of the fascist state, someone who would have been willing to turn her own parents over to the authorities. Moreover, the shots of the ordinary citizens in the film invariably show them in sanitary and affluent surroundings, implausibly spellbound by the crude propaganda spewing from their TV sets, without a hint of the remorseless hardships and agonizing losses that burden the everyday lives of the people in the comic. In other words, the Britain in the film version of *V for Vendetta* is essentially a prosperous, technologically advanced nation that merely happens to have a fascist government. No one is shot dead on the sidewalk by the authorities for trying to take cans of food from a looted store, as happens in the graphic novel. Likewise, no one in the film appears capable of screaming out, plunged into absolute despair, "We shouldn't have to live like this . . . I wish the bastard bomb had 'it bastard London . . . I wish we were all dead."[76]

These words are spoken by a once-powerful gangster reduced to utter despondency after vainly imploring the new chief of police to accept a bribe to spare the life of his aged mother. Indeed, the very existence of a home for the elderly in the film constitutes a significant deviation from the comic, where we learn through the despondent pleas of the hoodlum that the official policy of the government for the aging is to exterminate them. Thus, what the film misses—and what the graphic novel registers—is the atmosphere of unrelenting dread and the compensatory though increasingly futile viciousness that hovers over a society that has only recently inflicted the most brutal crimes against large segments of its own population. When Moore protests that the film completely "defangs fascism," noting that the script by the Wachowski brothers minimizes the racialist element in the ideology of the fascist ruling party, he also draws attention to the fact that the violence of genocide has left hardly a trace of guilt and revulsion, distress and terror on the society portrayed in the movie. Absent as well are the aggression and cruelty that would have to be drummed up on a regular basis to counteract these emotions, to justify the murderous policies of the past, and to instill in the population, whenever it should grow restive, the awareness of their possible exercise once again in the future. Instead, the people in the film are shown as thoroughly pacified and almost supernaturally untroubled, as though their state of deception and bovine immersion in the insipid and heavy-handed programming produced by the government were enough to substantiate their innocence in the atrocities committed on their behalf. Indeed, unlike in the original comic, none of the ordinary citizens in the film—those who were not directly involved with the liquidation of targeted minority groups—expresses sorrow and anguish for the victims of the regime, a rather gaping deficiency in the film's declared antifascist stance. But if the people could not be seen as blameless with respect to the crimes that have provided them with order, it would of course be that much harder for the audience to cheer at the finale when the film strives to reaffirm the value of democracy by having the masses rise up in collective protest against the fascist rulers who have lied to and deceived them.

Moore's critiques of the film accordingly display a double-edged character. On the one hand, the Wachowski brothers, along with director James McTeigue, drastically underplay the virulence of fascist society, the unceasing pressure of violence and cruelty it creates in everyday life. They thus end up with a vacuous and contradictory representation that is meant to topple over and collapse at the flimsiest caprice of the popular will. On

the other hand, the film does not portray the members of the fascist leadership with any degree of depth or nuance. The head of state is portrayed
as a simplistic, one-dimensional villain motivated purely by the desire for
power and by an uncomplicated hatred for anyone who does not share or
fit his ideology. But as Moore recognizes, such crude, caricatured portray-
als of evil do not shed any light on why large numbers of people, indeed
strong majorities of them, could embrace fascist rule or even settle on it
as a "rational choice," that is to say, as a choice impervious to other rational
arguments. So while the brutality and cruelty of fascist society requires
the depiction of realities too harsh and too ugly to be shown in the film,
the task of achieving a credible portrayal of the members of the fascist
leadership involves an imaginative act of sympathy, in which one sees the
world from within their perspective. For the least productive stance, both
aesthetically and ethically, is to treat fascism as an essentially alien and demonic phenomenon, devoid of any connection to recognizably human
motives and aspirations. Thus, for Moore, the fascist too must be accorded
the attention that arises from a conception of literary creation as an act
of love:

> the only [way] that you could ever understand [the child murderer]
> Myra Hindley, [serial killer] Fred West, a General Pinochet, is to in
> some way love them or at least suspend judgement, at least not hate,
> at least not draw back in revulsion from the very idea of these people.
> If you could in some way observe them with compassion, then you
> might actually learn something that was useful about them.[77]

Moore's determination to be "as fair as possible" in the depictions of
the fascists, his effort to achieve "rounded" characterizations,[78] reflects the
insight of Bauman, for whom "the most terrifying, and still most topical,
aspect of the 'Holocaust experience'" has to do with the fact "that in our
modern society people who are neither morally corrupt nor prejudiced
may also still partake with vigour and dedication in the destruction of
targeted categories of human beings."[79] What distinguishes the fascist is
not the absence of this or that identifiably human trait, but rather his or
her adoption of a perspective that regards as necessary and acceptable the
elimination of undesirable persons, often in accordance with a mythically
redemptive and rejuvenating historical struggle. Such a perspective can of

course exert a powerful attraction in times of severe deprivation as well as in periods of historical transition when the traditional channels of spiritual yearning have become abandoned or discredited. The Chancellor of Britain in Moore's comic, for example, is a far cry from the raving and rancorous bile-spitting fanatic of the film. Rather than a shrill and venomous monomaniac, he is instead revealed to be a deeply insecure man whose desire to serve his people is nevertheless sincere, and who grows increasingly delusional as his efforts to keep order come to grief.

Other members of the ruling elite are graced with similarly subtle touches, conveying their idiosyncrasies and insecurities, their competitive opportunism and constant antagonistic sniping. Derek Almond, the self-doubting head of the secret police (known as the "Finger"), comes from a comfortable middle-class background, having worked in insurance before the war. His anxieties over whether he is tough-minded and sharp enough for his job, as well as his frustrations at the petty insults heaped on him by the more predatory and ruthless members of the party, lead him to beat and abuse his wife. Helen Heyer, wife of the official who controls the media (called the "Eye"), matches Lady Macbeth in ambition and outdoes her in fortitude and resilience. Possessed of a keen and ruthless intellect, she recognizes a vital opportunity for advancement in the Chancellor's deteriorating mental condition. She relentlessly hectors her hapless and somewhat dimwitted husband, beating him and withholding sex, in order to goad him into seizing control of the state. Easily outmaneuvering and disposing of her husband's main rival, Heyer also risks throwing away all her gains by indulging in an affair with the Scottish gang leader she has bribed to clear the path for her husband's rise. Eric Finch, the capable chief of New Scotland Yard (also known as the "Nose"), cuts a grizzled, world-weary figure. Selflessly dedicated to his work and immune to the lure of ambition, he wins the unquestioning trust of the Chancellor. Finch is also shown still mourning the loss of his wife and son, who perished some years before in the epidemics after the war. The Finch of the film is the one member of the party who eventually joins the side of the antigovernment resistance—in hunting V, he uncovers the atrocities of Norsefire and, in moral horror and outrage, turns against the state. In the comic, Finch is struck by pangs of regret over the slaughter, not having borne any personal prejudice against blacks and Asians, or gays and lesbians, but he soberly concludes that even if he had known that Norsefire would murder so many innocent people, he would still have supported the movement, on the grounds that a terrible order is preferable to the ubiquitous and ceaseless violence of the war of all against all.

The absence from the film of Rosemary Almond, the wife of the head of the secret police who becomes widowed early in the narrative, likewise underscores the mutilated and anesthetized character of its portrayal of fascism. Shunned by the other members of her social circle, who see no point in maintaining contact with any person who has become useless for their ambitions, she is left without any means of supporting herself. Rosemary gives in to the advances of a man she utterly despises, Roger Dascombe, a former rival of her husband, who takes immense delight in sleeping with the wife of the man he enjoyed insulting. Once Dascombe follows his posthumous cuckold into death during the course of another operation mounted by V, she is then left with few choices as a middle class woman lacking in the right connections or adequate means. She becomes a burlesque dancer in a nightclub popular with members of the fascist party and the London underworld alike, where she is forced to cater to the appetites of the powerful. It is through the figure of Rosemary, and later through Finch, that Moore conveys the sense of remorse and regret among the ordinary citizens (as opposed to that of a direct participant like Dr. Delia Surridge) for the mass killings carried out by Norsefire in the name of their protection and security. While dancing in a chorus line, she reflects on the hopes and aspirations that died with the old world, when she and her husband were planning an ordinary middle-class life together, buying a house and having children. After the war, however, when Derek joined the party, she chose to do nothing when their neighbors, a nonwhite family that had helped them during the time of shortages, were rounded up and sent to their deaths: "Mrs. Rana next door loaned us food all through the war years. When they dragged her and her children off in separate vans we didn't intervene" (205). Having lost the man with whom she set out to build a future, for whose sake she was willing to sacrifice her conscience, she is now forced to gaze upon the vicious and pitiless face of a world divided between predators and scavengers, in which she is compelled every night to "offer [her] hindquarters in submission to the world." In the end, it is she, not V, who is responsible for assassinating the

Chancellor, in a suicidal act that takes place at the same time that V allows himself to be mortally wounded by Finch, his most dogged adversary.

It is within the context of this complex social reality, fascist as well as postapocalyptic, that the controversial turning points of the narrative must be addressed. The actions that have provoked the intense debate are not surprisingly the use of terrorism by V in his campaign of vengeance against the fascist state and his imprisonment of Evey, in which he starves and tortures her after tricking her into believing that she has become imprisoned in a government detention facility, all in the name of liberating her from her deepest fears. For V not only tracks down and kills the individuals who ran the concentration camp at Larkhill and who subjected him to scientific experiments, but his bombs also destroy the buildings housing the vital agencies of the government's security apparatus. In the film, these actions are portrayed as unambiguously legitimate, as borne out by the facile maxims that the screenplay places in V's mouth, but which are nowhere to be found in the comic: "violence can be used for good" and "blowing up a building can change the world," with the latter statement inadvertently raising the inconvenient specter of the Reichstag fire.[80] V's bombing of the Old Bailey and his takeover of the government-controlled TV station, in which he calls on the viewers to rise up against the fascist state, ultimately prove successful in rousing them out of their ideological stupor. At the end of the film, masses of outraged and resolute citizens, dressed in cloaks and sporting Guy Fawkes masks, spontaneously take to the streets and uneventfully swarm past the troops who miraculously hold their fire. The final sequence cuts between fireworks going off over the just-destroyed Houses of Parliament and the protestors, all of whom remove their masks in honor of the hero-martyr who summoned them to action. V, with his death, has brought about the revolution of the people and so becomes the apotheosis of their universalizing action—"he was all of us," says Evey to Finch.

As one can surmise by now, the uprising at the close of the graphic novel is far more frenzied, ugly, and chaotic, in an ending that displays a decidedly more open-ended character. Whereas in the film an immense throng of uniformly cloaked revolutionaries stride in good order toward an overawed and frightened column of soldiers and move past them with nary a jostle, in the graphic novel we find unruly and disruptive mobs, who wield truncheons and Molotov cocktails, set fires on the streets, and get drunk on looted alcohol. One of the panels shows a burning baby carriage. The outbreak of widespread strife at the conclusion of the narrative might be triggered by V's destruction of the surveillance mechanisms of the state, but the comic leaves ambiguous and unsettled the nature of the relationship between V and the people venting their frustration and fury on the streets. As Finch's assistant Dominic observes, "They're not the terrorist's followers or anything. They're just rioters... but [V]'s become a sort of all purpose symbol to them, hasn't he?" (252). For unlike in the film, V has not issued specific commands to the people to take to the streets. Rather, the speech he gives when he hijacks the TV station is artful, teasing, and ironic in tone, as opposed to the elementary didacticism with which the V of the film addresses a population that has been deceived by its leaders into acting against its true interests and giving up its liberties.

In the film, V reprimands the people for trading away their freedoms in exchange for the security offered by the fascist party. If they have grown weary, however, of the "cruelty and injustice, intolerance and oppression" perpetuated by the state, they should gather outside the Houses of Parliament on the next anniversary of the Gunpowder Plot to take back their liberties. V's speech closes by underscoring the unanimity between the people and himself: "if you feel as I feel, and if you would seek as I seek, then I ask you to stand beside me one year from tonight." In the graphic novel, on the other hand, there is in V's speech not even the pretense of unity or even symmetry with the people—after all, the survivors of this postapocalyptic Britain were the ones who looked the other way (or aided in the roundups) while those singled out by Norsefire as undesirables were sent off to the gas chambers. Thus, upon taking over the TV station, V mocks and needles his captive audience, adopting the persona of a boss fed up with the slacking of his employees:

I suppose you're wondering why I've called you this evening. Well, you see, I'm not entirely satisfied with your performance lately... I'm afraid your work's been slipping, and... and, well, I'm afraid we've been thinking about letting you go. I know, I know... you've been with the company a long time now. Almost... let me see. Almost ten thousand years! My word, doesn't time fly? It seems like only yester-day... I remember the day you commenced our employment, swing-ing down from the trees, fresh-faced and nervous, a bone clasped in your bristling fist... 'Where do I start, sir?' you asked, plaintively. I recall my exact words: 'There's a pile of dinosaur eggs over there, young-ster,' I said, smiling paternally the while. 'Get sucking.' (113)

The angry boss gives credit to human civilization where credit is due (the discovery of fire, the invention of the wheel, agriculture), but then casts a disapproving eye on their unwillingness to take the promotions that have been repeatedly offered to them (the image of a Buddha statue appearing behind V). The masked CEO then turns his ire against manage-ment and its shortcomings, "We've had a string of embezzlers, frauds, liars, and lunatics making a string of catastrophic decisions," as portraits of Hitler, Stalin, and Mussolini show up on the screen (116). The reproach that the employees have allowed their "workspace" to be filled with "dan-gerous and unproven machines" is accompanied by the photo of a mush-room cloud (117). Thus, in the graphic novel, V adopts a far more scathing tone toward the people, emphasizing that their rulers would have not been able to commit mass murder or continue their repressive policies without their cooperation and consent: "It was you! You who appointed these people! You who gave them the power to make your decisions for you!" Far from resorting to the tired and familiar leftist explanation that fear "corrupted [the people's] reason" and "common sense," V instead underscores how habits and reflexes instilled over centuries have laid the groundwork for the unconstrained tyranny of fascism: "While I'll admit that anyone can make a mistake once, to go on making the same lethal errors century after century seems to me nothing short of deliberate" (117). It is thus by means of a satirically all-encompassing vision, absurdly comprehen-sive in its breadth, that V brings to the fore the cataclysmic impact that a triumphant fascist totalitarianism would have on human civilization. By gazing back into the dim reaches of prehistory and evoking the simian ancestors of *Homo sapiens,* V underscores the fact that the success of this totalitarianism in vanquishing its opponents would have consequences as earth-shattering as the discovery of fire, the invention of the wheel, and the development of agriculture. It would be no less transformative than these leaps toward the emergence of civilization and the awakening of the spirit, but it would be a vault into the abyss in which morality would be abolished and evil turned into "innocence."[81]

Although the narrative never reveals any details about V's background or the reasons for his arrest, it implies that V might actually be the last surviving member of his kind, whether black, or Asian, or Jew, if it was indeed the case that he possessed certain tell-tale physical characteristics that were impossible to conceal. V is at any rate that subject whom the regime has irrevocably judged to be unworthy of life and who has to be liquidated regardless of whether he constitutes an actual threat to the state. There is accordingly never any question of the fascist state permitting V to lead a peaceful life within it, even in the event that he had never undertaken any sort of oppositional activity in the first place. Rather, he would in any case be hunted mercilessly simply on the basis of who he is, regardless of his actions. Thus, for V to live in fascist Britain is to exist in a permanent state of war against the fascist government. It would be for precisely this kind of politicized—and targeted—subject that the chaos of the state of nature—or what V calls the "land of take what you want" (195)—is manifestly preferable to a "terrifying order," which, as French political theorist Alain Joxe puts it, "makes you prefer death to life."[82]

At the end of his speech, V pointedly does not invite his audience to become his comrades and join his struggle to bring down the fascist state. Instead, he signs off with an ultimatum: the employees are given two years to improve their performance, or else face termination (118). The V of the graphic novel appears to be less a revolutionary liberator of the people than a kind of punisher, whose main purpose is to avenge himself and the other victims of Norsefire by wreaking havoc on the fascist state. But what keeps V from being wholly engulfed by his confrontation with the tyrannical regime, in which both endeavor to fulfill the verdict that the other is undeserving of existence, is his relationship with Evey Hammond, the girl he rescues from a group of security officials at the beginning of the story. Taking shelter with V in his underground headquarters, the "Shadow Gallery," Evey offers to help him in his struggle against the fascist state, after she reveals to him that her own father was arrested, and presumably executed, by Norsefire for having belonged to a socialist organization in his youth. But she reacts with anger and disapproval when V uses her to bait

the sexually dissolute Bishop Lilliman, the former chaplain of the internment camp where V had been tortured, and bring about his death. In the
film, Evey takes advantage of V's attack on the bishop to flee to the house
of a friend, a senior colleague at the TV station who conceals his homo-
sexuality from the state. In the comic, Evey is blindfolded and led by V out
of his personal underworld and abandoned on a desolate London street
lined by decrepit flats. She finds a lover, a petty criminal named Gordon,
and decides to forget about V, in order to enjoy her new life. In that respect, Evey behaves no differently than most people who have lived under
totalitarian or tyrannical regimes: resigned to the reality of unfreedom
and sensitized to the threat of repression, they try to make the best of terrible and trying circumstances by retreating into the realm of private life.
But Gordon soon loses his life to a feud with an upstart band of gangsters,
and Evey's sojourn in the predatory world of the living is cut short when
she attempts to avenge the murder of her lover. Before she can gun down
the ambitious Scottish gang leader, Harper, in front of a nightclub, her
protector once again intervenes, this time as her persecutor, by kidnapping her and subjecting her to starvation and torture.

THE LAST AND ONLY FREEDOM

The second major controversy surrounding the narrative involves V's
imprisonment of Evey, in which he makes her believe that she has been
arrested by the government. She is subjected to repeated interrogations in
which a guard forces her head into a basin of water, demanding that she
confess to her involvement with V in terrorist bombings and the killing of
security officers. Returned to her cell after one of these torture sessions,
Evey discovers a letter written on toilet paper stuck inside a hole in the
wall. The letter gives an account of the life of a woman prisoner in the ad-
jacent room, an actress named Valerie. Valerie writes of her childhood, her
break with her parents over her relationship with another girl, her successes
on the stage and in film, and then the war and the coming of the police
state. Her lover, Ruth, arrested by the agents of Norsefire, was tortured
into signing a statement accusing Valerie of having seduced her and subsequently committed suicide out of guilt over her betrayal. When Valerie
herself is caught in a roundup, her captors mock her with jokes about

lesbians and boast that all of her films will be destroyed. She writes of how the drugs she has been forced to take have drained all feeling from her tongue and left her unable to speak and how her flesh will soon be reduced to a lump of ashes. But Valerie notes that there is one part of her, that "last inch" of oneself, her integrity, which remains in her power: "It's small and it's fragile and it's the only thing in the world that's worth having. We must never lose it or sell it, or give it away. We must never let them take it from us" (160).

In Valerie's case the refusal to give up this "last inch" of herself takes the form of a love that flows out from her to the person in the next cell, a friend whom she will never know or see, but who she wishes will be able somehow to escape and live on: "I don't know who you are, or whether you're a man or woman . . . I will never hug you or cry with you or get drunk with you. But I love you . . ." Valerie has lost everyone she has loved, and her deteriorating physical condition attests to the imminence of her death, yet in spite of her realization that there is no escape or possibility of rescue for her, she experiences in the bleakest of circumstances a love and hope for others welling up within herself ("I hope that the world turns and that things get better, and that one day people have roses again"). The letter transforms Evey, who in the pit of her despair draws from it the courage to defy her captors and serenely choose execution over signing the confession prepared by her jailer. She chooses death over the offer of a shortened term of imprisonment followed by employment as an informer for the Finger, like so many of "her sort." But Evey's heroic resolve disintegrates on being confronted by the fact that it was V all along who tortured her and sought to break her will.

In the graphic novel, V justifies his deception and her ordeal with an explanation that stuns Evey with its flabbergasting perversity and gratu-itous cruelty—he did it out of "love" for her and the desire to "set her free." V moreover insists that she has been in prison her whole life, and all that he has done by torturing her is merely to "show her the bars" (169). Evey for her part violently rejects this idea, condemning his views as "warped and evil and wrong." For she has tasted happiness, experienced love, and therefore led a full life, one filled with its measure of joys and commitments as well as its burdens of grief and loss ("It's just life, that's all! It's what we've got to put up with . . . What gives you the right to de-

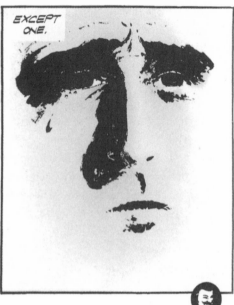

Alone in her cell, Evey reads the letter from Valerie. From *V for Vendetta;* copyright 1988 DC Comics; all rights reserved; reprinted with permission.

cide it's not good enough?"). Evey's commonsensical affirmation of life's value does not faze V in the slightest. Instead, V responds matter-of-factly that "happiness is the most insidious prison of all," followed by a curt and brutal clarification of why this is so:

> EVEY: When you threw me out I went to *live* with somebody. I...
>   I was in love with him. I was happy. If that's a prison, I don't care!
> V: Don't you? Your lover lived in the penitentiary that we are all born
>   into, and was forced to rake the dregs of that world for his living.
>   He knew affection and tenderness but only briefly. Eventually, one
>   of the other inmates stabbed him with a cutlass and he drowned
>   upon his own blood. Is that it, Evey? Is that the happiness worth
>   more than freedom?...
>   It's not an uncommon story, Evey. Many convicts meet with mis-

erable ends. Your mother, your father, your lover. One by one. Taken out by the chemical sheds . . . and shot. (169–70)

The fullness of a full life, according to V's standpoint, is condemned as radically deficient, in both political and ethical terms. Indeed, a full life stands exposed as merely the most extravagant costume for the perpetuation of bare life. Happiness, instead of supplying the brief and inspiring glimmers of utopian emancipation within a world defined by ruthless competition and predatory violence, in fact only serves to deepen one's condition of servitude and helplessness.

Evey persists in her denials, turning and running from her savior turned torturer, "You're mad! I don't want to hear it." Undeterred by her increasingly distraught protests, V makes the point that she refuses the truth because she can "feel freedom closing in upon" her, because "freedom" is "terrifying" (170). V towers over her, hounding her relentlessly in her distress: "Woman, this is the most important moment of your life, don't run from it." It is only when Evey collapses to the floor, tearfully crying out for her dead parents, that V kneels solicitously beside her, cradling her in his arms. As she lies across his lap in the manner of the *Pietà*, V asks her to remember how she felt when she chose fidelity to her principles over the life of the body, and at last Evey recovers herself, "I . . . felt . . . like . . . an angel" (171). Shocked by her recognition, and surprised by the memory of her sublime and unexpected defiance, Evey asks V to take her to the rooftop of his lair, without any more "blindfolds." There she exposes her emaciated body to the raging storm. "Five years ago, I too came through a night like this, naked under a roaring sky," says V. "This night is yours. Seize it . . . Encircle it within your arms. Bury it in your heart up to the hilt . . . Become transfixed . . . become transfigured . . . forever" (172).

Even more than V's willingness to engage in terrorism, which even many conservatives and right-wing nationalists recognize as a legitimate exercise of resistance against colonial occupation (the actress Natalie Portman prepared for the role of Evey by reading, among other books, the autobiography of Menachem Begin, who was a prisoner of the Soviet gulags before he became leader of Irgun), as well as against a tyranny or a totalitarian state, it is his imprisonment and deception of Evey that would be most difficult to justify. His act not only violates that most elementary precept of Kantian ethics—the injunction against treating other human beings as mere means—but it also suggests that V's own torture and ordeals at the hands of Norsefire have made him in effect as cruel and as remorseless as the totalitarian order he strives to destroy. No less than his enemies, V is ready and willing to exercise unrestrained power over other human beings. On the other hand, in the debates over the film that have taken place online, its principal participants have seen in Evey's ordeal an instantiation of Žižek's formula for achieving radical freedom by undergoing the process of "subjective destitution." Although the film nowhere makes reference to Žižek, and the graphic novel predates the publication of his earliest works in English, it nevertheless provides a compelling enactment of the traumatic renunciation at the core of the radical theorist's most contentious doctrines.[83] The narrative stages the double gesture associated with symbolic suicide, in which the act of giving up what is most precious to oneself is followed by the second renunciation whereby one recognizes that one has "nothing to lose in a loss." Nothing less than such a severe and ruthless break with one's own symbolic identity can enable a subject to break free of the spell of an overpowering sociopolitical domination.[84]

The militant revolutionary subject for Žižek is one who has passed through the "zero point" of "symbolic suicide"—having "renounced all symbolic ties," she is no longer to be deterred by an enemy who seeks to "hold [her] in check" by threatening what she holds to be "most precious" to herself.[85] Žižek thus endeavors to claim a type of subjectivization associated with mystical or military discipline for the practice of revolutionary politics. As political theorist Jodi Dean argues, apropos of the film, the characters who dare take action against the fascist state "have to give it all up" and "become excremental remainders."[86] It is by "going through the limit," recognizing themselves as objects and "jettisoning the biopolitics in which they are entrapped," that the "people as a whole acquire a capacity to act."[87] Along similar lines, the blogger K-punk describes Evey's dilemma of execution or cooperation with the authorities as the "existential choice in its purest form." She must decide between "defending her (old) identity—which, naturally, also amounts to a defence of the ontological framework which conferred that identity upon her—and affirming the evacuation of all previous identifications."[88] The passage to political action, the conditions under which one emerges as an authentically revolutionary subject, is thus identified with the psychic annihilation and rebirth of the subject *ex nihilo*, who undergoes a traumatic break with the forces and affections that have kept him bound to an oppressive existing reality. He thereupon makes the leap into a mode of existence wholly transfigured by a political commitment.

Steven Shaviro, on the other hand, takes a far more skeptical view of the "subjective destitution" Evey is forced to undergo. According to Shaviro, Žižek remains "too enamored of subjective destitution" and "invests negativity with a magical power of transformation."[89] For while "subjective destitution" might be a "necessary condition" for "radical change," it is by no means a "sufficient" one. Žižek's account of "revolutionary subjective transformation" ultimately relies on the Leninist fantasy of the "revolutionary act" to advance the linkage between the subject scourged by horrifying and traumatic ordeals and collective projects of radical sociopolitical action. As such, Žižek's theorization of militant revolutionary subjectivity as the outcome of the "traversal of fantasy" is undermined by his own refusal "to traverse and to give up" the fantasy of Leninist militancy, his chiliastic insistence that the justification of violent revolution resides above the realm of pragmatic and rational concerns.

Moreover, it could be pointed out that there is no rule according to which subjects who have undergone subjective destitution must thereafter engage in revolutionary politics. For instance, in the film *The Battle of Algiers* (1966), Gillo Pontecorvo's dramatization of urban guerilla warfare during the Algerian struggle for independence, the French colonel Mathieu, charged with crushing the terrorist insurgency of the National Liberation Front (FLN), defends his strategy of torturing suspected militants by appealing to the fact that some of his men ran grave risks to take part in the resistance to German occupation and paid the bitter price of imprisonment in the concentration camps: "Those who call us fascists forget the role many of us played in the Resistance. Those who call us Nazis don't know that some of us survived Dachau and Buchenwald."[90] Or to take an example from Alan Moore's own fictional universe, Rorschach, the rabidly right-wing vigilante of *Watchmen* who wages a lonely nocturnal struggle against evil—a struggle he nevertheless fully accepts as being both endless and futile—also exhibits the essential characteristics of the "destitute subject," from an unyielding commitment born of traumatic insight down to an ascetic's lack of concern for personal hygiene.

If it is indeed the case that the process of subjective destitution does not necessarily culminate in a commitment to the politics of a revolutionary Left, and thus cannot be grounded in specifically political terms, the question of the authority whereby V inflicts torture on Evey reveals far more troubling overtones. Shaviro asserts that the film justifies V's cruel deception according to the fantastic premise of superhero comics itself: "What authorizes V. to inhabit the superior perspective from which he is able, indeed, to torture Evey for her own good? It is precisely his superhero status, the fantasy that needs to be demystified, that grants him this authority."[91] V's actions are justified because, as a superhero, he possesses a different, higher ontological status than the rest of humanity. His behavior would recall Stalin's infamous description of the authentic communist and his privileged relationship to historical truth in the speech given at Lenin's funeral: "We, communists, are not like other people. We are made of special stuff."[92] V thus appears little different from other abusive charismatic leaders who claim for themselves the right to give and take life, whether by appealing to a retroactive justification or by insisting on the universality of the injuries and indignities that he has borne personally. Even the defense of V's actions on the grounds that he only imposes on others what he himself has personally endured points the way to the self-righteous and self-destructive despotism of Melville's Ahab, another survivor branded by terrible suffering who is convinced that his own ordeals entitle him to compel his crew to share in his own woeful fate. Ahab in effect brandishes his state of agony in order to dissuade and deter the less scarred and less tormented sailors from taking action to avert the catastrophe that will overtake them all because of his unyielding hunt for the titanic beast.

So if V's act of deceiving and torturing Evey is wholly immoral and altogether indefensible, what are we then to make of its outcome, whereby Evey emerges from her ordeal determined to take on the arduous task of rebuilding a more human society upon the ruins of the fascist dictatorship—a task, it should be noted, that V himself is not capable of undertaking? Is her personal transformation then as philosophically flawed and ethically reprehensible—and as politically dubious—as the Leninist project of achieving revolutionary change through the violent seizure of state power by a militant elite? Or might her experience of imprisonment and torture indicate the embrace of other kinds of commitment, as well as an awakening to elusive and arduous forms of knowledge? After all, the depiction of Evey's ordeal contains familiar elements drawn from the literature of testimony recounted by those forced to endure inhuman treatment, such as the shaving of her head, the message of consolation from a fellow prisoner, extended periods of solitude interrupted only by the brutality of interrogation under torture, and the exploitation of her physical powerlessness by her captors who make a game of uncovering the limits of her endurance. The difference, of course, is that *V for Vendetta* provides a speculative twist to the ordeal of undergoing inhuman suffering, a projective framework the fantastic character of which some are certain to reject as trivializing. On the other hand, one could assert that it is precisely the speculative trappings of the narrative that endow it with uncanny and unexpected force. Because *V for Vendetta* does not refer to a reality that has become identifiably historical, in which the categories of villain and victim can be deployed with the brisk and breezy assurance of hindsight, its depiction of a postapocalyptic fascism provokes the interpretive encounter that Voegelin associates with Greek tragedy, whereby the reader is compelled to ask how he or she might act when thrown into similarly harsh and unrelenting circumstances.

Shaviro takes Žižek's theories as well as the narrative of *V for Vendetta* to task for "romanticizing" the crushing ordeal of "subjective destitution." He thereby raises the fundamental question of the kind of effect such a demand for authentic commitment—the injunction to overcome the fear of death—actually produces: "what does it mean for me to say that subjective destitution is a necessary precondition (for either a 'revolutionary act' or a 'cure'), when I have not actually undergone such a process?" Rejecting the idea that there are ordinary correlatives for extraordinary ordeals, the line of critique developed by Shaviro underscores the gap that the reader of a text like *V for Vendetta* is forced to endure between the relative security of his or her present circumstances and the exceptional situation depicted in the narrative. For does this speculative narrative not compel the typical First World reader to become conscious of his or her historical, or rather posthistorical, perspective, which has been both shaped and constrained by scientific rationality, an expanding market economy, and the humanistic values of a secularized Christianity? These elements have combined to make possible a way of life free of the adversities and hardships that have afflicted humankind for most of its history. Would not such a reader take for granted the material abundance, political liberties, and technological advancements enjoyed by prosperous industrialized democracies and yet also suspect that the social reality he or she inhabits might in fact be a historical aberration, a brief interlude in the normal cycle of destruction and renewal, and that civilized restraint might in fact be a flimsy artifice easily discarded once history resumes its operations as a slaughter bench?

The reader is thus caught between the certainties of the present and upheavals that are fictional but also surely historical and thus may yet in some form be futural. The ignorance perpetuated by abundance has yet to become transmuted into the wisdom of privation. But this knowledge, which is not to be attained through the mediation of fictional (or philosophic) ordeals, nevertheless exerts an irresistible pull toward that horizon beyond which one would in effect become transformed into an entity unrecognizable to oneself. The reader, borne along by a self-resisting momentum in which one's compassion with the victims of genocide and torture clashes with dread at the prospect of sharing their fate, is thus brought to the threshold of the decision that anticipates—without predicting or ensuring—the inward movements of those trapped by unremittingly harsh ethical and political dilemmas. Again, it is Weil who approaches with unparalleled rigor and lucidity the strange but common enough predicament of reflecting on what one fears while hesitating about what one knows:

A man whose whole family had died under torture, and who had himself been tortured for a long time in a concentration camp; or a sixteenth-century Indian, the sole survivor after the total extermination of his people. Such men if they had previously believed in the mercy of God would either believe in it no longer, or else they would conceive of it quite differently from before. I have not been through such things. I know however, that they exist; so what is the difference?[93]

Weil strives to wrap her mind around events that she knows would transfigure or derange beyond recognition her character, her faith, and her conception of the world. Her concern falls foremost not on physical suffering but rather on the death of the soul—the abandonment of moral restraints and the disintegration of spiritual life in those formerly free individuals who find themselves under extreme situations, in which life and well-being come to depend entirely on the will and whims of the cruel and pitiless. Would she seek to survive at any cost, even at the cost of bringing harm to her fellow inmates? Or would she be able to preserve her integrity in the midst of unrelenting hunger and constant danger, as well as maintain the presence of mind to give help to others in their need? Would she be capable of choosing physical death over the loss of her spiritual freedom, and thereby avoid the fate of living death, of being reduced to the mere "state of matter"?[94] In confronting these questions and thus countenancing her own vulnerability to spiritual destruction, Weil draws a crucial distinction between suffering, in which pain and death stop short of transfixing and breaking the psyche, and affliction, which by contrast "stamps the soul to its very depths with the scorn, the disgust, and even the self-hatred and sense of guilt and defilement" that according to conventional morality should have stricken the perpetrators of violence but torment instead their innocent victims.[95]

For Weil, affliction presents the overriding mystery of human existence. Whereas a glance at history suffices to establish the frequency, if not the routine nature, of the wars and invasions in which the "innocent are killed, tortured, driven from their country, made destitute, or reduced to slavery, imprisoned in camps or cells," it nevertheless remains mystifying as to why affliction should have "the power to seize the very souls of the innocent and to take possession of them as their sovereign lord."[96] Affliction demoralizes its victims by stripping them of personality and imposes on them a state of dire helplessness. The martyrs who go joyfully to the deaths prepared for them by contrast do not suffer affliction, inasmuch as they accept their persecution as an expression of the will of God. Affliction operates through a "blind mechanism" that turns people into "things." Thus, it does not produce martyrs but "quasi-damned souls" in whom the "vital instinct," torn from all other bonds and commitments, "blindly fastens itself" to the objective of survival, even when life has become "in no way preferable" to death.[97] Under such conditions, acts of compassion and friendship quickly become rare, for the afflicted are "in no state to help anyone at all, and they are almost incapable of even wishing to do so."[98] Moreover, those under the sway of a desolation at once physical and spiritual find themselves increasingly subject to the pressure of an inertia that "goes so far as to prevent [them] from seeking a way of deliverance" and drives the afflicted to the point where they might no longer be able even to wish for deliverance but instead refuse it altogether when the chance arrives.[99] As V tells the thunderstruck Evey, after revealing himself as her captor, "You've been in a prison so long, you no longer believe there's a world outside" (170).

Some will of course assert that it is futile or senseless to bother about transformations that cannot be anticipated, to brace for traumas that one might never have to endure, or to meditate on afflictions that are impossible to survive physically or morally. Michael André Bernstein, for example, rejects outright the view that truth is to be found in extreme conditions, that it is terrible affliction that most readily discloses the truth about an individual: "I believe that very little about human nature or values can be learned from a situation *in extremis* except the virtual tautology that extreme pressure brings out extreme and extremely diverse behavior."[100] For the belief that "the truth lies in the extreme moments which 'ordinary bourgeois life' covers over" bears an uncomfortable proximity to "envisaging murder as the final and potentially most purifying confrontation with 'the destructive element' in humankind."[101] While Bernstein is entirely justified in his warning that the fascination with genocide and an obsession with the experience of victimhood can easily promote a "compensatory urge to tyrannize over others," his insistence that "beliefs, ideas, values, and people are tested best in the daily, routine actions and habits of normal life, not in moments of extraordinary crisis" opens itself to the charge of bearing far too sanguine a trust in the firmness and stability of the normal.[102]

In Weil's view, by contrast, conventional social restraints—premised as they are on notions of rational self-interest, the fairness of legal institutions, and the accountability of elected representatives—are among the first things to be discarded under the harsh conditions of wartime and military occupation. Ordinary restraints are too flimsy and feeble to forestall the prevalence in daily life of ruthless self-concern in the struggle to survive or to hamper collaboration with the occupying authorities. Weil recognizes that for too many individuals, it is the pressure of social conformity alone that "keeps one from falling naturally into the most atrocious kinds of vice or crime,"[103] hence the ease with which so many of her countrymen were able to collaborate with the Nazi occupiers and the heroic endurance that they were routinely able to muster for the sake of securing a single egg but not for defense of their country in battle.[104] Weil's observations on the fate of France under Nazi occupation would bear out Gray's recognition that "weakness of civilisation" lies in how it "encourages the illusion that it is the normal human condition, and when this is punctured barbarism can return almost unnoticed."[105] Such an illusion, moreover, is never more widespread than in a "culture that prefers psychological comfort above anything else."[106] Indeed, an anxious confidence in the durability of normal conditions, or a desperate clinging to their continued existence, has the effect of rendering one all the more vulnerable to becoming demoralized and broken once apparently stable and formerly trustworthy social structures begin to totter and give way.

The rejection of the formula "in extremis veritas" would therefore categorically deprive us of any meaningful inquiry into the most needful of questions, of how to confront the spiritual destruction that catches off guard above all those who have placed themselves at the mercy of fortune. Such a task, to be sure, necessarily comes across as elusive, quixotic even, in a scientifically advanced, economically prosperous liberal capitalist society, for it entails a radical break with the psychic equivalent of the dominant technological paradigm of "maximizing efficiency," whereby one would expend only that minimum level of effort, whether moral or physical or economic, required to avoid disaster. On the other hand, is it not rather the case that life in extraordinary times, during periods of transition and upheaval when increasing numbers of persons are thrown back on necessity, would demand a stance toward contingency akin to the elementary working principles of ancient Roman engineers who, "operating in a world of unknown unknowns," deliberately "overbuilt their arches and the like," which "helped the structures better withstand unexpected shocks"?[107] Indeed, the effort of preparing for the testing of one's principles might appear too high a price to pay for those who trust in the indefinite continuation of the present with the status quo distribution of geopolitical and economic advantages. Yet is there not something irrefutably "dismal," as Kierkegaard puts it, about taking refuge in the desperate and pitiful hope that one will be spared by chance from ordeals that innumerable others were forced to endure without choice?[108]

Of course, reading a literary narrative is no substitute for actually undergoing imprisonment and torture, nor does the fact of having endured extreme hardship necessarily ensure the attainment of wisdom. Yet, the question of how one ought to orient oneself toward the reality of inhuman suffering and extreme situations is one that a speculative narrative such as *V for Vendetta*, no less than the notebooks of Weil, insistently raises. The risk of such a text succumbing to a kind of politically dubious didacticism is not to be underestimated, as the embrace of the film's leftist-liberal posturing as a straightforward illustration of the militant subjectivization theorized by Žižek bears out. Žižek himself in a recent book moves to repudiate such a linkage when he presents a haphazardly argued case for the underlying identity between the fascist leader and the rebel against his own extermination: "So when Evey is imprisoned and tortured by V in order to learn how to overcome fear and be free, is this not parallel to what Sutler [the name of the fascist leader in the film] does to the entire English population, terrorizing them so that they become free and rebel?"[109] Moreover, the original comic, as opposed to its ethically and ideologically facile adaptation, confronts the ambitious task of depicting credibly the first steps of a character toward the elusive lesson that not all those—indeed, perhaps not a great many—subjected to inhuman treatment ever manage to reach. In my view, the graphic novel succeeds in this task, whereas the film fails pathetically at it. The comic underscores the contingent character of Evey's release from the prison of the world and her acceptance of the radical spiritual freedom that can only be attained beyond the pleasure principle. The original narrative does so with a portrayal of V that suggests dimensions of his character far more disturbing than the adaptation allows.

As with other key instances in the narrative, there are significant and telling divergences between the film and the original comic in their respective treatments of Evey's imprisonment. While in the film, V apologizes for deceiving Evey, insisting that "every day I wanted to end it," the V of the comic is by contrast detached and almost cold-blooded. When Evey rails at him for driving her to the edge of madness, V dryly replies, "If that's what it takes" (168). The film softens considerably the matter of torture by allowing V to resort to the explanation that he is only doing what Evey herself said she wanted—in the beginning of the film Evey explicitly tells V that she wants to "live without feeling afraid all the time." In the comic, by contrast, there is no pretense of consent, nor is it possible for V to avail himself of the excuse that Evey gave him permission, however implied, to teach her how to live free from fear. Whereas the V of the film is a verbose and somewhat pitiful figure, given to bombastic speechifying and lugubrious self-revelations, the V of the graphic novel is forbidding and laconic, displaying at almost every turn a keen and bitter sense of irony. Not only does he refuse to apologize to Evey, but the combination of sardonic aloofness and utter conviction he displays toward her upon unveiling the illusion also suggests an array of unnerving possibilities had Evey actually broken under torture and signed the confession. In an eminently disquieting instance of what Bernstein has ingeniously called "sideshadowing," whereby the reader is confronted with a "present dense with multiple, and mutually exclusive, possibilities for what is to come," we are obliged to ask what V would have done to Evey had she decided to give him up to the secret police.[110] Would V have then killed her? If Evey were confronted with the truth after betraying V, wouldn't she be filled with a sense of shame so overpowering as to drive her to suicide? In the harsh world of the comic, it is clear that such extremes are included in the stakes willingly accepted by V in the particular course of education he elects for his protégée.

Unlike his more amiable screen double, the V of the comic would not have intervened to rescue Evey the moment he sensed her spirit was under immediate threat of breaking. Thus, Evey's liberation, her sublime defiance of death, is revealed as a contingent outcome, one that could yet be undone by a resurgence of resentment or self-righteous indignation. For, it can be the case that those who have survived terrible ordeals presume that their travails confer on them the authority to justify the ruthless pursuit of domination and the unconstrained exercise of force. On the other hand, what is striking about Evey's ordeal and reawakening is that her breakdown comes *after* she recognizes that her imprisonment was a charade carried out by V, that is to say, once she realizes she is no longer in any danger of being executed or tortured. Her frantic attempts to defend the "mere life" that had provided her with moments of passing and transitory happiness take place after she has renounced her claims to happiness in defending her principles. So what is it that shocks her back into fearlessness and freedom, and steels her for the labors of building where V has destroyed? For Weil, it is only in the elusive instants marked by the "acceptance of the moral void" that human beings ever break free from the pitiless laws of mechanistic necessity. In these moments in which one is forced to endure a "moment of the void," one "either receives the supernatural bread" of grace or "falls."[111] The receptivity to grace, however, arises from the detachment that comes from "passing through a kind of death,"[112] the terrible scourging in which love, becoming severed from attachment, that is to say, from the illusory operation of filling the void in oneself with "things," takes on an impersonal and gratuitous character.[113]

Valerie's letter, as a form of "supernatural bread," flows from her faith that her own death will not prevent her from giving hope to another. Her message fixes itself upon Evey's destiny once the latter comes to grips with the fact that her own suffering is not unique, that what V has forced her to endure has been imposed on incalculable millions who, moreover, never came to receive grace from their persecutors or their fellow prisoners. The outpouring of anonymous love, which Evey received gladly in her imprisonment, thus carries her to the arduous threshold of an impersonal truth. She moves from outrage at the brutal treatment of her own person ("you did this to me?") to the impersonal universality of the recognition—and the ineluctable terror to which such a recognition is bound—that "this was done to countless individuals, none of whom possessed any less of a claim upon life than I" (167). Such an attitude undoubtedly strikes us as forbidding and dauntingly difficult to sustain—we shrink from it as we would from those truths that, though valid and even supremely practical in certain demarcated instances, are too extreme to be of use in daily life. And so we tell ourselves to put this subjective stance aside within the free-floating limbo of our indecision, next to other ideas we as proper liberals would rather not think about, such as the *amor fati* of Nietzsche and the resolution of Kierkegaard "to live as though dead," inexorable commitments that we feel free to dismiss as eccentricities peculiar to repressed nineteenth-century recluses, rather than accept as vital and essential elements of their thought. For the power that V has until this point wielded over Evey—a power he himself seeks to dispel—stems precisely from her paralyzing dread at the unbearable thought of having to share his fate. Her fantasy that V might in fact be her father, after all, speaks to her desire for protection from the outside world, for a heroic parent who would do everything in his power to shield her from the terrors of a ruthless and amoral universe. Notably, this fantasy is left out by the film.

The horrors portrayed in *V for Vendetta* evoke the historical realities that have preponderantly shaped the thinking of ethics and politics from the end of the Second World War to the present: concentration camps, the threat of nuclear annihilation, and the disintegration of democratic states into totalitarian regimes. Yet the depiction in the graphic novel of the catastrophes and pressures under which a shattered and traumatized society comes to accept state terror and internment camps reveals an unsettling resonance with respect to the perilous crises of the present time. The competition for scarce resources and the threat of environmental destruction collide with the capitalist imperative of growth so vital to the legitimacy of industrialized states. The prospect of collective action to forestall environmental disaster grows increasingly chimerical in affluent and fragmented societies deadlocked by the pursuit of enjoyment. Indeed, a society inured to the expectation of future abundance is prone to chafe at making the sweeping and often painful adjustments necessary to avoid even worse hardships in the future. Such neglect, carried beyond a certain threshold, can make the resort to inhuman policies appear necessary and inevitable, once a society loses the capacity to distinguish reasonable self-preservation from a destructive and futile defense of unjustifiable expectations. As Voegelin observes, Nietzsche's vision of the last men, for whom psychological and physical comfort become the supreme good, must be recognized as a prophecy of total war. For such an epoch is to be wracked by wars such "as there never have been" on this globe.[114]

V for Vendetta unfolds on the other side of that threshold, in which a liberal democratic society, having been dealt too many devastating blows, has succumbed to the forces of inhuman will and unforgiving necessity. Against the nightmare of totalitarian barbarism, the task that Evey undertakes in salvaging a civilized community from its ruins radiates a clarity of purpose. Those, who, in the daylight of the present age, strain to breathe life back into dashed and disappointed hopes for a better sociopolitical order may find this clarity enviable, even as they shrink from the arduous nature of the trials that are the source of its illumination. On the other hand, the model of political subjectivization that emerges in the narrative would appear to rely on the condition that the worst must first come to pass. But the ordeal of opening oneself to grace is not a process that is reducible to the political state of emergency, nor can its central question, whether one is capable of receiving and giving sublime love, be subsumed under the categories of the political. Rather, these movements whereby one clears within one's soul the space for transfiguration are indistinguishable from the effort to confront the worst, setting out from the wager that there is a hope that abides beyond the rule of oblivion and death.

ACKNOWLEDGMENTS

I would like to thank my friends and colleagues whose wisdom and generosity were essential to the completion of this book. Roy Swanson and Rachel Skalitzky welcomed me to Milwaukee and provided a congenial atmosphere in which to begin my work, helping to straighten a path that I had once expected to be more circuitous. Robin Pickering-Iazzi encouraged me in my decision to embark in a new direction of research, shifting temporarily away from my earlier work in literary modernism, in part to reflect more intensively on transformed political realities.

A fellowship from the Center for Twenty-first Century Studies at the University of Wisconsin–Milwaukee helped me to initiate this project, and I remain grateful to its then-director, Dan Sherman. A second grant from the Institute for Research in the Humanities at the University of Wisconsin–Madison was vital for getting me to the midpoint of the manuscript, and for this support I thank David Sorkin and Claudia Card. I would also thank the Korean Film Council (KOFIC) for its extraordinary generosity in providing foreign scholars with resources for the study of Korean cinema.

Writing this book brought me into contact with fellow scholars whose kindness and insights were an unfailing source of inspiration. I am especially grateful to Michael Shin, Amy Elias, Phillip Wegner, Frenchy Lunning, Wendy Goldberg, Gregg Lambert, Marianna Torgovnick, Paul Maltby, Martin Kevorkian, and Matthew Biberman. Amy Elias introduced me to the debates over postmodern theory taking place within theology. Phillip Wegner helped me to broaden the scope not only of this project but also my future research by engaging the scholarship of utopian studies. Gregg Lambert has my gratitude for concluding his careful reading of the manuscript with a challenge that was crucial for giving shape to its concluding chapter. Frenchy Lunning invited me to present a section of my manuscript at the Minneapolis College of Art and Design; it was both an honor and a delight to talk about the work of Alan Moore and Hayao Miyazaki at its annual conference on anime and manga. Michael Shin gave me a chance to test out my ideas about Korean cinema at the East Asian Studies Colloquium at Cornell University. A second visit to Cornell offered the occasion for a stimulating discussion of the theoretical debates engaged by my book. For this rigorously invigorating dialogue, I am grateful to Natalie Melas, Walter Cohen, Jonathan Culler, Debra Castillo, Jonathan Monroe, Sue Besemer, and the graduate students in the Department of Comparative Literature. Lastly, I am indebted to Robert and Sabine Doran, co-organizers of the Colloquium on Violence and Religion in 2008. This conference—and the spirited exchanges that took place there—ignited the spark necessary to see the manuscript to its end.

To my colleagues at the University of Wisconsin–Milwaukee I owe a large measure of thanks. Tasha Oren took time from her many responsibilities to read portions of the manuscript. Bill Bristow generously shared his knowledge of philosophical ethics in ways that were always illuminating and instructive. Ihab Hassan gently redirected me when my writing was headed in a false direction. I owe a special debt of gratitude to Patrice Petro, whose tireless generosity and sagacious counsel were indispensable in the development of this project from manuscript to book.

I appreciate the steadfast and unwavering support I received from the University of Minnesota Press and its inspiring editor, Doug Armato. I am deeply honored and touched by his commitment to my project, and his confidence in my work provided both inspiration and incentive to finish the manuscript after an unexpected delay. I thank Danielle Kasprzak for her dedication and attentiveness in preparing the manuscript. I am grateful for the words of praise and encouragement expressed in the reader's report by Steven Shaviro: I hope that some day I will be able to encourage a younger scholar with the eloquent precision and warm insight with which he has inspired me.

To my wife, Nan Kim, and my son, Elijah, I owe the deepest thanks for their patience during the many occasions this manuscript compelled me to draw back into my study.

NOTES

INTRODUCTION

1. See Darko Suvin, *Metamorphoses of Science Fiction: On the Poetics and History of a Literary Genre* (New Haven, Conn.: Yale University Press, 1979); Fredric Jameson, *Archaeologies of the Future: The Desire Called Utopia and Other Science Fictions* (London: Verso, 2005); and Carl Freedman, *Critical Theory and Science Fiction* (Hanover, N.H.: Wesleyan University Press, 2000).

2. Istvan Csicsery-Ronay Jr., "Marxist Theory and Science Fiction," in *The Cambridge Companion to Science Fiction*, ed. Edward James and Farah Mendlesohn (Cambridge: Cambridge University Press, 2003), 120.

3. Suvin, *Metamorphoses of Science Fiction*, 49.

4. Ibid., 58.

5. Darko Suvin, "Locus, Horizon, and Orientation: The Concept of Possible Worlds as a Key to Utopian Studies," *Utopian Studies* 1, no. 2 (1990): 77.

6. Freedman, *Critical Theory and Science Fiction*, 69.

7. Ibid., 17.

8. Thomas More, *Utopia*, trans. and ed. Robert M. Adams, 2nd edition (New York: W. W. Norton, 1992), 31.

9. Eric Voegelin, *Modernity without Restraint: The Political Religions; The New Science of Politics; and Science, Politics and Gnosticism*, vol. 5 of *The Collected Works of Eric Voegelin*, ed. Manfred Henningsen (Columbia: University of Missouri Press, 2000), 305.

10. Eric Voegelin, *History of Political Ideas, Volume VI: Renaissance and Reformation*, vol. 22 of *The Collected Works of Eric Voegelin*, ed. David L. Morse and William M. Thompson (Columbia: University of Missouri Press, 1998), 129, 128.

11. Eric Voegelin, *Renaissance and Reformation*, 129.

12. Carl Schmitt, *The Concept of the Political*, trans. George Schwab (Chicago: University of Chicago Press, 1996), 79.

13. Georges Sorel, *Reflections on Violence*, ed. Jeremy Jennings and trans. T. E. Hulme (Cambridge: Cambridge University Press, 2004), 10.

14. See for example, John Lukacs, *Democracy and Populism: Fear and Hatred* (New Haven, Conn.: Yale University Press, 2005). Lukacs maintains that fascism and Nazism cannot truly be considered conservative or even reactionary movements, as both Hitler and Mussolini had a "progressive" faith in technology to transform the world in accordance with their respective ideological plans.

15. John Gray, "Introduction," to *Heresies: Against Progress and Other Illusions* (London: Granta Books, 2004), 4.

16. Freedman, *Critical Theory and Science Fiction*, 64.

17. Ernst Bloch, *The Principle of Hope, Volume One*, trans. Neville Plaice, Stephen Plaice, and Paul Knight (Cambridge, Mass.: MIT Press, 1986), 305.

18. Stanley Rosen, *G. W. F. Hegel: An Introduction to the Science of Wisdom* (South Bend, Ind.: St. Augustine's Press, 2000), 217. See Hegel, *The Phenomenology of Spirit*, trans. A. V. Miller (Oxford: Oxford University Press, 1977), 463, 666–67.

19. Reinhart Koselleck, *Critique and Crisis: Enlightenment and the Pathogenesis of Modern Society* (Cambridge, Mass.: MIT Press, 1988), 146, 185.

20. Sorel, *Reflections on Violence*, 11.

21. Freedman, *Critical Theory and Science Fiction*, 122.

22. Ibid., 127.

23. My argument here owes much to the recent writings of Slavoj Žižek, though I differ with him in taking the view that the revolutionary destruction of the old regime results in a situation resembling the Hobbesian state of nature, which as a consequence poses insuperable limitations on the expansion and intensification of militant passion in the postrevolutionary order. See Slavoj Žižek, *Did Somebody Say Totalitarianism? Five Interventions in the (Mis)Use of a Notion* (London: Verso, 2001), 153–54 and "Robespierre, or, 'The Divine Violence' of Terror," in Maximilien Robespierre, *Virtue and Terror*, trans. John Howe (London: Verso, 2007), xxxv.

24. Jacques Derrida, *Specters of Marx: The State of the Debt, the Work of Mourning, and the New International*, trans. Peggy Kamuf (New York: Routledge, 1994), 88.

25. Koselleck, *Critique and Crisis*, 186.

26. Simon Critchley, for example, defines radical politics as the "continual questioning from below of any attempt to impose order from above." See *Infinitely Demanding: Ethics of Commitment, Politics of Resistance* (London: Verso, 2007), 13.

27. Umberto Eco, "The Myth of Superman," in *Arguing Comics: Literary Masters on a Popular Medium*, ed. Jeet Heer (Jackson: University of Mississippi Press, 2004), 164.

28. Ibid., 163.

29. See Frank Miller and Bill Sienkiewicz, *Elektra: Assassin* (New York: Marvel Comics, 1987).

30. Alan Moore and John Totleben, *Miracleman Book 3: Olympus* (Forestville, Calif.: Eclipse Books, 1990), 122–23.

31. Schmitt, *Political Theology*, 36.

32. Ibid., 7.

33. See Carl Schmitt, *The Nomos of the Earth*, trans. Gary Ulmen (New York: Telos Press, 2003), 59–60.

34. Schmitt, *Political Theology: Four Chapters on the Concept of Sovereignty*, trans. George Schwab (Chicago: University of Chicago Press, 2006), 66. See also Heinrich Meier, *The Lesson of Carl Schmitt: Four Chapters on the Distinction between Political Theology and Political Philosophy*, trans. Marcus Brainard (Chicago: University of Chicago Press, 1998), 74–75.

35. Meier, *The Lesson of Carl Schmitt*, 76.

36. Boris Groys, *The Total Art of Stalinism: Avant-Garde, Aesthetic Dictatorship, and Beyond*, trans. Charles Rougle (Princeton, N.J.: Princeton University Press, 1992), 12. Further references are cited parenthetically in the text.

37. See John Gray, "The New Wars of Scarcity," in *Heresies*, 121.

38. Moore and Totleben, *Miracleman Book 3: Olympus*, 80–81.

39. Ibid., 84.

40. G. K. Chesterton, "The Secret of Father Brown," in *The Penguin Complete Father Brown* (New York: Penguin, 1981), 466.

1. UTOPIA ACHIEVED

1. J. G. A. Pocock, *The Machiavellian Moment: Florentine Political Thought and the Atlantic Republican Tradition* (Princeton, N.J.: Princeton University Press, 1975), 170–71.

2. Ibid., 190.

3. See Paul Ricoeur, "The Political Paradox," in *History and Truth*, trans. Charles Kelbley (Evanston, Ill.: Northwestern University Press, 1965), 262, and Sheldon Wolin, *Politics as Vision: Continuity and Innovation in Western Political Thought*, expanded ed. (Princeton, N.J.: Princeton University Press, 2004), 197–200.

4. Ricoeur, "The Political Paradox," 262.

5. Simone Weil, *Oppression and Liberty*, trans. Arthur Wills and John Petrie (Amherst: The University of Massachusetts Press, 1973), 58.

6. This is an idea explored by Moore in his earlier revisionist comic, *Miracleman: Olympus*. See the introduction to this book.

7. Alan Moore and Dave Gibbons, *Watchmen* (New York: DC Comics, 1986) Book XI, iii. Further references are cited parenthetically in the text, with the issue or chapter number followed by the page number.

8. Hannah Arendt, *On Revolution* (New York: Penguin, 1965), 82.

9. Roz Kaveney also notes these connections between the character of Ozymandias, the Roman emperor, and the silent film star in her recent study of *Watchmen*. See her informative discussion of the comic in *Superheroes! Capes and Crusaders in Comics and Films* (London: I.B. Tauris, 2008), 130.

10. Slavoj Žižek, *The Ticklish Subject: The Absent Centre of Political Ontology* (London: Verso, 1999), 237.

11. See Slavoj Žižek, *Welcome to the Desert of the Real! Five Essays on September 11 and Related Dates* (London: Verso, 2002), 30.

12. Niccolò Machiavelli, *The Prince*, trans. George Bull (New York: Penguin, 2003), 25.

13. Kurt Vonnegut, *The Sirens of Titan* (New York: Delta, 1998), 177.

14. Ibid., 177.

15. Thomas Hobbes, *Leviathan*, ed. C. B. Macpherson (New York: Penguin, 1988), 160.

16. E. M. Cioran, *History and Utopia*, trans. Richard Howard (Chicago: University of Chicago Press, 1988), 109.

17. Leo Strauss, *Thoughts on Machiavelli* (Chicago: University of Chicago Press, 1958), 230.

18. Niccolò Machiavelli, *The Discourses*, trans. Leslie J. Walker, S. J. and Brian Richardson (New York: Penguin, 1970), 163.

19. See Žižek, *The Ticklish Subject*, 379–80.

20. In reference to the misguided efforts to read Kojève as a conventional Hegel scholar, Stanley Rosen, while not approving his former teacher's political program, describes the posthistorical order as the positive achievement of historical violence, the sacrificial outcome of wars and massacres: "Kojève is entitled to argue that 'philological correctness' is a historical triviality, like the murder of millions of innocent persons in fulfillment of Hegel's observation that history is a slaughter-bench, a bench, in other words, upon which are prepared the feasts of the gods: the residents of the posthistorical utopia." See Stanley Rosen, *Hermeneutics as Politics* (Oxford: Oxford University Press, 1987), 94.

21. It should be noted that Moore himself remains skeptical of any gesture that ascribes validity to a system of values simply by virtue of its having been historically repressed or subjugated. Far from didactically advocating a return to matriarchal values, or the worship of the goddesses suppressed by the emergence

of patriarchy, the narrative in *From Hell* makes clear the constructed nature of the mystical and mythic feminine that furnishes the negative pole in Gull's brutal cosmology, to which he opposes the rational discipline and rigid hierarchies of the patriarchal order. Yet the patriarchal order for Gull is itself a flagrantly heterodox conception that deploys a syncretic, Masonic symbolism associated with the worship of a trinity of male solar deities consisting of Apollo, Christ, and "Jahbulon" or Baal.

22. Alan Moore and Eddie Campbell, *From Hell* (Marietta, Ga.: Top Shelf Productions, 2004), chapter 10: 21–22.

23. Hegel, *The Phenomenology of Spirit*, 407.

24. Alexandre Kojève, *Introduction to the Reading of Hegel*, ed. Allan Bloom, trans. James H. Nichols Jr. (Ithaca, N.Y.: Cornell University Press, 1980), 159n.

25. Ibid., 68.

26. Rosen, *Hermeneutics as Politics*, 92.

27. Not surprisingly, the ubiquity of these inconspicuous alterations of real-world phenomena has spawned a comprehensive annotation of the novel by Doug Atkinson, which can be accessed on a variety of Web sites, such as at http://www .capnwacky.com/rj/watchmen and http://www.enjolrasworld.com.

28. Apropos of Ozymandias's decision to stage an encounter with an alien life-form as the means to bring about world peace, Ronald Reagan was known to dismay members of his cabinet by speaking longingly of an alien invasion that would have the effect of putting an end to the rivalry between the superpowers.

29. See Alain Badiou, *Saint Paul: The Foundation of Universalism* (Stanford, Calif.: Stanford University Press, 2003), 58–59, and Žižek, *The Ticklish Subject*, 228–29.

30. See Doug Atkinson, "The Annotated *Watchmen*," http://www.capnwacky .com/rj/watchmen/chapter8.html.

31. Geoff Klock, *How to Read Superhero Comics and Why* (New York: Continuum, 2003), 66.

32. See Žižek, *The Ticklish Subject*, 363.

33. Machiavelli refers to the tyrant of Perugia, Giovampagolo Baglioni, as his example of the baffling and recurrent failure to take advantage of an unambiguously favorable turn of events to dispose of one's adversary, such as would be provided by a rash mistake on the part of the opponent: "Thus Giovampagolo, who thought nothing of incest or of publicly murdering his relatives, knew not how, or better, did not dare, to avail himself of an excellent opportunity to do what would have caused everyone to admire his courage and would have gained for him immortal fame, since he would have been the first to show prelates how little men are

respected who live and rule as they do, and would have done a thing the greatness of which would have obliterated any infamy and any danger that might arise from it." See Machiavelli, *The Discourses*, 178.

34. Machiavelli, *The Discourses*, 178.

35. The second issue of *Watchmen* portrays the meeting from the perspective of Ozymandias (II: 11), while the sixth issue gives Rorschach's commentary on the event (VI: 15). The Comedian's act of burning the map of the United States, on which have been stuck the ills plaguing the nation in the mid-1960s, is in fact an event pivotal for both Veidt, who is thereby provoked into devising his bloody scheme to save the earth, and Rorschach, whose crime fighting comes to take on a pervasively nihilistic character under the shadow of nuclear annihilation as well as against the pervasive reality of human wantonness.

36. The Comedian also mentions Byron Lewis (Mothman), who has been committed to an insane asylum, and "Jon Goddamn Walking H-bomb Osterman" (Dr. Manhattan) in his diatribe.

37. It should be noted that the caption appears right above the hands of Ozymandias, which have just hurled the Comedian through the shattered window. If Veidt and Rorschach have one thing in common, it is the fact that they both possess a heightened sense of irony but do not see a need for laughter, and are never shown laughing. They thus appear as less warm-bloodedly human than their former teammates Nite Owl, the Silk Spectre, and even the Comedian.

38. Brent Fishbaugh, "Moore and Gibbons's *Watchmen*: Exact Personifications of Science," *Extrapolation* 39, no. 3 (1998): 198.

39. Schmitt, *The Concept of the Political*, 54; italics mine.

40. For a treatment of the significance of disavowed trauma and transgressive rituals for the formation of community, see Slavoj Žižek, "The Act and Its Vicissitudes," http://www.lacan.com/symptom6_articles/zizek.html.

41. See Slavoj Žižek, *On Belief* (London: Routledge, 2001), 13–15.

42. Žižek, "The Act and Its Vicissitudes."

43. See for example, Lukacs, *Democracy and Populism*.

44. Žižek, *On Belief*, 11.

45. The irreversible demythologizing of sacrificial violence takes place with the narrative of Christ, which according to Girard reveals the truth of the victim's innocence: "The text of persecution reveals an inability to produce true myths that characterizes the modern Western world as a whole. The modern ability to pursue and demystify subtle modes of persecution, which may be hidden not only behind very transparent accusations but also behind texts that appear to be innocent, can only correspond to a more advanced phase of an evolution that progresses in the

form of a spiral, with the deciphering of cultural mechanisms leading to more decomposition, and vice versa." See René Girard, *Things Hidden Since the Foundation of the World,* trans. Stephen Bann and Michael Metteer (Stanford, Calif.: Stanford University Press, 1987), 130.

46. Ibid., 36–37.

47. Ibid., 287.

48. Giorgio Agamben, *Homo Sacer: Sovereign Power and Bare Life,* trans. Daniel Heller-Roazen (Stanford, Calif.: Stanford University Press, 1998), 171.

49. Ibid., 169.

50. Giorgio Agamben, *The State of Exception,* trans. Kevin Attell (Chicago: University of Chicago Press, 2005), 22.

2. THE DEFENSE OF NECESSITY

1. Leo Strauss, "Restatement on Xenophon's Hiero," in *On Tyranny,* ed. Victor Gourevitch and Michael S. Roth (Chicago: University of Chicago Press, 2000), 209.

2. See Kojève, *Introduction to the Reading of Hegel,* for his account of the "universal and homogeneous state."

3. Strauss, "Restatement," 209.

4. Rosen, *Hermeneutics as Politics,* 93.

5. See Rosen, *Hermeneutics as Politics,* 93–95.

6. John Rawls, *The Law of Peoples; with, The Idea of Public Reason Revisited* (Cambridge, Mass.: Harvard University Press, 1999), 63.

7. Derrida, *Specters of Marx,* 70–71.

8. Rosen, *Hermeneutics as Politics,* 94.

9. Kojève, *Introduction to the Reading of Hegel,* 83.

10. Alain Badiou, *Ethics: An Essay on the Understanding of Evil,* trans. Peter Hallward (London: Verso, 2001), 30.

11. Francis Fukuyama, *The End of History and the Last Man* (New York: The Free Press, 1992), 46. Emphasis in the original.

12. Žižek, *Welcome to the Desert of the Real,* 60.

13. Rosen, *Hermeneutics as Politics,* 90.

14. This turn in theory owes much to Giorgio Agamben's *Homo Sacer.*

15. See Tzvetan Todorov, *The Fantastic: A Structural Approach to a Literary Genre,* trans. Richard Howard (Ithaca, N.Y.: Cornell University Press, 1975).

16. Schmitt, *The Concept of the Political,* 79.

17. Eric Voegelin, "The Order of Power: Erasmus and More," in *Renaissance and Reformation,* 128–29.

18. Derrida, *Specters of Marx*, 65.

19. I am drawing here on Slavoj Žižek's idea of "actively assuming passivity," that is, of a subject deriving an obscene pleasure from the very experience of his or her subjection. Such a traumatic form of enjoyment gives rise, in Žižek's account, to an overpowering sense of humiliation, self-revilement, and, ultimately, suicidal despair. See Žižek, *Did Somebody Say Totalitarianism?* 188.

20. Žižek, *Welcome to the Desert of the Real*, 152.

21. Machiavelli, *Discourses*, 178.

22. Philip Lamy and Devon Kinne, "Alien Invasion: Ufology and the Millennial Myth," in *Fear Itself: Enemies Real and Imagined in American Culture*, ed. Nancy Lusignan Schultz (West Lafayette, Ind.: Purdue University Press, 1999), 415.

23. In his incarnation as Lord of the Dance, which governs the cycle of destruction and renewal, Shiva typically possesses four arms, but when his movements attain a cosmic scale of power, they multiply to eight. Shiva is often depicted trampling a dwarf representing ignorance and obliviousness; it is noteworthy in this regard that after he has strangled Byung-Gu, Kang stamps on his unconscious body with his feet, bringing him back to consciousness.

24. For an elaboration of the thesis that hegemonic power serves as a condition for the production of science-fiction narratives, see Isvtan Csicsery-Ronay, "Dis-Imagined Communities," in *Edging into the Future: Science Fiction and Contemporary Cultural Transformation*, ed. Veronica Hollinger and Joan Gordon (Philadelphia: University of Pennsylvania Press, 2002).

25. Simone Weil, *Gravity and Grace*, ed. Gustav Thibon and trans. Emma Crawford (London: Routledge, 1992), 147–48.

3. THE SAINTLY POLITICS OF CATASTROPHE

1. See Susan Napier, *Anime from "Akira" to "Howl's Moving Castle": Experiencing Contemporary Japanese Animation*, 2nd ed. (New York: Palgrave Macmillan, 2005), 234–35.

2. *Princess Mononoke (Mononoke-hime)*, screenplay by Hayao Miyazaki. Dir. Hayao Miyazaki. Perfs. Yôji Matsuda, Yuriko Ishida, and Yûko Tanaka. Studio Ghibli, 1997.

3. See the afterword, "On *Nausicaä*," in Hayao Miyazaki, *Nausicaä of the Valley of Wind: Volume 1*, trans. David Lewis and Toren Smith (San Francisco: Viz Media, 2004), 135. In the previous edition published in 1995, it appears on 262–63. See *Nausicaä of the Valley of Wind: Perfect Collection, Volume 1*, trans. David Lewis and Toren Smith (San Francisco: Viz Communications, 1995), 262–63.

4. Andrew Osmond, "Nausicaä and the Fantasy of Hayao Miyazaki," *Foundation* 72 (Spring 1998): 70.

5. Hayao Miyazaki, *Nausicaä of the Valley of Wind: Volume 3*, 105; *Nausicaä of the Valley of Wind: Perfect Collection, Volume 2*, 110. Further references are cited parenthetically in the text, with the volume number followed by the page number. The seven-volume Viz Media edition of 2004 is cited first, followed by references to the four-volume *Perfect Collection* published in 1995.

6. Osmond, "Nausicaä and the Fantasy of Hayao Miyazaki," 70.

7. Edith Wyschogrod, *Saints and Postmodernism: Revisioning Moral Philosophy* (Chicago: University of Chicago Press, 1990), xxiii.

8. Simone Weil, "The *Iliad*, Poem of Might," in *The Simone Weil Reader*, ed. George Panichas (Wakefield, R.I.: Moyer Bell, 1999), 181.

9. Emmanuel Lévinas, "Substitution," in *The Levinas Reader*, ed. Séan Hand (Oxford: Blackwell, 1989), 111–12.

10. John Milbank, *Being Reconciled: Ontology and Pardon* (London: Routledge, 2003), 203.

11. Catherine Pickstock, "Postmodern Theology?" *Telos* 110 (1998): 174.

12. Weil, *Gravity and Grace*, 70.

13. Weil, "The *Iliad*, Poem of Might," 181.

14. Osmond, "Nausicaä and the Fantasy of Hayao Miyazaki," 71.

15. See Takeuchi Yoshinori, "Centering and the World Beyond," trans. James W. Heisig, in Alfred Bloom, ed., *Living in Amida's Universal Vow: Essays in Shin Buddhism* (Bloomington, Ind.: World Wisdom, 2004), 54.

16. Osmond, "Nausicaä and the Fantasy of Hayao Miyazaki," 73.

17. Frederik Schodt, *Dreamland Japan* (Berkeley, Calif.: Stone Bridge Press, 1996), 281.

18. Osmond, "Nausicaä and the Fantasy of Hayao Miyazaki," 74.

19. "I Understand Nausicaä a Bit More Than I Did a Little While Ago," interview with Hayao Miyazaki, *Comic Box* (January 1995); http: www.comicbox.co.jp/e-nau/e-nau.html.

20. Margaret Atwood, *Oryx and Crake* (New York: Nan A. Talese, 2003), 305.

21. See John Gray, *Straw Dogs: Thoughts on Humans and Other Animals* (London: Granta, 2002), 6–7.

22. Bill McKibben, *Enough: Staying Human in an Engineered Age* (New York: Times Books, 2003), 113.

23. Albert Camus, *The Rebel: An Essay on Man in Revolt*, trans. Anthony Bower (New York: Vintage, 1991), 304.

24. I owe this point to Anthony Lioi. See also Osmond, "Nausicaä and the Fantasy of Hayao Miyazaki," 73.

4. BETWEEN TRAUMA AND TRAGEDY

1. Slavoj Žižek, *The Fragile Absolute, or, Why Is the Christian Legacy Worth Fighting For?* (London: Verso, 2000), 10, and *The Parallax View* (Cambridge, Mass.: The MIT Press, 2006), 301.

2. For a valuable account of how the political Right took over the utopian dreams typically associated with the Left, see John Gray, *Black Mass: Apocalyptic Religion and the Death of Utopia* (New York: Farrar, Straus and Giroux, 2007), 29.

3. Meghnad Desai, *Marx's Revenge: The Resurgence of Capitalism and the Death of State Socialism* (London: Verso, 2004), 313–14.

4. Žižek, *The Parallax View*, 315.

5. Slavoj Žižek, "Reloaded Revolutions," in *More Matrix and Philosophy: Revolutions and Reloaded Decoded*, ed. William Irwin (Chicago: Open Court, 2005), 206.

6. Žižek, *The Parallax View*, 316. Žižek makes the case that Smith, in his "negatively heroic" role of serving as the ultimate antagonist whose very presence prevents peace and reconciliation between the classes, contains anti-Semitic resonances: "Smith is a proto-Jewish figure, an obscene intruder who multiplies like a rat, runs amok and disturbs the harmony of Humans and Machines, so that his destruction makes possible a (temporary) class truce."

7. Ibid.

8. *The Matrix Reloaded*, screenplay by Andy Wachowski and Larry Wachowski. Dir. Andy Wachowski and Larry Wachowski. Perfs. Keanu Reeves, Laurence Fishburne, Carrie-Anne Moss, and Hugo Weaving. Warner Bros., 2003.

9. See William Rodney Allen, ed., *Conversations with Kurt Vonnegut* (Jackson: University Press of Mississippi, 1988), 159–60.

10. Simone Weil, *Formative Writings: 1929–1941*, ed. Dorothy Tuck McFarland and Wilhemina Van Ness (Amherst: University of Massachusetts Press, 1987), 227. Quoted in John Lukacs, *The Duel: The Eighty-Day Struggle between Churchill and Hitler* (New Haven, Conn.: Yale University Press, 1990), 15. Emphasis mine.

11. See Žižek, "Reloaded Revolutions," 207.

12. Žižek, *The Parallax View*, 317.

13. Theodore Schick Jr., "Choice, Purpose, and Understanding," in Irwin, ed., *More Matrix and Philosophy*, 79–80.

14. John Gray, "Faith in the Matrix," in *Heresies: Against Progress and Other Illusions*, 54–55.

15. Gray, *Straw Dogs*, 109–10.

16. *The Second Renaissance, Part I*, in *The Animatrix*. Screenplay by Andy

Wachowski and Larry Wachowski. Dir. Mahiro Maeda. Perf. Julia Fletcher. Warner Bros., 2003.

17. Aristotle, *Poetics*, 9.1–4. Quoted in Eric Voegelin, "Tragedy," in *Order and History, Volume 2: The World of the Polis*, vol. 15 of *The Collected Works of Eric Voegelin*, ed. Athanasios Moulakis (Columbia: University of Missouri Press, 2000), 320.

18. *The Second Renaissance, Part II*.

19. Strauss, *Thoughts on Machiavelli*, 240.

20. Simone Weil, "Analysis of Oppression," in *Oppression and Liberty*, trans. Arthur Wills and John Petrie (Amherst: University of Massachusetts Press, 1973), 66, 69.

21. Quoted in Adrian Poole, *Tragedy* (Oxford: Oxford University Press, 2005), 62.

22. See ibid.

23. Martha Nussbaum, *The Fragility of Goodness: Luck and Ethics in Greek Tragedy and Philosophy* (Cambridge: Cambridge University Press, 1986), 13, 388.

24. Judith Butler, *Precarious Life: The Powers of Mourning and Violence* (London: Verso, 2004), 32–33.

25. Terry Eagleton, "Commentary," in *Rethinking Tragedy*, ed. Rita Felski (Baltimore: The Johns Hopkins University Press, 2008), 344. John Gray notes that Homeric *arete* and Christian *agape* are mutually exclusive virtues in *Two Faces of Liberalism* (New York: New Press, 2000), 38, 51.

26. Eagleton, "Commentary," 345.

27. Terry Eagleton, *Sweet Violence: The Idea of the Tragic* (Oxford: Blackwell, 2003), 52.

28. Voegelin, "Tragedy," 321.

29. Ibid., 325, and *The New Science of Politics*, 146.

30. Voegelin, "Tragedy," 325.

31. Ibid., 321.

32. Voegelin, *The New Science of Politics*, 144.

33. See Slavoj Žižek, *Violence* (New York: Picador, 2008), 35.

34. See Gray, "Introduction," in *Heresies*, 2–3.

35. Žižek, *Welcome to the Desert of the Real*, 60.

36. Koselleck, *Critique and Crisis*, 50.

37. Žižek, *Did Somebody Say Totalitarianism?* 97.

38. See Žižek, *Violence*, 191–92.

39. Timothy Reiss, *Tragedy and Truth: Studies in the Development of a Renaissance and Neoclassical Discourse* (New Haven, Conn.: Yale University Press, 1980), 290.

40. Rosen, *Hermeneutics as Politics*, 19.

41. Susan Neiman, *Moral Clarity: A Guide for Grown-up Idealists* (Orlando: Harcourt, 2008), 156.

42. See Michael Hardt and Antonio Negri, *Empire* (Cambridge, Mass.: Harvard University Press, 2000).

43. Derrida, *Specters of Marx*, 65.

44. See Jacques Derrida, "Force of Law: The 'Mystical Foundation of Authority,'" in *Deconstruction and the Possibility of Justice*, ed. Drucilla Cornell, Michel Rosenfeld, and David Gray Carlson (New York: Routledge, 1992), especially 19–29.

45. Rosen, *Hermeneutics as Politics*, 3, 5.

46. Derrida, *Specters of Marx*, 167.

47. Gray, "The New Wars of Scarcity," 116.

48. Gray, "Joseph Conrad, Our Contemporary," in *Heresies*, 106.

49. Morris Berman, *Dark Ages America: The Final Phase of Empire* (New York: W. W. Norton, 2006), 239–40.

50. Leo Strauss, "What Is Political Philosophy?" in *What Is Political Philosophy? and Other Studies* (Chicago: University of Chicago Press, 1988), 47.

51. Ibid., 49.

52. Eric Voegelin, "Hobbes," in *History of Political Ideas, Volume VII—The New Order and the Last Orientation*, vol. 25 of *The Collected Works of Eric Voegelin*, ed. Jürgen Gebhardt and Thomas A. Hollweck (Columbia: University of Missouri Press, 1999), 61.

53. Strauss, "What Is Political Philosophy?" 49.

54. Ibid.

55. Gray, "The Dark Side of Modernity: Europe's New Far Right," in *Heresies*, 176.

56. John Gray, *Two Faces of Liberalism* (New York: The New Press, 2000), 91, 104.

57. Neiman, *Moral Clarity*, 29.

58. See Giorgio Agamben, *Remnants of Auschwitz: The Witness and the Archive*, trans. Daniel Heller-Roazen (New York: Zone Books, 2002), 41–45.

59. Ibid., 69.

60. Zdzislaw Ryn and Stanislaw Klodzinski, *An der Grenze zwischen Leben und Tod: Eine Studie über die Erscheinung des "Muselmanns" im Konzentrationslager, Auschwitz-Hefte*, vol. 1 (Weinheim and Basel: Beltz, 1987), 127. Quoted in Giorgio Agamben, *Remnants of Auschwitz*, 43. Note that in this passage, the terms "Muselmann" and "Muslim" are being used interchangeably.

61. Slavoj Žižek, *The Puppet and the Dwarf: The Perverse Core of Christianity* (Cambridge, Mass.: The MIT Press, 2003), 158.

62. Ibid., 157.

63. Ibid., 158–59.

64. Gray, *Straw Dogs*, 89.

65. Ibid., 100.

66. Varlam Shalamov, "Quiet," in *Kolyma Tales*, trans. John Glad (New York: Penguin, 1995), 442. Quoted in Gray, *Straw Dogs*, 100.

67. John Keegan, *Intelligence in War: Knowledge of the Enemy from Napoleon to Al-Qaeda* (New York: Alfred A. Knopf, 2003), 345.

68. Edward Luttwak, "Dead End: Counterinsurgency as Military Malpractice," *Harper's*, February 2007: 40.

69. Zygmunt Bauman, *Modernity and the Holocaust* (Ithaca, N.Y.: Cornell University Press, 2000), 206.

70. Gray, *Straw Dogs*, 90. Gray cites the memoir of Roman Frister, who had been an inmate in a concentration camp while a teenager. After being raped by a guard, Frister discovered that his abuser had stolen his cap. The penalty for prisoners lining up in the morning without a cap being immediate execution, the sixteen-year-old stole the cap of another prisoner, a stranger. The teenager, writing years later, describes his feelings upon hearing the man's body crumple to the ground: "I was delighted to be alive."

71. Neiman, *Moral Clarity*, 342.

72. Bauman, *Modernity and the Holocaust*, 177.

73. Slavoj Žižek, *The Fragile Absolute; or, Why Is the Christian Legacy Worth Fighting For?* (London: Verso, 2000), 149.

74. Cesare Casarino and Antonio Negri, "It's a Powerful Life: A Conversation on Contemporary Philosophy," *Cultural Critique* 57 (Spring 2004): 175.

75. See "Alan Moore: The Last Angry Man," interview on MTV.com, http://www.mtv.com/shared/movies/interviews.

76. Alan Moore and David Lloyd, *V for Vendetta* (New York: DC Comics, 1989), 127. Further references are cited parenthetically in the text.

77. Barry Kavanagh, "The Alan Moore Interview: *V for Vendetta*," http://blather.net/articles/amoore/v1.html.

78. "A for Alan, Part I," interview with Alan Moore, http://www.comicon.com/thebeat/20..._moore.html.

79. Bauman, *Modernity and the Holocaust*, 250.

80. *V for Vendetta*. Screenplay by Larry and Andy Wachowski. Dir. James McTeigue. Perfs. Natalie Portman, Hugo Weaving, John Hurt, and Stephen Rea. Warner Bros., 2006.

81. Weil, *Gravity and Grace*, 71.

82. Alain Joxe, *Empire of Disorder*, trans. Ames Hodges (Los Angeles: Semiotext(e), 2002), 123.

83. I explore the parallels between Moore's comic and Žižek's ideas on revolutionary subjectivization in "The Pessimist Rearmed: Žižek on Christianity and Revolution," *Theory and Event* 5, no. 4 (2005), http://muse.jhu.edu/journals/theory_and_event/v008.8.2paik.html. The following analysis expands some of the points made in that article while diverging from it on other matters.

84. Slavoj Žižek, *Enjoy Your Symptom! Jacques Lacan in Hollywood and Out* (New York: Routledge, 1992), 43.

85. Žižek, *Enjoy Your Symptom*, 43, and *The Fragile Absolute*, 150.

86. Jodi Dean, "V with and against Z," http://jdeanicite.typepad.com/i_cite/2006/03/v_with_and_agai.html.

87. Ibid.

88. K-punk, "Dis-identity Politics," http://k-punk.abstractdynamics.org/archives/007709.html.

89. Steven Shaviro, "K-punk on 'Dis-identity Politics,'" *The Pinocchio Theory*, http://www.shaviro.com/Blog/?p=492.

90. *The Battle of Algiers*. Screenplay by Gillo Pontecorvo and Franco Solinas. Dir. Gillo Pontecorvo. Perfs. Brahim Haggiag, Jean Martin, Yacef Saadi, and Fusia El Kader. Criterion, 2004.

91. Steven Shaviro, "V for Vendetta," *The Pinocchio Theory*, http://www.shaviro.com/Blog/?p=488.

92. Quoted in Žižek, *The Parallax View*, 149.

93. Weil, *Gravity and Grace*, 104.

94. Ibid., 74.

95. Simone Weil, *Waiting for God*, trans. Emma Craufurd (New York: Harper, 2001), 69–70.

96. Ibid., 69.

97. Weil, *Gravity and Grace*, 25. See also Weil, *Waiting for God*, 73, and *The Notebooks of Simone Weil: Volume One*, trans. Arthur Wills (New York: G. P. Putnam, 1956), 223.

98. Weil, *Waiting for God*, 69.

99. Ibid., 71.

100. Michael André Bernstein, *Foregone Conclusions: Against Apocalyptic History* (Berkeley and Los Angeles: University of California Press, 1994), 89. Quoted in Gary Weissman, *Fantasies of Witnessing: Postwar Efforts to Experience the Holocaust* (Ithaca, N.Y.: Cornell University Press, 2004), 78.

101. Bernstein, *Foregone Conclusions*, 91.

102. Ibid., 88, 89.

103. Weil, *Notebooks: Volume One*, 109.

104. Simone Weil, *The Need for Roots*, trans. Arthur Wills (London: Routledge, 2002), 253.

105. John Gray, "The Savage Within," *The New Statesman*, August 21, 2006; http:// www.newstatesman.com/200608210037.

106. Gray, *Black Mass*, 193.

107. Thomas Homer-Dixon, *The Upside of Down: Catastrophe, Creativity, and the Renewal of Civilization* (Washington, D.C.: Island Press, 2006), 283.

108. Søren Kierkegaard, *Either/Or, Part II*, ed. and trans. Howard V. Hong and Edna H. Hong (Princeton, N.J.: Princeton University Press, 1987), 343.

109. Slavoj Žižek, *In Defense of Lost Causes* (London: Verso, 2008), 193.

110. Bernstein, *Foregone Conclusions*, 1.

111. Weil, *Gravity and Grace*, 11.

112. Weil, *The Need for Roots*, 218.

113. Weil, *Gravity and Grace*, 13.

114. Eric Voegelin, "Nietzsche, the Crisis, and the War," in *Published Essays 1940–1952*, vol. 10 of *The Collected Works of Eric Voegelin*, ed. Ellis Sandoz (Columbia: University of Missouri Press, 2000), 129.

INDEX

Agamben, Giorgio, 66, 150, 191, 196;
on the figure of the *Muselmann*,
150–51; *Homo sacer*, 67
Animatrix: The Second Renaissance
(film), 132, 136
apocalypse, 21, 42; and historical
change, 13, 123–24; and the impossibility of retaliatory violence,
41; the *katechon*, 15; in *Miracleman: Olympus* (Moore), 10–15,
20; in *Nausicaä of the Valley of
Wind*, 98, 100, 109–10, 113–17,
119–22; in *Oryx and Crake*
(Atwood), 119–20; in *Princess
Mononoke* (film), 94; in *Save the
Green Planet* (film), 85–86, 88–
89, 91–92; in *The Second Renaissance* (film), 133–36; in *V for
Vendetta* (Moore), 156–59, 162–
65, 173; in *Watchmen* (Moore),
30, 38, 60, 64
Arendt, Hannah, 36, 188
Aristotle, 133, 195
Atkinson, Doug, 189
Atwood, Margaret, 119–20, 123, 193
avant-garde: Soviet, 16. *See also*
Groys, Boris

Badiou, Alain, 58, 75, 125, 154, 189, 191
Bakunin, Mikhail, 15
Barthes, Roland, 137
Battle of Algiers, The (film), 171, 198
Bauman, Zygmunt, 152, 159, 197
beautiful soul, 6, 141. *See also* Hegel,
Georg Wilhelm Friedrich; Žižek,
Slavoj
Begin, Menachem, 169
Benjamin, Walter, 74
Berman, Morris, 147, 196
Bernstein, Michael André, 176, 198,
199; on sideshadowing, 179
Bloch, Ernst, 2, 3, 6, 186
Borgia, Cesare, 37, 38
Brave New World (Huxley), 120
Bukharin, Nikolai, 142
Butler, Judith, 138, 195

Cabinet of Dr. Caligari, The (film), 37
Campbell, Eddie, 189
Camus, Albert, 121, 193
capitalism, 7, 9, 67, 119, 123, 125, 141,
181; and apocalypse, 123–24; liberal, 5, 18, 75, 124, 126, 127, 147,
148; neoliberal, 6, 18–19, 125. *See
also* globalization; neoliberalism

Peter Y. Paik is associate professor of comparative literature at the University of Wisconsin–Milwaukee.